D0930309

Royal Navy Frigates
since 1945

Above:
**HMS *Venus*, a Type 15 frigate converted from a wartime
destroyer, leads the postwar Type 12, HMS *Torquay*, and
two other Type 15s in the summer of 1963. The four ships
formed the 17th Frigate Squadron which doubled as the
Dartmouth Training Squadron.**
Imperial War Museum (IWM) MH30512

Royal Navy Frigates
since 1945
Second Edition
Leo Marriott

LONDON

IAN ALLAN LTD

Acknowledgements

One of the joys of writing a book like this is the realisation that there are a wide variety of people who are only too willing to take the time and effort to help out by providing photographs, information and personal knowledge. It gives me great pleasure, therefore, to take this opportunity to thank the following people and organisations who have contributed in some way to the compilation of this book and hope that they will find the end result worthy of their efforts: Wright and Logan, Naval Photographers, Portsmouth; Mike Lennon; Mr T. C. Bickerton, Public Relations Manager, British Aerospace Dynamics Group, Bristol Division; Fleet Photographic Unit, HMS *Excellent*; Photographic Unit, HMS *Osprey*, Portland; Mr J. Baird, Public Relations Department, Westland Aircraft Ltd, Yeovil; Mr D. K. Brown FRINA, RCNC (for information relating to frigate type designations listed in Appendix 1); Cdr F. E. R. Phillips RN, Naval Assistant to the Director of Public Relations (Navy); Mr Tom Goyer, Assistant Publicity Manager, Short Bros Ltd, Belfast; Mr Charles Hamilton, Managing Director, Skyfotos; Mr W. C. McMillan, Executive Manager, Yarrow (Shipbuilders) Ltd; Lt-Cdr E. H. Featherstone, HMS *Fearless*; Officers and Crew, HMS *Brighton*; Elaine Lawson, Yarrow Shipbuilders Ltd; Lt L. Smallman, PRO HMS *Phoebe;* Adrian Vicary, Maritime Photo Library; Paul Kemp, Department of Photographs, Imperial War Museum; CPO(A) Phot R. Forbes, HMS *Osprey* Photographic Section; Staff Public Relations Officer, Flag Officer Plymouth; John Thornton, British Aerospace; Lt J. R. H. Clink, PRO HMS *Active*; Anne McNicol, Deputy Staff PRO, FOSNI; Cdr T. Morton, Officer Commanding HMS *Sirius*; Sub-Lt R. E. Blackwell, HMS *Brilliant*; Lt M. Ewers, PRO HMS *London*; Hugh F. Graham, Staff PRO, C-in-C Fleet; Sub-Lt M. R. McGinley, HMS *Sheffield*; Sub-Lt R. S. Hatcher, HMS *Scylla*; Lt M. A. Hart, HMS *Charybdis*; Lt M. D. Blowers, HMS *Juno*; Cdr S. V. Mackay, Officer Commanding HMS *Ambuscade*; Sub-Lt M. D. Power, HMS *Argonaut*; Lt-Cdr J. L. Wakeling, HMS *Brazen*; Lt-Cdr D. I. Lister, HMS *Cleopatra*.

Leo Marriott

First published 1983
Second edition 1990

ISBN 0 7110 1915 0

Published by Ian Allan Ltd, Shepperton, Surrey; and printed by Ian Allan Printing Ltd at their works at Coombelands in Runnymede, England

Contents

Above:
Modern naval warfare is, first and foremost, an electronic battle. HMS *Phoebe*, a 'Leander' class frigate modified to carry a towed array sonar, bristles with aerials and antennae as she manoeuvres off Portland. *HMS Osprey*

Glossary and Abbreviations

AA	Anti-Aircraft	IN	Indian Navy
AAW	Anti War Warfare	kg	Kilogram
ADAWS	Action Data Automation Weapon System	kW	Kilowatt
		Limbo	See Squid
AIO	Action Information Organisation	LSH	Landing Ship, Headquarters
AS	Anti-Submarine	MATCH	Manned Torpedo Carrying Helicopter
ASR	Admiralty Standard Range	MGB	Motor Gunboat
ASW	Anti-Submarine Warfare	mm	Millimetre
ASWE	Admiralty Surface Weapons Establishment	MRS	Medium Range System
		MAD	Magnetic Anomaly Detector. An airborne device for detecting submerged submarines by measuring disturbances in the earth's magnetic field
ATW	Ahead Throwing Weapon		
bhp	Brake horsepower		
CAAIS	Computer Assisted Action Information System		
CACS	Computer Assisted Command System	MW	Megawatt
CIWS	Close In Weapon System	NATO	North Atlantic Treaty Organisation
CODLAG	Combined Diesel Electric and Gas Turbine	NGS	Naval Gunfire Support
		oa	Overall
CODOG	Combined Diesel or Gas Turbine. An integrated ship's propulsion system where the ship can be driven by either diesel or gas turbine power, but not both together	PDMS	Point Defence Missile System
		RDN	Royal Danish Navy
		RCN	Royal Canadian Navy
		R Nor N	Royal Norwegian Navy
		RN	Royal Navy
COGOG	Combined Gas turbine or Gas Turbine. An integrated propulsion system consisting of two or more gas turbine units where the ship can be driven by a combination of some, but not all, units	RNVR	Royal Navy Volunteer Reserve
		shp	Shaft horsepower
		SCOT	Satellite Communication Terminal
		Squid	Three-barrelled AS mortar firing depth charge projectiles to a range of about 400yd. Loaded manually. Postwar development led to the Limbo system which fired a heavier projectile over a longer range. Could be loaded, aimed and fired by remote control
COSAG	Combined Steam and Gas Turbine. An integrated propulsion system consisting of both steam and gas turbines and where the ship can be driven by either or both turbines together		
CRBFD	Close Range Blind Fire Director	SSM	Surface to Surface Missile
DF	Direction Finding	STAAG	Stabilised Tachymetric Anti-Aircraft Gun
DP	Dual Purpose		
ECM	Electronic Countermeasures	STD	Simple Tachymetric Director
ECCM	Electronic Counter Countermeasures	STWS	Ship's Torpedo Weapon System
ESM	Electronic Surveillance Measures	TACAN	Tactical Aid to Navigation. System whereby a ship or aircraft can determine its bearing and distance from a beacon which may be land-based or installed in another ship or aircraft
EW	Electronic Warfare		
Foxer	An acoustic decoy towed astern of a ship to counteract acoustic homing torpedoes		
GRP	Glassfibre Reinforced Products	TAS	Towed Array Sonars
GWS	Guided Weapon System	UHF	Ultra High Frequency
HF/DF	High Frequency Direction Finding	UK	United Kingdom
IFF	Identification Friend or Foe. A radar system designed to identify co-operating targets on a radar screen	US	United States
		VDS	Variable Depth Sonar
		VLF	Very Low Frequency
ihp	Indicated horsepower. Measure of power output of steam reciprocating machinery	VLS	Vertical Launch System

Introduction

It is 45 years since the end of World War 2. In that time political and technical changes have altered the status of Great Britain and the role of the Royal Navy in ways which could not have been foreseen amid the rejoicing at the coming of peace in 1945. At that time Britain was an equal partner with the other two great powers, the United States and Soviet Russia, and her Empire and Commonwealth stretched around the globe. Her navy was second only to the vast fleet possessed by the United States Navy and was tasked with worldwide commitments. Most important of all, Britain was privy to the technical secrets which shortly enabled her to construct and test her own nuclear and thermonuclear weapons.

The effort of fighting and winning a second world war within a period of 30 years had left its mark, however, and in the years immediately following the end of the war the armed forces were inevitably run down. No money was available for the furtherance of new weapons, and, rightly, the government of the time gave priority to the domestic front, where the rehousing and resettlement of a population disrupted by nearly six years of war was a major task. Industry and transport systems needed to be re-equipped and revitalised, and in this period the welfare state was introduced in the form that we know it today.

Abroad an irresistible tide of nationalism led to the break-up of the Empire, a process which had already started before the war, and even independent Commonwealth countries such as Australia and Canada were far less dependent on the mother country than they had been before 1939. Thus, in the late 1940s, both political and economic factors pointed to a steady decline in the strength of the Royal Navy and it was obvious that it would never again hold the pre-eminent position it had held before the start of World War 2. Nevertheless, several factors contributed towards a temporary halt in the reduction of the effective strength of the Royal Navy in the late 1940s and early 1950s. The start of the so-called 'Cold War', signalled by the blockade of Berlin by the Russians in 1948, was followed by Chinese communist aggression in the Far East, which in turn led to the Korean War in 1950-53. Against this background, the North Atlantic Treaty Organisation was set up in 1949 and, apart from military aid, the United States also pledged financial assistance for European rearmament. The Mutual Defense Assistance Pact (MDAP) provided funds for the purchase of weapons by NATO countries and enabled the Royal Navy to go ahead with the development and construction of new ships to meet an increasingly threatening international situation. Although many ships of the wartime navy continued their expected progress to the scrapyard, the 1950s saw the laying down of many new classes of warships and the completion of major ships laid down or designed during the war. Thus, for example, the carriers *Ark Royal* and *Eagle* passed into service during this period.

Following the end of the Korean War, the urgency for re-equipment of military forces lessened and the Defence White Paper of 1957 contained many sweeping measures which effectively cut the plans of all three services for future equipment and also established the guided missile as the prime aerial defence system. The policies of the Wilson Labour government, elected in 1964, led to a review of Britain's position in the world and a realistic appreciation of her financial abilities to follow various defence policies. This led to a decision in 1968 to withdraw all military forces from positions east of Suez by 1971 and a similarly timed announcement led to the decision to run down the expensive aircraft carrier force. This latter decision, hotly contested at the time, was possibly the most retrograde step taken in respect of the Royal Navy by any postwar government. In the event, a Conservative government elected in 1971 decided to retain the *Ark Royal* in service as long as possible and also authorised the construction of three through-deck cruisers which became the current 'Invincible' class. Obviously, the foregoing decisions had a major impact on the size and structure of the Royal Navy. In 1970, the Wilson government had set a target of approximately 70 destroyers and frigates as the front line strength and by 1980 this figure had fallen to approximately 60. The defence review announced by John Knott, the Conservative Defence Minister in 1981, cut the numbers to only 50. This decision was made in the teeth of fierce protests that the Navy would be unable even to carry out its NATO commitments in the Eastern Atlantic which represent its current major task.

At the moment, the Royal Navy is the world's third most powerful navy in terms of effectiveness if not in terms of actual ship numbers. It is, however, only a fraction of the size of the powerful American and Russian navies, and may well be overtaken in the near future by other navies such as the French (which currently operates two modern fixed-wing aircraft carriers as well as a force of six ballistic missile submarines with a seventh vessel approved).

It is against the foregoing background that this book sets out to study the development of the frigate in the Royal Navy during the period in question. Apart from political and financial influences, the overwhelming factor affecting warship design has been the technological revolution in virtually all fields of warship construction. The greatest advances have been in electronics and sensor systems, weapons and propulsion systems. The changes undergone in warship design since the end of World War 2 are probably as fundamental and as varied as those experienced by the Victorian navy when steam supplanted sail and iron hulls replaced the traditional 'wooden walls'.

At the end of the war, steam represented the major propulsion system in most RN escorts and frigates, using either turbines or reciprocating machinery to drive the screws. In the early postwar designs for the 'Whitby' and 'Blackwood' classes, higher operating pressures and temperatures resulted in greater fuel economies and lighter machinery. However, the Navy was ready to investigate and use alternative systems and the first to see widespread adoption was the diesel engine which was chosen for the 'Salisbury' and 'Jaguar' classes in the early 1950s. Again fuel economy and increased range was the objective but the resulting ships were relatively slow for their role as major fleet escorts (although considerably faster than wartime frigates). Both the steam turbine and the diesel were eventually replaced by an entirely new propulsion system which took its technology from the aircraft industry — the gas turbine. Introduced into operational service with the 'Tribal' class frigates of the early 1960s, the gas turbine proved to be a reliable and effective warship propulsion system and all major warships constructed for the Royal Navy since the early 1970s have been powered by this system. Adoption of the gas turbine has had many effects on warship design as it requires large intake and exhaust trunkings and filters. Most importantly, gas turbine-powered ships can be started from cold and be under way within a matter of minutes compared with the hours required to raise steam from a boiler. Another consideration is that the turbines are usually installed in modular form which means that they can be removed as a complete unit for major repairs and another unit substituted. Thus ships need to spend less time in dockyard hands. Most designs incorporate two or more separate gas turbines which means that the chances of a ship having a total power failure due to battle damage is considerably reduced. Finally, the modern gas turbine lends itself to remote and electronic

control which in turn reduces the numbers of staff required to operate it.

Mention of electronics brings us to the greatest revolution, not only in warship design, but in the world as a whole. Computers have changed our lives and they have certainly taken over warships. Computers take up space in a warship, not because of their actual size but because of the need to protect them from shock damage and to provide them with adequate ventilation and cooling. The Type 21 was the first design to be provided with a modern digital control system for the ship and its weapons, and the Type 22 has gone a stage further. Ships of the 'Leander' class have been equipped with computer-assisted action information systems during their rebuilding and no self-respecting warship can take to the seas these days without its own electronic brain. As well as controlling and operating weapon systems, computers are also found in engine control systems, communications and other departments.

Another development in the electronic field is, of course, radar. Although developed to a high state during World War 2, new research and techniques have brought continuous improvements. Again technology, in the shape of the transistor, has had a major impact on warship design. Although transmitters and receivers are much more compact and reliable than they used to be for a given power, the increase in tasks allocated to frigates has meant that these ships have to carry a greater array of radar equipment than before. The ultimate in this respect was probably the Type 61 aircraft direction frigate which carried a bewildering array of radar equipment to the exclusion of virtually everything else. The huge 'double bedstead' aerial carried by these ships weighed nearly two tons and, being mounted at the top of a tall mast, must have caused great problems to the ship designers trying to keep stability within reasonable limits.

Transmissions from any radar, as well as detecting other targets, can also be received by other ships and the direction of the signals plotted. This means that any ship using its radar can be detected and possibly located by an enemy vessel which is not using its own radar and therefore remains undetected. This has the result that strict procedures have to be enforced with regard to the use of radar and all modern frigates (and other warships) are equipped with the means to detect and locate other ships' radar and radio transmissions. This is known as electronic surveillance measures (ESM) and is something else for which the overworked ship designer has to find room.

Radar systems can be rendered useless by various methods of jamming, and modern radar systems are designed to try to overcome this. Thus a whole new field of electronic countermeasures and electronic counter-countermeasures (ECM and ECCM) has come into existence. The steady increase in aerials and black boxes which have equipped postwar frigates are witness to the increasing effect of electronics in sea warfare.

The original function of frigates was to attack and sink submarines, and their main weapons were depth charges and the early ahead throwing weapons (ATW) such as Hedgehog and Squid. As the underwater speed of submarines and the range of sonar has increased, so the range of AS weapons has also improved. The first development was the Limbo mortar, an improvement of the Squid, but this has been supplanted and replaced by other weapons such as the Ikara missile system and helicopter-carried homing torpedoes. The helicopter has wrought a major change on the shape and layout of the modern frigate, as all designs now include a hangar and flightdeck for the carriage and operation of this vital piece of equipment.

Since the invention of gunpowder, the main armament of any ship had been its guns but, initially against airborne targets, and then almost universally, the gun was slowly replaced by the guided missile. Already under development at the end of World War 2, the guided missile appears in a variety of forms on most modern frigate designs culminating in the latest Type 22 design where missiles are the main means of defence against both air and surface targets. On the other side of the coin is the necessity for ships to be able to defend themselves against missile attack and while this has usually meant attempting to jam or disrupt the missiles' guidance systems, the Seawolf missile system now in service is capable of intercepting other missiles in flight.

Thus the modern Royal Navy frigate carries extensive radar and electronic equipment, is armed with guided missiles, carries one or more helicopters, is powered by products of the aerospace industry, and the whole thing is run by computers. Compare this with the typical late war frigate which carried relatively simple radar equipment, was armed with a couple of 4in guns and depth charge mortars, was propelled by reciprocating steam machinery, and was controlled by weatherbeaten men exposed to the elements whilst standing on an open bridge: the difference between these two images is what this book is about.

The conflict in the Falkland Islands threw the characteristics of our modern warships into the spotlight of topical discussion. The informed layman probably knew more about Royal Navy warships than he ever did in the past and, for a while, names such as Exocet, Seawolf, Sea Dart, *Antelope*, *Sheffield*, *Coventry* and *Ardent* were household words. Although the memory of the war is already fading in some quarters, the professionals of the Royal Navy and the warship designers have taken a close look at the lessons which have been learnt and these are reflected in the form of new ships and modifications to existing vessels. Some of the lessons, however, were painfully relearnt after being forgotten in the years since World War 2. Foremost amongst those was that, historically, a force of surface warships has never been able to defend itself effectively against concentrated air attack unless provided with sufficient carrier-based air power of its own. When the Task Force sailed for the South Atlantic many observers wondered if the development and deployment of sophisticated surface-to-air guided missiles would change this basic situation. It did not.

Although surface-based missiles took a terrible toll of attacking aircraft, enough got through to cause severe losses of ships and lives amongst the British fleet. Sea Harriers operating from the two carriers were more successful than could reasonably have been hoped in the circumstances, but were handicapped by lack of any airborne early warning system.

Another lesson to be absorbed was the surprising usefulness and effectiveness of the gun in modern warfare. The medium calibre guns of the destroyers and frigates were essential in the shore bombardment role and one frigate even claimed to have shot down an Exocet with its 4.5in gun. Light automatic weapons were shown to be still a very effective means of countering close-range air attack.

The first edition of this book appeared in 1983, only a year after the end of hostilities and too early to reflect the changes brought about to the Navy's frigate force as a result of the war. Today, the results are clearly visible on many ships — notably improved electronic warfare devices, increased light AA armament, new CIWS gun-based systems, medium calibre guns introduced on the later Type 22s and greater attention to fire and damage control facilities in all ships.

In the anti-submarine role the introduction of the sensitive towed array sonars, together with improved computerised signal processing equipment, has placed much greater emphasis on the passive detection of submarines. In turn, this has led to new and quiet propulsion systems wherein diesels and electric motors have partly replaced the gas turbine in the latest ships.

Mention of computers reminds us that, although essential to the operation of the modern frigate, such systems have become so all-embracing that they are in danger of being swamped by the amount of data being fed to them. A major crisis in the British frigate building programme has arisen due to the inability of the current series of

Computer Assisted Command Systems to perform at the advanced level deemed essential in today's sophisticated threat environment. Great efforts are being made to overcome this deficiency, but it will be several years before completely satisfactory systems are available.

Another disturbing trend, despite the Falklands experience, is the steady decline in the size of the Royal Navy's destroyer and frigate fleet. Since the start of 1983, the Navy has taken delivery of only 12 new ships of these types and during 1989 will receive the last Type 22 and the first Type 23 — an average of two ships a year. Against this, the rundown of the fleet has continued at a much greater rate. In the same period all the remaining 'County' class destroyers have been sold and the remaining active 'Tribal' and 'Rothesay' class frigates have been sold, scrapped or laid up. In addition, substantial numbers of the formerly ubiquitous 'Leander' class have been withdrawn from service and have suffered similar fates. There

is no doubt that the new ships are considerably more powerful and sophisticated than their predecessors, but numbers of hulls still count and the Royal Navy is becoming increasingly unable to meet even its basic commitments to NATO.

Despite these problems, the greatest lesson which we can learn from the past, shown time and again in the history of the Royal Navy, is that the finest ships and weapon systems in the world are of no use unless they are manned, maintained and operated by human beings. Although this book is a history of the ships themselves, it should not be forgotten that the most important factor in their success or failure is the men that sail in them. It is because of such men that the rest of us are able to go about our daily lives in peace and security.

Below:
HMS *Ghurka* passes under the Forth Bridge on her way to Rosyth to pay off in 1980. Note the VDS gear on the stern. *MoD Navy*

1 The Wartime Frigates

Frigate Development in World War 2

The first warship in modern times to be termed a frigate was the 'River' class of escorts which came into service in late 1942. They were purpose-built vessels intended to escort and protect ocean convoys against submarine attack and they were the first vessels to be designed specifically for this particular role. There were, of course, several other classes of warship which were being used to escort convoys but none of them had been specifically designed for the particular purpose of defending ocean-going convoys against concentrated submarine attacks. It is instructive to look more closely at these escorts, because the omissions and deficiencies in their design led to the development of the first frigates.

Perhaps the most successful ships in service in 1942 was the 'Black Swan' class sloops of which 31 were eventually completed for the Royal Navy. Displacing 1,300 tons and equipped with steam turbines to give a speed of 20kt, they were heavily armed with six 4in guns in three twin high-angle mountings, and several light AA guns. They were excellent ships in every way and they shared in the destruction of 28 U-boats as well as shooting down several enemy aircraft; but, despite this, they suffered from two main drawbacks. In the first place their very excellence arose partly from the fact that they were designed to full naval warship standards and therefore could only be built in yards familiar with the construction of warships. Even then building could take up to two years and consequently the type could not be rapidly produced in the numbers required at that stage of the war. Secondly, the design could not easily be adapted to carry the new AS weapons such as Hedgehog and Squid unless part of the main armament was removed. The Admiralty was loath to do this as the ships' AA armament was sorely needed at the time.

Also in service were several prewar-built sloops of the 'Bridgwater', 'Hastings' and 'Grimsby' classes, which had preceded the 'Black Swan' design. With a displacement of just over 1,000 tons and a speed of only 16½kt they were both smaller and slower than the 'Black Swans' and carried a lighter armament. Although useful ships, they suffered from the drawbacks of the 'Black Swan' class to an even greater extent and were not built in very large numbers.

The escort available in greatest numbers in 1942 was the famous 'Flower' class corvette, which had been developed from a commercial whaler design just prior to the outbreak of the war. On a standard displacement of 950 tons the 'Flowers' made 16kt and carried a 4in gun, a few light AA guns and depth charges. They were intended mainly for use in coastal regions and short-range escort work, and were never intended for the mid-ocean work in which they were soon employed. Although excellent seaboats they were very lively and the accommodation standards for the wartime crews were cramped, cold and damp. Their small size made it difficult to fit new weapons and radar, and although a modified version was eventually produced it could do no more than nibble at the problems. The outstanding advantage of the type was that it could be produced quickly and in large numbers by normal commercial shipyards — and ultimately a total of 145 was built in UK yards with others being built in Canada. The large number built, and the rate at which they were introduced into service in the early part of the war, was a vital factor in holding off the expanding U-boat menace despite the operating deficiencies of the class.

Against the experience gained with the prewar escort vessels in the early part of the war, the Admiralty decided that a new class of vessel was required to provide effective defences for the ocean convoys. Thus plans were drawn up in 1940 for a 'twin screw corvette', which became the 'River' class and was later redesignated 'frigate'. The 'River' class, displacing 1,400 tons, was considerably larger than the 'Flower' class and was armed with two single 4in guns and several light AA. Anti-submarine armament comprised the usual depth charge racks and throwers, while Hedgehog was fitted on the foredeck in front of the forward 4in gun. The large open quarterdeck gave plenty of room for depth charge stowage (over 200 were carried eventually) and later for handling acoustic torpedo decoy gear (Foxer). The increase in size meant that accommodation standards for the crew were improved and the ship was better able to carry improved radar as it became available. Being designed to commercial standards, the 'Rivers' could be built by normal shipyards; a total of 57 was built in the UK, more

Top:
**The precursor of the modern frigate was the prewar sloop
which was built in limited numbers in the decade before
1939. Typical of these was HMS *Dundee* launched in 1932
which displaced 1,060 tons, made 16kt and was armed
with twin 4in guns and a multiple 2pdr.** *Wright & Logan*

Above:
**The 'River' class was designed as an ocean going escort in
the light of experience gained in the early part of the war
and was the first Royal Navy ship in modern times to be
designated as a 'Frigate'. HMS *Meon* was refitted after
the war as an LSH(S), as shown here, and served on until
1965.** *Real Photographs*

Below:
**Although most of the Royal Navy's 'River' class ships
were laid up after the war, the Canadian Navy carried out
an extensive modernisation programme on some of its
ships in the 1950s as shown in this view of HMCS *New
Glasgow*. The forecastle deck was extended right aft and
two Squid mortars were mounted in an enclosed well on
the quarterdeck. Armament was increased to a twin 4in
forward and six 40mm AA guns, while the radar and
sonar outfit was updated.** *Real Photographs*

were built in Canada and the design was also adopted by the United States Navy.

Due to the increase of size in the 'River' class, several yards which had been building 'Flower' class corvettes were unable to build the new design. In order to plug this gap an updated and modernised design was produced to replace the 'Flowers'. The new type was known as the 'Castle' class frigate and was 50ft longer than the corvettes to give a displacement of 1,100 tons. Gun armament was similar with a single 4in and several AA guns, but the major improvement was the inclusion of a Squid AS mortar just forward of the bridge and enclosed from the weather by protective bulwarks. Speed remained at 16½kt. Although the first vessels of the class were not laid down until 1943 a total of 26 had been completed for the Royal Navy by the end of the war and others had been completed for the Canadian and Allied navies.

The final product of wartime experience was the 'Loch' class frigate, the first of which was completed in mid-1944. Although of a similar size to the earlier 'River' class, the new design was optimised for large scale production and provision was made to incorporate new weapons and equipment coming into service. Thus the armament consisted of a single 4in gun, a large number of light AA guns and, most significantly, two Squid mortars mounted just forward of the bridge. As soon as the design was finalised, all contracts for the 'River' class were cancelled and replaced by orders for 'Loch' class vessels. The efficiency of the new type can be gauged from the fact that, despite their late entry into the war, ships of the 'Loch' class were involved in the sinking of 16 U-boats.

In 1944 a requirement arose for AA escort vessels, particularly for the British Pacific Fleet which was forming at the time. The answer to this requirement was an adaptation of the 'Loch' class, involving the removal of the single 4in gun and the Squid mortars, and their replacement by four 4in AA guns in two twin mountings installed in B and X positions. The new variant was designated the 'Bay' class and a total of 19 vessels of this class was completed for the Royal Navy.

Finally, mention should be made of one other class of escort vessel which, although numerically very important, lies rather out of the scope of this book. This is the 'Hunt' class of escort destroyers, a total of 86 of which was produced between 1939 and 1943. Designed mainly as fleet AA escorts with a limited AS capability, over 60 survived the war and were redesignated as frigates in 1948. During and after the war, several were transferred to foreign navies and the rest were scrapped in the 1950s. No major modifications were made to the class after the end of the war to adapt them for modern AS warfare and they therefore played no part in the evolution of the postwar frigate. In passing, however it is worth mentioning the two 'Hunt' Type IV destroyers *Brecon* and *Brissenden*. These two vessels were designed by Thornycroft and were completely different from the other 'Hunt' class types in that the forecastle deck was extended right aft to give virtually a flush deck appearance instead of the traditional destroyer layout. A fuller hull section was adopted and a pronounced knuckle was incorporated on either side of the bow. The net result of these changes was improved sea riding qualities with no loss of performance. The extra stability of the fuller hull allowed the full 'Hunt' class armament of six 4in guns and a triple set of torpedo tubes. The Type I and III 'Hunts' had had to sacrifice one twin 4in mounting due to stability problems. In many ways these two vessels were ahead of their time and experience with some of the features of this class was invaluable in the design of postwar vessels. In particular, the extended forecastle deck became a standard feature of many postwar designs and conversions.

It is not the intention of this book to go into great detail concerning the design and development of the wartime frigates as this aspect has been well recorded and documented in other publications. However, the following pages set out general details of those classes which saw significant postwar service and details of their eventual fates.

'Black Swan' Class AA Frigates

This famous class of escorts had its origin in a Naval Staff Requirement of 1937 for ocean-going escorts having good AA and AS qualities. The result, a development of earlier sloop designs, produced a vessel of 1,300 tons standard displacement carrying a heavy armament of six 4in AA guns in three twin mountings as well as a quadruple pom-pom mounting and a number of 20mm single guns. Thirteen vessels were built to the original 'Black Swan' design (including four for the Indian Navy) but wartime experience and the need to fit extra equipment resulted in 24 further vessels completed to a modified design and known (naturally enough!) as the Modified 'Black Swan' class. Several of the later vessels were not completed until after the end of the war.

The modified vessels featured better provision for the light AA armament, a slight increase in beam, stabilisers and other detail improvements. As the war progressed, continual modifications and additions of new and extra equipment eroded the differences between the two versions and by 1945 they could be considered as one class for all practical purposes. Radar equipment varied but, again by 1945, the standard outfit consisted of a Type 291 air warning radar at the very top of the mast, with a Type 293 'cheese' aerial mounted at the top of the lattice structure of the mast. The lattice mast, a feature of the last few ships to complete, was retrospectively fitted to all the class where it replaced the original tripod mast. *Pheasant* was the last vessel to be so fitted, the work not being carried out until some time after the end of the war. A Type 285 gunnery radar was installed on top of the director tower above the bridge. In the original design the sole AS armament consisted of depth charge throwers and rails on the quarterdeck. Later in the war those ships originally fitted with the quadruple pom-pom mounting on the quarterdeck had it removed in order to carry more depth charges and their equipment. A split Hedgehog spigot mortar was fitted forward in most ships to increase their AS effectiveness.

By the end of the war the class was regarded mainly as an AA escort due to their combination of a heavy AA armament coupled with a radar-controlled fire control system as well as a substantial secondary battery. The stabilisers fitted to the Modified 'Black Swan' class made them exceptionally good gun platforms. Because of these features, a large number of the class were sent to the British Pacific Fleet in the Far East where their excellent AA capabilities were needed against the Japanese. Thus by VJ-Day in August 1945, no less than 17 of the class were in Far Eastern waters.

Of the 37 vessels of both groups completed, six had been delivered to the Indian Navy and a further six were lost during the war which left the Royal Navy with a balance of 25 at the end of hostilities. Five of these (*Acteon, Modeste, Nereide, Snipe, Sparrow*) were not completed until after the end of the war. Indeed the last of the class to be commissioned, *Sparrow*, was not finally completed until December 1946.

With the end of the war, some of the vessels were adapted for peacetime roles. *Redpole* and *Starling* were disarmed and converted to act as navigational training ships. *Redpole* retained her original tripod foremast but a new lattice mast, carrying a Type 277 radar aerial, was stepped aft and extra deckhouses were constructed on the quarterdeck and in the position vacated by X turret. She continued in her training role until she

finally paid off in 1958 and was scrapped in 1960. *Starling* retained the lattice foremast with which she had been fitted and also the Type 293 and 291 radars mounted thereon. Like *Redpole* she also had extra accommodation erected aft and a lattice mainmast installed on the quarterdeck. This new mast was taller than that fitted to *Redpole* and carried mainly communication equipment. Following a refit in the mid-1950s, extra equipment was installed on the mainmast for trials but, following completion of the trials, the mainmast and its associated aerials were removed in 1957. *Starling*, of course, had a distinguished wartime record when she was leader of the 2nd Escort Group led by the famous Capt F. J. Walker, who was probably the most proficient AS tactician of the whole war. Sadly, he died of illness brought on by overwork before the end of the war but his memory lived on at the paying-off ceremony when the ship ended her last commission in November 1959. Following a period in reserve she was put up for disposal in 1961 but was not finally scrapped until 1965.

Another ship of the class to undergo substantial modification was *Wild Goose*, one of the original 'Black Swans'. In the course of a refit during 1945-46 she had X turret removed and extra accommodation installed on the quarterdeck. The twin 40mm Hazemeyers which she had previously carried were replaced by the standard Mk V twin mounting with an STD for each position. The original tripod mast was replaced by a lattice structure and an up-to-date radar outfit installed. Finally, 3pdr saluting guns were added and the ship was repainted in the prewar standard Far East colours, comprising a white hull and superstructure and a buff funnel. Thus equipped she was allocated to the Persian Gulf division of the East Indies Station where she served with only short breaks until 1954 when she was placed in reserve. Apart from *Wild Goose*, several ships served in the Gulf area including *Wren*, which was also repainted in the white and buff colour scheme, although for several years she was not otherwise modified. However, in April 1949 she commenced a refit at Malta dockyard which involved the removal of the AS gear on the quarterdeck and also the twin 40mm guns and their sponsons from the waist. Again extra accommodation was installed on the quarterdeck but X turret was not removed. *Flamingo* was similarly altered prior to 1949 and both vessels also served for many years in the Gulf area.

Many of the ships of the class in commission in the Far East at the end of the war remained in the area to assist in the maintenance of a British presence. One of these, *Amethyst*, became a household name following her famous exploit on the Yangtse river in late 1949. Trapped by the

Above:
The numerous 'Hunt' class escort destroyers were redesignated as AA frigates in the postwar era. HMS *Brocklesby* was the last survivor in Royal Navy service and acted as a trials and training ship until decommissioned in 1963. *Wright & Logan*

Below:
HMS *Brissenden*, shown at Malta in 1946, was one of only two Type IV 'Hunt' class frigates. Their distinctive feature was the hull form with the forecastle deck extended aft, a characteristic which was to be copied in many postwar frigate designs. *Wright & Logan*

Bottom:
The 'Black Swan' class frigates evolved from the preceding 'Egret' class of three ships of which HMS *Pelican* was the only one to survive the war. In this 1945 view she retains her tripod foremast, and the multiple 2pdr mounting aft has been supplemented by four single 40mm guns. *Wright & Logan*

advancing Chinese communist forces at Nanking, where she was acting as guardship for the British diplomatic community, she was heavily shelled and trapped in the river nearly 200 miles from the sea. After months of diplomatic activity had failed to obtain the ship's release, Lt-Cdr J. Kerrans led the ship on an epic and dramatic night-time dash along the heavily-guarded river to the freedom of the sea. The exploit caught the imagination of the country and the ship was given a warm welcome when she returned to Devonport in November 1949, still bearing the scars of her action. Following a refit, she sailed again for the Far East in July 1950, where she rejoined the 3rd Frigate Flotilla in time to see more action in the Korean War. *Black Swan*, the name ship of the class, had been one of the ships waiting anxiously off the mouth of the Yangtse for the *Amethyst* to make her breakout and was later in action herself. In June 1950 she was assigned to Task Group 96.5 stationed off the east coast of Korea and later was involved in an action when five out of six attacking North Korean gunboats were sunk. During the course of the Korean War several ships of the class had their light AA armament modernised and increased. *Modeste*, for example, by 1952 carried no less than eight 40mm guns disposed as two single mountings in the bridge wings, two twin mountings amidships and two more single guns on the quarterdeck.

Following the end of the Korean War and the rundown of forces in the Far East, several vessels returned to the UK and were laid up prior to disposal and scrapping. While the activity in the Far East had held the limelight, other 'Black Swans' were carrying out arduous duties in other parts of the world. In the confused situation following the setting up of an independent state of Israel, British ships were involved in patrols designed to prevent the flow of unauthorised refugees and arms into the area. The 3rd Frigate Flotilla, consisting of *Pelican* (one of the forerunners of the 'Black Swan' class), *Peacock*, *Magpie* and *Mermaid*, took part in the so-called Haifa Patrol and later in the Red Sea patrolled the Gulf of Aqaba before finally returning home in 1952. In the South Atlantic *Snipe* found herself in an encounter with an Argentine gunboat as she was engaged in re-establishing British posts at Port Lockroy and Admiralty Bay on King George Island in the South Shetlands.

In 1949, *Whimbrel* was sold to the Egyptian Navy and was renamed *El Malek Farouq*. In 1954, following the deposing of King Farouq and the rise of Col Nasser, the ship was again renamed and became the *Tarik*. The only other vessels to be transferred to foreign navies were four ships which went to the newly reformed West German Navy in 1958 and 1959. The four vessels concerned (*Mermaid*, *Flamingo*, *Hart*, *Acteon*) were renamed *Scharnhorst*, *Graf Spee*, *Scheer* and *Hipper* respectively. While these were, no doubt, cherished names in the German Navy, there seemed something incongruous about small escort vessels carrying names previously borne by famous battlecruisers and heavy cruisers. However, they

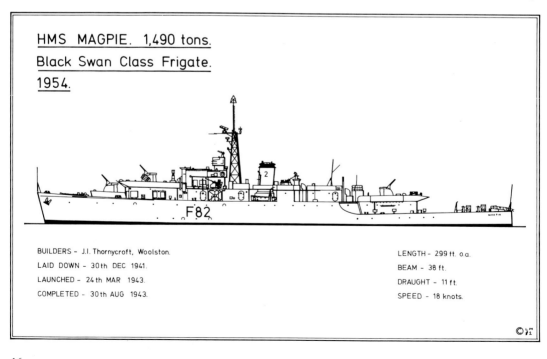

HMS MAGPIE. 1,490 tons.
Black Swan Class Frigate.
1954.

F82

BUILDERS – J.I. Thornycroft, Woolston.
LAID DOWN – 30th DEC 1941.
LAUNCHED – 24th MAR 1943.
COMPLETED – 30th AUG 1943.

LENGTH – 299 ft. o.a.
BEAM – 38 ft.
DRAUGHT – 11 ft.
SPEED – 18 knots.

proved useful training vessels for the new navy and served for many years with their new owners, the last being scrapped in 1972.

Erne, one of the original 'Black Swans', was allocated to the Wessex division of the Royal Navy Volunteer Reserve as a drill ship in 1951 and served in this role until 1965 when she was sold and scrapped.

Others continued in service, particularly with the 3rd Frigate Flotilla in the Far East, until the late 1950s and early 1960s. As the new frigates came into service they were gradually withdrawn until the last ship in Royal Navy service, *Crane*, paid off at Portsmouth in 1961.

Like most of the other wartime frigates, the 'Black Swan' class saw much useful service after the war in all corners of the world where their heavy gun armament on a relatively small ship provided an economic projection of British seapower. In the postwar ASW situation their limitations as anti-submarine vessels were recognised and in 1951 it was proposed to modify some vessels to improve their AS capabilities. The modifications involved the removal of B turret to make room for a single Squid mortar and the fitting of updated radar and sonar gear. Such a modification would not have been particularly effective due to the relatively slow speed (18kt) of the 'Black Swan' type and in any case by this time all resources were involved in the construction of new types and the conversion of destroyers to fast AS frigates.

Name	Number	Builder	Laid Down	Launched	Completed	Remarks
Acteon	U07/F07	J. I. Thornycroft, Woolston	15/5/44	25/7/45	24/7/46	W. German Navy 1958. For disposal 1964.
Alacrity	U60/F60	W. Denny and Bros, Dumbarton	5/4/43	1/9/44	13/4/45	Sold Arnott Young. Arrived Troon 3/11/56 for scrapping after hull stripped at Dalmuir.
Amethyst	U16/F116	Alex Stephens and Sons, Linthouse	25/3/42	7/5/43	2/11/43	Sold Demmelweek and Redding. Arrived Plymouth 18/1/57 for scrapping.
Black Swan	L57/F57	Yarrow and Co, Scotstoun	20/6/38	7/7/39	27/1/40	Sold West of Scotland Sbkg. Arrived Troon 13/9/56 for scrapping.
Crane	U23/F123	W. Denny and Bros, Dumbarton	13/6/41	9/11/42	10/5/44	Sold Lacmonts. Arrived Queenborough 1965 for scrap.
Cygnet	U38/F38	Cammell Laird, Birkenhead	30/8/41	28/7/42	1/12/42	Sold Sbkg Industries. Arrived Rosyth 16/3/56 for scrapping.
Erne	U03	Furness Shipbuilding, Haverton Hill	26/5/38	5/8/40	26/4/41	RNVR drillship (Solent), 1951. Broken up Antwerp, 1965.
Flamingo	L18/F18	Yarrow and Co, Scotstoun	26/5/38	18/4/39	3/11/39	W. German Navy 1959. Broken up 1965.
Hart	U58/F58	Alex Stephens and Sons, Linthouse	27/3/42	7/7/43	12/12/43	W. German Navy 1958. Broken up 1969.
Hind	U39/F39	W. Denny and Bros, Dumbarton	31/8/42	30/9/43	11/4/44	Sold Clayton and Davie. Arrived Dunston 10/2/58 for scrapping.
Magpie	U82/F82	J. I. Thornycroft, Woolston	30/12/41	24/3/43	30/8/43	Sold Hughes Bolckow. Arrived Blyth 12/7/59 for scrapping.
Mermaid	U30/F30	W. Denny and Bros, Dumbarton	8/9/42	11/12/43	12/5/43	W. German Navy 1958. Broken up 1958.
Modeste	U42/F42	Chatham Dockyard	15/2/43	29/1/44	3/9/45	Sold J. A. White. Arrived St Davids on Forth 11/3/61 for scrapping.
Nereide	U64/F64	Chatham Dockyard	15/2/43	29/1/44	6/5/46	Sold P. and W. McLellan. Arrived Bo'ness 18/5/58 for scrap.

Top:
HMS *Snipe*, a 'Modified Black Swan' class frigate, was serving with the West Indies squadron when this photograph was taken in 1948. Ships of this class were extensively deployed overseas on patrol duties in the postwar years. *Maritime Photo Library*

Above and below:
HMS *Starling* (F66) and *Redpole* (F69) were converted for use as navigation training ships in 1948/49 entailing the removal of all armament and the erection of various deckhouses. While both stepped new mainmasts, *Redpole* retained her tripod foremast. *Real Photographs*

Name	Number	Builder	Laid Down	Launched	Completed	Remarks
Opossum	U33/F33	W. Denny and Bros, Dumbarton	28/7/43	30/11/44	16/1/45	Sold Demmelweek and Redding. Arrived Plymouth 24/6/60 for scrapping.
Peacock	U96/F96	J. I. Thornycroft and Co, Woolston	29/11/42	11/12/43	10/5/44	Sold Sbkg Industries. Arrived Rosyth 7/5/58 for scrap.
Pheasant	U49/F49	Yarrow and Co, Scotstoun	17/3/42	21/12/42	12/5/43	Sold West of Scotland Sbkg. Arrived Troon 15/1/63 for scrapping.
Redpole	U69/F69	Yarrow and Co, Scotstoun	18/5/42	25/2/43	24/6/43	Sold J. A. White. Arrived St Davids on Forth 20/11/60 for scrapping.
Snipe	U20/F20	W. Denny and Bros, Dumbarton	21/9/44	20/12/45	9/9/46	Sold J. Cashmore. Arrived Newport 23/8/60 for scrap.
Sparrow	U71/F71	W. Denny and Bros, Dumbarton	30/11/44	18/2/46	16/12/46	Sold Sbkg Industries. Arrived Rosyth 26/5/58 for scrap.
Starling	U66/F66	Fairfield Shipbuilding Co, Govan	21/10/41	14/10/42	1/4/43	Sold Lacmonts. Arrived Queenborough 6/7/65 for scrapping.
Whimbrel	U29	Yarrow and Co, Scotstoun	31/10/41	25/8/42	13/1/43	Transferred to Egyptian Navy 1949.
Woodcock	U90/F90	Fairfield Shipbuilding Co, Govan	21/10/41	26/11/42	29/5/43	Sold Sbkg Industries. Arrived Rosyth 28/11/55 for scrapping.
Wren	U28/F28	W. Denny and Bros, Dumbarton	27/2/41	11/8/42	4/2/43	Sold Sbkg Industries and arrived Rosyth 2/2/56 for scrapping.
Wild Goose	U45/F45	Yarrow and Co, Scotstoun	28/1/42	14/10/42	11/3/43	Sold P. and W. McLellan. Arrived Bo'ness 27/2/56 for scrapping.

Data: HMS *Opossum*, 1949
Displacement: 1,490 tons standard; 1,925 tons full load
Length: 299ft oa
Beam: 38ft
Draught: 11ft full load
Guns: 6 × 4in Mk XVI (3 × 2) in Mk XIX mountings, 8 × 40mm AA (2 × 2, 4 × 1) in Mk V twin and Mk VII single mountings
AS weapons: Split Hedgehog multiple spigot mortar mounted on B gundeck
Machinery: 2 × Admiralty three-drum boilers operating at 250lb/sq in. Parsons geared turbines driving two shafts giving a total of 4,300shp
Speed: 18kt
Oil fuel: 415 tons
Complement: 192

Note: Considerable variation in close range armament occurred throughout the class

'Castle' Class AS Frigates

The pressing need for escort vessels in World War 2 led to the maximum utilisation of shipbuilding capacity in the United Kingdom. Although the 'River' class frigates and their later derivatives, the 'Loch/Bay' class, represented the ideal type of escort vessel for the Royal Navy, it was decided that there was still a requirement for a smaller and simpler vessel which could make use of the capacity of the smaller shipyards. Accordingly the design team at Smith's Dock, which had been responsible for the original 'Flower' class corvette design, drew up plans for a new and larger corvette. The new type, to be named after British castles, was nearly 50ft longer than the preceding 'Flower' class and featured improved accommodation, more oil fuel and a modernised armament.

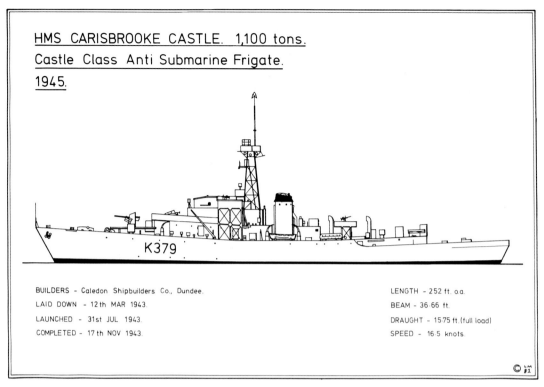

HMS CARISBROOKE CASTLE. 1,100 tons.
Castle Class Anti Submarine Frigate.
1945.

K379

BUILDERS - Caledon Shipbuilders Co., Dundee.

LAID DOWN - 12th MAR 1943.

LAUNCHED - 31st JUL 1943.

COMPLETED - 17th NOV 1943.

LENGTH - 252 ft. o.a.

BEAM - 36.66 ft.

DRAUGHT - 15.75 ft. (full load)

SPEED - 16.5 knots.

© LM

The first vessel, *Hadleigh Castle*, was laid down in April 1943, and was completed in the amazingly short time of just over five months. The 'Castles' were good-looking ships with well proportioned lines and a workmanlike look about them. Main armament comprised a single 4in gun on the forecastle with a single Squid three-barrelled AS mortar mounted behind it, just in front of the bridge. Initially the light AA armament consisted of six 20mm guns mounted as two singles in the bridge wings and two twin mountings aft. Extra 20mm guns were fitted in some vessels. At the top of the lattice mast was the aerial of the Type 272 radar with HF/DF mounted above it. Machinery was the same as the 'Flower' class corvettes but speed rose by half a knot, to 16½kt, as a result of the greater hull length.

Following approval of the design, a vast programme was put in hand in early 1943 with 59 vessels being ordered from British yards and further orders being placed in Canada. In December 1943, a reappraisal of the whole frigate and corvette building programme was carried out. This was occasioned by the fact that the Battle of the Atlantic, while not won outright, was definitely running in the Allies' favour and that, as a result, the amount of new construction required could be safely reduced. The facilities thus freed could be used for other priority work such as the construction of landing craft. One result of this

review was that future construction would concentrate on frigate types and no more corvettes would be ordered. Accordingly 15 of the ships ordered from UK yards were cancelled as were all those ordered from Canadian yards. Of the remainder, five were completed as mercantile rescue ships, one was transferred to the Norwegian Navy on completion, 12 were commissioned into the Royal Canadian Navy, which left a total of 26 completed for the Royal Navy. Two vessels, *Denbigh Castle* and *Hurst Castle*, were sunk in action so that at the end of the war in 1945 only 24 remained in service.

Following the end of hostilities most of the class paid off into reserve. Already their small size and slow speed made them obsolescent as front line AS vessels, although they proved useful in various roles such as training and coastal patrol. In 1948 they were redesignated 'Frigates (2nd Rate)' and their pendant number changed to Flag F superior in common with other wartime escort classes. Also in 1948 a scheme was put forward to modernise the class. Changes would have included the replacement of the single 4in gun with a Mk XIX twin mounting, replacing the previous radar with a Type 293Q and the addition of AS homing torpedoes which were under development at that time. In the event this scheme was not proceeded with, probably on the grounds of limited cost effectiveness. Modification to the class in the postwar period was limited mainly to fitting an

Above:
For their size the 'Black Swan' class were heavily armed. Shown serving with the 2nd Training Squadron in 1953, HMS *Cygnet* carries mountings for eight 40mm guns as well as the six 4in and is fitted with a Type 293 radar on the foremast, a Type 291 on the pole mainmast and Type 285 on the gunnery director. *Skyfotos*

Below:
HMS *Bamborough Castle* entering Portsmouth in 1946 is little altered from her wartime appearance. A Type 272 radar with its distinctive 'lantern' is carried at the top of the lattice foremast and the light AA armament consists of only four 20mm guns. *Wright & Logan*

improved radar and replacing the twin 20mm guns by two single 40mm mountings. The original Type 272 radar was replaced in most vessels by the later Type 277 as fitted to the 'Loch' class. This programme had in fact already started before the end of the war. In the 1950s those ships in commission were fitted with the new Type 974 navigation radar, with the aerial installed on a small platform projecting forward from the lattice mast.

In 1951, the only ships in commission were *Flint Castle*, *Hedingham Castle*, *Leeds Castle*, *Oakham Castle* and *Tintagel Castle*. A few years later the class was represented at the Coronation Review by *Caistor Castle*, *Carisbrooke Castle*, *Knaresborough Castle*, *Hedingham Castle*, *Leeds Castle*, *Flint Castle* and *Tintagel Castle*. Those vessels temporarily out of reserve, such as *Caistor Castle*, appeared with their armament cocooned and were really only there to make the numbers up.

Oakham Castle was converted to an Atlantic weather ship by James Lamont and Co, Port Glasgow, and was commissioned under Air Ministry ownership as the *Weather Reporter* on 16 May 1958; she replaced a 'Flower' class weather ship conversion named *Weather Explorer*. That left three other 'Flower' class conversions remaining in service and these were later replaced by three more 'Castle' class vessels in 1960. The three new ships were *Weather Monitor* (ex-*Pevensey Castle*), *Weather Adviser* (ex-*Amberley Castle*) and *Weather Surveyor* (ex-*Rushen Castle*) and all four weather ships gave sterling service well into the 1950s before the advent of satellites made them redundant.

The vessels converted to weather ships were the last of the class to survive, the rest have been withdrawn and scrapped by 1960. One of the first to go was *Berkeley Castle* which was damaged when she capsized in dry dock at Sheerness during the disastrous East Coast floods in February 1953. Up for disposal in 1955, she was scrapped in 1956 along with *Caistor Castle* and *Knaresborough Castle*. By 1958 only eight vessels remained with the Royal Navy and all of these were in reserve and due for disposal. Except for those converted to weather ships, they were all scrapped in the next two years.

Although a useful type at the time of building, the 'Castle' class was rapidly outmoded in the postwar era and had little effect on mainsteam frigate development.

Name	Number	Builder	Laid Down	Launched	Completed	Remarks
Allington Castle	K689/F89	Fleming and Ferguson, Paisley	22/7/43	29/2/44	19/6/44	Broken up Sunderland, 1958.
Alnwick Castle	K405/F105	Geo Brown and Co, Greenock	12/6/43	23/5/44	11/11/44	Broken up Sunderland, 1958.
Amberley Castle	K386/F286	S. P. Austin and Son, Sunderland	31/5/43	27/11/43	24/11/44	Air Ministry *Weather Adviser*, 1960.
Bamborough Castle	K386/F12	J. Lewis and Sons, Aberdeen	1/7/43	11/1/44	30/5/44	Broken up Llanelly, 1959.
Berkely Castle	K387/F387	Barclay Curle and Co, Glasgow	23/3/43	19/8/43	18/11/43	Broken up Grays, 1956.
Caistor Castle	K690/F690	J. Lewis and Sons, Aberdeen	28/8/43	22/5/44	29/9/44	Broken up West of of Scotland Sbkg, Troon, 1956.
Carisbrooke Castle	K379/F379	Caledon Shipbuilding Co, Dundee	12/3/43	31/7/43	17/11/43	Broken up Industries, Faslane, 1958.
Dumbarton Castle	K388/F388	Caledon Shipbuilding Co, Dundee	6/5/43	28/9/43	25/2/44	Broken up Gateshead, 1961.
Farnham Castle	K413/F413	John Crown and Sons, Sunderland	26/6/43	25/4/44	31/1/45	Broken up Gateshead, 1960.
Flint Castle	K383/F383	H. Robb, Leith	20/4/43	1/9/43	31/12/43	Broken up Faslane, 1958.
Hadleigh Castle	K355/F355	Smiths Dock, Middlesbrough	4/4/43	21/6/43	18/9/43	Broken up Gateshead, 1959.
Hedingham Castle	K529/F386	John Crown and Sons, Sunderland	2/11/43	30/10/44	12/5/45	Broken up Granton, 1958.
Kenilworth Castle	K420/F420	Smiths Dock Co Ltd, Middlesbrough	7/5/43	17/8/43	22/11/43	Broken up Llanelly, 1959.

**HMS *Leeds Castle* was one of several 'Castle' class used
for training purposes in the postwar years with the 2nd
Training Squadron based at Portland. The Squid mortar
can be clearly seen just forward of the bridge and also
visible are the rocket rails on the side of the 4in gun shield
for launching illuminating flares.** *Skyfotos*

Below:
**HMS *Carisbrooke Castle* (F379) and *Caistor Castle* at the
Coronation Review off Spithead in 1953. Both ships carry
a Type 277 radar and two single 40mm guns have
replaced the original 20mm guns aft of the funnel.**
Skyfotos

Name	Number	Builder	Laid Down	Launched	Completed	Remarks
Knaresborough Castle	K389/F389	Blyth Shipbuilding Co	22/4/43	28/9/43	5/4/44	Broken up Port Glasgow, 1956.
Lancaster Castle	K691/F691	Fleming and Ferguson, Paisley	10/9/43	14/4/44	15/9/44	Broken up Gateshead, 1960.
Launceston Castle	K397/F397	Blyth Shipbuilding Co	27/5/43	27/11/43	20/6/44	Broken up St Davids on Forth, 1959.
Leeds Castle	K384/F384	Wm Pickersgill and Sons, Sunderland	22/4/43	12/10/43	15/2/44	Broken up T. W. Ward, Grays, 1968.
Morpeth Castle	K693/F693	Wm Pickersgill and Sons, Sunderland	23/6/43	26/11/43	13/7/44	Broken up E. Rees, Llanelly, 1960.
Oakham Castle	K530/F530	A. and J. Inglis, Pointhouse	30/11/43	20/7/44	10/12/44	Air Ministry *Weather Reporter*, 1958.
Oxford Castle	K692/F692	Harland and Wolff, Belfast	21/6/43	11/12/43	10/3/44	Broken up T. W. Ward, Briton Ferry, 1960.
Pevensey Castle	K449/F449	Harland and Wolff, Belfast	21/6/43	11/1/44	10/6/44	Air Ministry *Weather Monitor*, 1960.
Portchester Castle	K362/F362	Swan Hunter, Wallsend	17/3/43	21/6/43	8/11/43	Broken up West of Scotland Sbkg, Troon, 1958.
Rushen Castle	K372/F372	Swan Hunter, Wallsend	8/4/43	16/7/43	24/2/44	Air Ministry *Weather Surveyor*, 1960.
Tintagel Castle	K399/F399	Ailsa Shipbuilding Co, Troon	29/4/43	13/12/43	7/4/44	Broken up West of Scotland Sbkg, Troon, 1958.

Data: Postwar service
Displacement: 1,100 tons standard; 1,580 tons full load
Length: 252ft oa
Beam: 36¾ft
Draught: 14ft
Guns: 1 × 4in Mk XIX on Mk XXIV mounting
2 × 40mm AA (2 × 1)
2 × 20mm (2 × 1)

AS weapons: 1 × Squid three-barrelled AS mortar.
2 × depth charge throwers and one rail (15 depth charges)
Machinery: 2 × Admiralty three-drum boilers.
Four-cylinder triple expansion reciprocating engine driving one shaft giving a total of 2,880ihp
Speed: 16½kt
Oil fuel: 480 tons
Complement: 96

'Loch' Class AS Frigates

The 'Loch' class of AS frigates represented the final product of wartime experience in frigate design and operation. It was basically a redesigned version of the successful 'River' class and was optimised for mass production on dispersed sites. To facilitate this, the ship was built up of prefabricated sections which could be constructed at the dispersed sites and moved by road or rail to an assembly slipway. Each section had maximum dimensions of: length 29ft; width 8ft 6in; and height 8ft 6in. Maximum weight of each section was set at 2½ tons to suit crane capacity at the shipyards. Eighty per cent of the hull and superstructure was made up of prefabricated units, the rest of the structure being worked in by the assembly yard. The setting up of the organisation

necessary to run a widely dispersed production system was a massive task, and took some time. However, once in operation, the time required to complete a frigate was drastically reduced. Whereas the average time taken to complete a conventionally constructed 'River' class frigate was in the order of 15 to 18 months, a prefabricated 'Loch' class frigate was completed in an average time of 10 or 11 months. Had the war continued past 1945, building times would probably have fallen even more as the tempo of production increased. As it was, of the 110 ships ordered under the original programme, only 28 'Loch' class were completed although a further 19 were completed as 'Bay' class AA frigates (qv) and eight converted to non-frigate uses. In order to simplify

Above:
As originally completed the 'Loch' class was armed with a
single 4in gun forward, a quadruple 2pdr aft, and varying
numbers of 20mm guns. This arrangement is illustrated in
this view of HMS *Loch Alvie*. *Real Photographs*

Right:
Loch Fada was one of seven ships modernised in the
mid-1950s. Armament was changed to one twin 4in
Mk XIX mounting, one Mk V twin 40mm aft, and four
single 40mm guns. The Squid mortars were retained and
can be clearly seen just forward of the bridge. A
Type 277Q radar is carried on the lattice foremast.
Real Photographs

Below:
Several of the modernised 'Loch' class were further
modified by an extension of the bridge structure to
incorporate an enlarged operations room. This can be
seen in this 1959 view of HMS *Loch Insh*.
Wright & Logan

production, curved structures were eliminated wherever possible and one noticeable result of this was that the deck sheer was reduced to three straight lines instead of a continuous and more graceful curve from bow to stern. This introduced a distinct kink in the upper deck just in front of the foremast, although the revised hull form showed no adverse performance features compared with the previous 'River' class.

As completed the ships displaced 1,435 tons (standard) on a length of 307ft (oa), a beam of 38½ft and a full load draught of 12ft. Machinery consisted of four-cylinder triple-expansion reciprocating engines driving two shafts and giving 5,500ihp, which in turn gave revolutions for 19½kt. (*Loch Tralaig* and *Loch Arkaig* were fitted with double reduction geared turbines with an output of 6,500shp.) Armament consisted of a single Mk V 4in gun, a quadruple 2pdr pom-pom and several single 20mm guns. For anti-submarine use two Squid AS mortars were mounted forward of the bridge with an all-round screen protecting the operating crews from the worst of the weather, and a depth charge thrower and rail on the quarterdeck. Sonar Type 144 was fitted for search purposes and to assist accurate Squid attacks, Sonar Type 147b depth-finding sonar was carried.

A strong lattice foremast provided the platform for the Type 277 search radar which could detect surface targets out to 15 or 20 miles and aerial targets out to 40 miles. A pole extension to the mast carried the standard HF/DF aerial and IFF interrogators and responders were also fitted.

Of the 28 vessels completed, three were transferred on completion to the South African Navy and never served with the Royal Navy. The three vessels concerned, *Loch Ard*, *Loch Boisdale* and *Loch Cree* were renamed on transfer and became *Transvaal*, *Good Hope* and *Natal* respectively. A further three vessels (*Loch Achanalt*, *Loch Alvie*, *Loch Morlich*) were transferred to the Royal Canadian Navy but returned to Royal Navy ownership after the end of the war.

Following the end of hostilities against Japan most of the class paid off into reserve with the exception of *Loch Glendhu* and *Loch Quoich* which remained active in the Far East, and *Loch Arkaig*, *Loch Fada*, *Loch Tralaig* and *Loch Veyatie* at home. In 1948 six of the laid-up ships were taken out of reserve, refitted and transferred to the New Zealand Navy. The ships concerned, together with their new names and final disposal are listed below:

Loch Achanalt (Pukaki)	F424	Transferred 3/9/48. Broken up Hong Kong, 1966.
Loch Achray (Kaniere)	F426	Transferred 7/7/48. Broken up Hong Kong, 1967.
Loch Eck (Hawea)	F422	Transferred 1/10/48. Broken up Hong Kong, 1966.
Loch Katrine (Rotoiti)	F625	Transferred 7/7/49. Broken up Hong Kong, 1967.

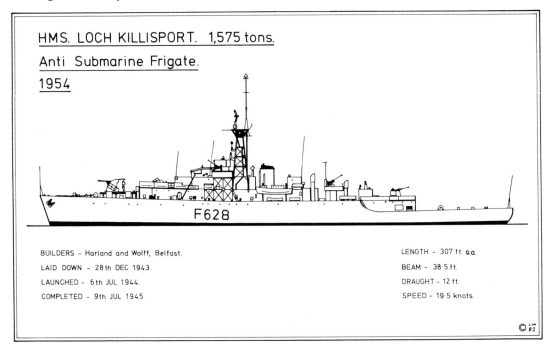

HMS. LOCH KILLISPORT. 1,575 tons.

Anti Submarine Frigate.

1954

F628

BUILDERS - Harland and Wolff, Belfast.	LENGTH - 307 ft. o.a.
LAID DOWN - 28th DEC 1943.	BEAM - 38·5 ft.
LAUNCHED - 6th JUL 1944.	DRAUGHT - 12 ft.
COMPLETED - 9th JUL 1945.	SPEED - 19·5 knots.

© 72

Top:
HMS *Loch Ruthven* at the 1953 Coronation Review with the Type 16 frigate HMS *Orwell* and two 'Castle' class in the background. At this time the ship was serving with the Londonderry-based anti-submarine training squadron (3rd TS). *Skyfotos*

Above:
In the early 1960s HMS *Loch Killisport* was fitted with an experimental glassfibre gunshield for the twin 4in

mounting and subsequently this material was used in the gunhouse of the Mk 8 automatic 4.5in gun mounted on the Type 21 and later ships. *Loch Killisport* decommissioned in 1965. *IWM 30518*

Below:
HMS *Loch Insh* was sold to Malaya in 1964 and was renamed *Hang Tuah*. She was modified by the erection of an extended deckhouse covered by a helicopter landing deck right aft. *Wright & Logan*

Loch Morlich (Tutira)	F517	Transferred 11/4/49. Broken up Hong Kong, 1962.
Loch Shin (Taupo)	F421	Transferred 3/9/48. Broken up Hong Kong, 1962.

Hawea and *Taupo* served with the Mediterranean Fleet in 1950 on an exchange basis.

The start of the Korean War saw the reactivation of several ships from the reserve fleet, including nine 'Loch' class which were formed into two frigate squadrons. *Loch Craggie, Loch Dungevan, Loch Lomond, Loch More* and *Loch Scavaig* were recommissioned for service in the Mediterranean where they replaced the destroyers *Chaplet, Childers* and *Cheviot*. At home, *Loch Alvie, Loch Fyne, Loch Insh* and *Loch Killisport* displaced the destroyers *Barrossa, Alamein, Aisne* and *Jutland*. The new frigate squadrons remained active until 1952 when the ships were paid off, although seven were retained in service and were earmarked for a modernisation programme which commenced in 1953. Also in 1953, two vessels represented the class at the Spithead Coronation Review — *Loch Ruthven* and *Loch Veyatie*.

The modernisation programme referred to involved mainly changes in armament. The single 4in gun was replaced by a Mk XVI twin 4in mounting with its associated director positioned on the after end of the bridge. The previous mixed light AA armament was removed and replaced by a uniform battery of six 40mm guns consisting of a Mk V twin mounting in the position formerly occupied by the pom-poms, and four single mountings. The single guns were positioned in the bridge wings and on either beam abaft the funnel. The Type 277 radar was retained but improved communication equipment was fitted. The seven ships to undergo modernisation were *Loch Alvie, Loch Fada, Loch Fyne, Loch Insh, Loch Killisport, Loch Lomond* and *Loch Ruthven*.

The modernised ships saw extensive service, particularly in the Middle and Far East where their general handiness and adequate gun armament made them suitable for peacetime policing and patrolling, as well as the traditional showing-the-flag duties. To assist her in the discharge of these duties, a detachment of Royal Marines was embarked in *Loch Killisport* in July 1956. She thus became the first Royal Navy frigate to carry Royal Marines as part of her normal complement, a practice which was later applied to other frigate classes. The original detachment consisted of one officer, four NCOs and 17 marines.

While the modernised ships continued in service, other ships of the class were being paid off and scrapped. First to go were *Loch Glendhu* and *Loch Quoich* in 1957, followed by *Loch Scavaig*

and *Loch Tarbert* in 1959. The other unmodernised ships were scrapped in the 1960s.

Of the modernised ships, *Loch Alvie, Loch Fyne, Loch Ruthven* and *Loch Insh* were withdrawn in 1960/61 and subsequently scrapped with the exception of *Loch Insh* which was sold to the Malaysian Navy in 1964 and saw several years' useful service before being withdrawn from service in 1977. The three remaining ships (*Loch Lomond, Loch Fada* and *Loch Killisport*) underwent a major refit to suit them for service east of Suez. Work done included improvements to accommodation and air conditioning of some of the internal spaces. Following this refit the vessels continued in service for a few more years with *Loch Lomond* paying off in 1964, *Loch Killisport* in 1965, and finally *Loch Fada* in 1967. *Loch Fada* was the last of the wartime-built frigates in service with the Royal Navy and her passing finally severed the connection between the wartime frigate types and the entirely different postwar types.

Of the 28 'Loch' class vessels completed, three were transferred on completion to the South African Navy and later a further six were transferred to the New Zealand Navy. The fate of the remaining 19 vessels of the class is listed below:

Loch Alvie Broken up, in the Far East (possibly Singapore), 1965.

Loch Arkaig Sold to J. J. King and arrived Gateshead 28/1/60 for scrapping.

Loch Craggie Sold to Dantos Leal and arrived Lisbon 25/10/63 for scrapping.

Loch Dunvegan Sold to T. Ward and arrived Briton Ferry 25/8/60 for scrapping.

Loch Fada Sold to Shipbreaking Industries Ltd and arrived Faslane 1970 for scrapping.

Loch Fyne Sold to J. Cashmore and arrived Newport, Wales, for scrapping 6/8/70.

Loch Glendhu Sold to Clayton and Davie and arrived Dunston, Gateshead, for scrapping 14/11/57.

Loch Gorm Sold to Kavounides Shipping Co, Greece, in 1961 and converted to passenger ship. Scrapped Yugoslavia in 1966.

Loch Insh Malaysian Navy *Hang Tuah* 1964. Withdrawn from service 1977, and scrapped.

Loch Killin Sold to J. Cashmore and arrived Newport 24/8/60 for scrapping.

Loch Killisport Sold to Hughes Bolckow and arrived Blyth 18/3/70 for scrapping.

Loch Lomond Sold to Shipbreaking Industries and broken up at Faslane in 1968.

Loch Quoich sold to Clayton and Davie and arrived Dunston, Gateshead for scrapping 13/11/57.

Loch Ruthven Sold to Davies and Cann and broken up at Plymouth commencing November 1966.

Loch Scavaig Broken up by Italian shipbreaker at Genoa, arrived 5/9/59.

Loch Tarbert Sold to Italian shipbreaker and arrived Genoa 18/9/59 for scrapping.

Loch Tralaig Sold to P. and W. McLellan and arrived Bo'ness for scrapping 24/8/63.

Loch Veyatie Sold to W. H. Arnott Young and arrived Dalmuir 12/8/65 for scrapping.

Two other vessels, *Loch Assynt* and *Loch Torridon*, were completed in 1945 as Coastal Forces depot ships and were respectively renamed *Derby Haven* and *Woodbridge Haven*. In 1949 *Derby Haven* was reconverted to a frigate and was sold to Iran where she was renamed *Babr*. She served until 30 October 1969, when she was paid off and subsequently scrapped a few years later. *Woodbridge Haven* remained with the Royal Navy and was variously used as a training and target ship before being scrapped by Hughes Bolckow at Blyth, arriving there on 12 August 1965. Her final role before paying off was as a minesweeper support vessel.

Vessel	No	Builder	Laid Down	Launched	Completed
Loch Achanalt	F424 (K424)	H. Robb, Leith	14/9/43	23/3/44	11/8/44
Loch Achray	F426 (K426)	Smiths Dock, Middlesbrough	13/12/43	7/7/44	1/2/45
Loch Alvie	F428 (K428)	Barclay Curle, Whiteinch	31/8/43	14/4/44	21/8/44
Loch Arkaig	F603 (K603)	Caledon Shipbuilding Co, Dundee	1/11/44	7/6/45	17/11/45
Loch Assynt (Derby Haven)	K438	Swan Hunter and Wigham Richardson, Tyne	11/2/44	14/12/44	2/8/45
Loch Craggie	F609 (K609)	Harland and Wolff, Govan	28/12/43	23/5/44	23/10/44
Loch Dunvegan	F425 (K425)	Charles Hill and Sons, Bristol	29/9/43	25/3/44	30/6/44
Loch Eck	F422 (K422)	Smiths Dock, Middlesbrough	25/10/43	25/4/44	7/11/44
Loch Fada	F390 (K390)	J. Brown, Clydebank	8/6/43	14/12/43	10/4/44
Loch Fyne	F429 (K429)	Burntisland Shipbuilding Co	8/12/43	24/5/44	9/11/44
Loch Glendhu	F619 (K619)	Burntisland Shipbuilding Co	29/5/44	18/10/44	23/2/45
Loch Gorm	F620 (K620)	Harland and Wolff, Govan	28/12/43	8/6/44	18/12/44
Loch Insh	F433 (K433)	H. Robb, Leith	17/11/43	10/5/44	20/10/44
Loch Katrine	F625 (K625)	H. Robb, Leith	31/12/43	21/8/44	29/12/44
Loch Killin	F391 (K391)	Burntisland Shipbuilding Co	22/6/43	29/11/43	12/4/44
Loch Killisport	F628 (K628)	Harland and Wolff	28/12/43	6/7/44	9/7/45
Loch Lomond	F437 (K437)	Caledon Shipbuilding Co, Dundee	7/12/43	19/6/44	16/11/44
Loch More	F639 (K639)	Caledon Shipbuilding Co, Dundee	16/3/44	3/10/44	24/2/45
Loch Morlich	F517 (K517)	Swan Hunter and Wigham Richardson, Tyne	15/7/43	25/1/44	2/8/44
Loch Quoich	F434 (K434)	Blyth Shipbuilding Co	3/12/43	2/9/44	11/1/45
Loch Ruthven	F645 (K645)	Charles Hill and Sons, Bristol	4/1/44	3/6/44	6/10/44
Loch Scavaig	F648 (K648)	Charles Hill and Sons, Bristol	31/3/44	9/9/44	22/12/44
Loch Shin	F421 (K421)	Swan Hunter and Wigham Richardson, Tyne	6/9/43	23/2/44	10/10/44
Loch Tarbert	F431 (K431)	Ailsa Shipbuilding Co, Troon	30/11/43	19/10/44	22/2/45
Loch Torridon (Woodbridge Haven)	K654	Swan Hunter and Wigham Richardson, Tyne	2/5/44	13/1/45	19/10/45
Loch Tralaig	F665 (K665)	Caledon Shipbuilding Co, Dundee	26/6/44	12/2/45	4/7/45
Loch Veyatie	F658 (K658)	Ailsa Shipbuilding Co, Troon	30/3/44	8/10/45	13/7/46

Data: as modified
Displacement: 1,575 tons standard, 2,400 tons full load
Length: 307ft oa
Beam: 38½ft
Draught: 12ft
Guns: 2 × 4in Mk XIV (1 × 2)
6 × 40mm AA (1 × 2, 4 × 1)
AS weapons: 2 × Squid three-barrelled AS mortars

Machinery: 2 × Admiralty three-drum boilers operating at 225lb/sq in. Four cylinder triple expansion reciprocating engines driving two shafts for total ihp of 5,500 tons (*Loch Arkaig* and *Loch Tralaig* had double reduction geared turbines giving 6,500ihp)
Speed: 19½kt
Oil fuel: 735 tons
Complement: 124-140 (originally 103)

Above:
Two 'Loch' class ships were converted during building to act as depot ships for coastal forces and submarines. One of these was *Woodbridge Haven* (ex-*Loch Torridon*) which is shown here in 1953 when she was attached to the 3rd Submarine Squadron. *Wright & Logan*

'Bay' Class AA Frigates

In 1944, as the emphasis of the war at sea moved from Europe and the North Atlantic to the Far East, a requirement arose for an escort vessel with a heavy AA firepower to accompany the British Pacific Fleet into Japanese waters. The simplest way to meet this requirement was to modify some of the 'Loch' class frigates then being built in large numbers. Accordingly plans were drawn up to modify 26 of the 'Loch' class to a new AA configuration: the new design to be designated the 'Bay' class.

The hull, machinery, superstructure and basic layout of the new class was the same as that for the 'Loch' class frigates, and the ships could be built by the same production centres. The main changes were in the armament, which consisted of two twin 4in AA mountings and two twin 40mm AA mountings. The 4in guns were carried in B position (replacing the two Squid mortars of the 'Loch' class) and 'X' position (replacing the multiple pom-pom) while the two 40mm mountings were carried on the upper deck just forward of the break in the forecastle. Fire control for the main armament was provided by a Mk V director equipped with Type 285 gunnery radar, and the 40mm guns were provided with a simple tachymetric director for each mounting. For anti-submarine use a Hedgehog mortar was situated on the forecastle in the position occupied by the 4in gun in the 'Loch' class, while aft were the usual depth charge rails and throwers.

Other radars fitted included a Type 293 with its 'Cheese' aerial on a platform at the top of the lattice mast and a Type 291 with its aerial on a pole extension above the lattice mast platform. IFF transponders and interrogators were also carried, as was medium and high frequency DF equipment. The Type 291 acted as a general air warning radar while the Type 293 was used as a target-indicating radar providing information for the Type 285 on the director to acquire the target. Altogether, the 'Bay' class frigates were effective AA platforms and were easily produced from the basic 'Loch' class design. The only serious problem to arise during the building programme was the provision of the twin 4in gun mountings, as production facilities were already fully stretched. In the event some vessels were equipped with mountings taken from other vessels which were being withdrawn from service or had been too badly damaged to be repaired.

The Admiralty originally planned to build 26 'Bay' class vessels but in fact only one was completed before VE-Day and only another seven before VJ-Day. As most of the vessels were in an advanced stage of construction, only one was cancelled and 19 were completed as designed. A further six were completed to different designs, two as despatch vessels and four as surveying ships. Of the 19 completed as frigates, all were completed by the autumn of 1946 with the exception of *Morecambe Bay* and *Mounts Bay*. Launched by the builders, W. Pickersgill of Sunderland, in 1944 and 1945 respectively, they were not finally completed until 1949 by other shipbuilders. *Morecambe Bay* was completed by J. Samuel White at Cowes and *Mounts Bay* by J. I. Thornycroft at Woolston, Southampton.

Following the end of hostilities, several of the class were consigned to the Reserve Fleet, but others continued in commission, particularly in the Far East where their heavy gun armament made them ideal for peacetime patrol work. Their excellent seakeeping qualities were demonstrated on several occasions when they rode out the fierce typhoons which were a common hazard in that area.

In 1950 *Carnarvon Bay*, *Cawsand Bay*, *Enard Bay*, *Largo Bay*, *Padstow Bay*, *Porlock Bay*, *Start Bay*, *Widemouth Bay* and *Wigtown Bay* were in reserve, while *Tremadoc Bay* was being used for training purposes. The class was represented at the Coronation Review by *Burghead Bay*, *Enards Bay*, *Largo Bay*, *Start Bay* and *Widemouth Bay*. *Start Bay* was still part of the Reserve Fleet at this time and appeared at the rerview with her armament cocooned.

By the mid-1950s the usefulness of the class as front line warships was declining. The 4in guns and World War 2 fire control system were no match for the new generations of jet aircraft and the ships' relatively low speed and rudimentary AS equipment was of little effective use against modern submarines. The modernisation of the 'Loch' class had produced ships with adequate firepower for peacetime patrolling while at the same time their twin Squid mortars still retained a useful AS capability. In consequence it was no surprise when *St Austell Bay* and *Whitesand Bay* went to the breakers in early 1956 having seen only 10 years' service since their completion. The next year two more of the class, *Enards Bay* and *Widemouth*

Bay, also went to the breakers. At the same time other vessels of the class were still active with, for example, *Burghead Bay* commissioned in May 1957 for service in the South Atlantic, *Mounts Bay* commissioning in October 1956 also for the South Atlantic, and *Cardigan Bay* commissioning at Singapore in November 1956 for further service in the Far East.

Several ships of the class were sold abroad. *Bigbury Bay* and *Burghead Bay* were transferred to the Portuguese Navy on 11 May 1959 and renamed *Pacheco Pereira* and *Alvares Cabral* respectively. Two years later, following a refit by J. I. Thornycroft, *Mounts Bay* and *Morecambe Bay* were also transferred to the Portuguese Navy and renamed *Vasco da Gama* and *Dom Francesco de Almeida*. In 1962 *Porlock Bay*, one of the last two remaining Royal Navy vessels, was transferred to the Finnish Navy and renamed *Matti Kurki*. The other vessel, *Cardigan Bay*, went to the scrapyard in 1962 as well.

As previously mentioned, several uncompleted hulls were adapted for other uses following the end of the war. Two of these, *Dundrum Bay* and *Gerrans Bay*, were completed as despatch vessels and renamed *Alert* and *Surprise*. As completed, the forward half of the ship was identical to the frigate, including the forward 4in gun mounting. Aft of the funnel all armament was deleted and extra accommodation was added on the quarter-

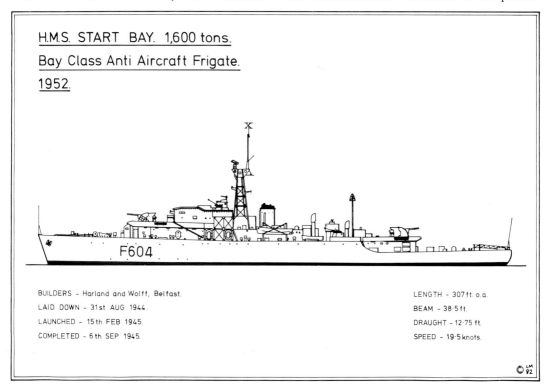

H.M.S. START BAY. 1,600 tons.

Bay Class Anti Aircraft Frigate.

1952.

F604

BUILDERS - Harland and Wolff, Belfast.	LENGTH - 307 ft. o.a.
LAID DOWN - 31st AUG 1944.	BEAM - 38·5 ft.
LAUNCHED - 15th FEB 1945.	DRAUGHT - 12·75 ft.
COMPLETED - 6th SEP 1945.	SPEED - 19·5 knots.

© LM 92

Top:
The 'Bay' class AA frigates used the same hull and machinery as the 'Loch' class and the family resemblance is clearly shown in this 1947 view of HMS *Widemouth Bay* when she still carried her wartime pendant number. The obvious alterations are to the main armament which now comprises four 4in guns in two Mk XIX twin mountings. *Maritime Photo Library*

Above:
Standard radar outfit in the 'Bay' class was a Type 293 atop the lattice foremast, Type 285 on the gunnery director and a Type 291AW on a polemast aft, although on some ships the latter was originally mounted on a pole extension to the foremast. This is HMS *Morecambe Bay* shortly after her completion in 1949. *Wright & Logan*

Below:
HMS *Largo Bay* was the first 'Bay' class ship to be launched, but was not completed until after the war. She spent most of her subsequent career in reserve except for two years from 1952 to 1954 when she was with the Rosyth-based 4th Training Squadron. *Skyfotos*

deck. Above this the forecastle deck was extended to the stern giving a large open platform. Following their completion the two ships were allocated as commander-in-chief's yachts; *Alert* to the China Station and *Surprise* to the Mediterranean. In 1953, *Surprise* returned to the United Kingdom where she underwent modifications to act as Royal Yacht at the Fleet Coronation Review in 1953. Her forward gun mounting was removed and a special platform constructed in its place for Her Majesty to use as a reviewing stand. During the review she flew the Royal Standard as well as the flag of the Flag Officer, Royal Yachts, Vice-Adm E. M. C. Abel Smith CB, CVO. Following this occasion she reverted to her original configuration and returned to the Mediterranean.

The open deck aft was useful for the ceremonial occasions associated with the presence of a commander-in-chief but, in later years, was used as a helicopter landing deck for transferring visitors and stores. Although not strictly frigates, the two vessels retained their frigate pendant numbers (F647 *Alert* and F436 *Surprise*) until their disposal in 1965 and 1971. By this time of course, the Royal Navy had shrunk to a size where luxuries such as commander-in-chief's yachts could not be justified or afforded.

Four other vessels (*Herne Bay*, *Luce Bay*, *Pegwell Bay*, *Thurso Bay*) were completed as survey ships and were renamed *Dampier*, *Dalrymple*, *Cook* and *Owen*. The conversion of the incomplete hulls was carried out by Chatham Dockyard in the case of *Dampier* and *Owen*, while the other two were completed by Devonport Dockyard. All four vessels were commissioned between 1948 and 1950.

The importance of the 'Loch/Bay' class to postwar frigate development lay not in their capabilities. Indeed, in the early 1950s they were officially classed as 'Second Rate Frigates' in recognition of the fact that they were eclipsed by the new postwar designs. Their unique feature was that they demonstrated that it was possible to produce by a dispersed organisation a range of specialised frigates based on a common hull and machinery produced to standard design criteria. The success of this concept, which was amply demonstrated by the wide variety of uses the standard hull was put to, resulted in a determined effort to produce a new range of bigger, faster and more capable frigates based again on a common hull. This was to lead to the 1945 frigate concept, to which reference will be made in the following chapters.

Above:
A stern view of HMS *Bigbury Bay*. On the quarterdeck are two single 40mm guns and depth charge throwers and racks. This ship spent most of her postwar career on the West Indies and South Atlantic stations before being sold to Portugal in 1959. *IWM MH30505*

Name	Number	Builder	Laid Down	Launched	Completed	Remarks
Bigbury Bay	K606/F06	Hall Russell (Aberdeen)	30/5/44	16/11/44	10/7/45	Portuguese Navy 1959. Sold 6/7/70 and scrapped.
Burghead Bay	K622/F622	Charles Hill and Sons, Bristol	21/9/44	3/3/45	20/9/45	Portuguese Navy 1959. Sold 23/6/71 and scrapped.
Cardigan Bay	K630/F630	H. Robb, Leith	14/4/44	28/12/44	25/6/45	Sold West of Scotland Shipbreaking. Arrived Troon for scrapping 5/3/62.
Carnarvon Bay	K636/F636	H. Robb, Leith	8/6/44	15/3/45	20/9/45	Sold Italy. Arrived La Spezia 28/8/59 for scrap.
Cawsand Bay	K644/F644	Blyth Shipbuilding Co	24/4/44	26/2/45	13/11/45	Sold Italy. Arrived Genoa 5/9/59 for scrapping.
Enards Bay	K435/F35	Smiths Dock, Middlesbrough	27/5/44	31/10/44	4/1/46	Sold Shipbreaking Industries. Arrived Faslane 15/11/57 for scrapping.

Name	Number	Builder	Laid Down	Launched	Completed	Remarks
Largo Bay	K423/F423	W. Pickersgill, Sunderland	8/2/44	3/10/44	26/1/46	Sold to T. W. Ward. Arrived Inverkeithing 11/7/58 for scrapping.
Morecambe Bay	K624/F624	W. Pickersgill, Sunderland	30/3/44	1/11/44	22/2/49	Portuguese Navy 1961. Sold 7/9/70 and scrapped.
Mounts Bay	K627/F627	W. Pickersgill, Sunderland	23/10/44	8/6/45	11/4/49	Portuguese Navy 1961. Sold 2/12/71 and scrapped.
Padstow Bay	K608/F608	H. Robb, Leith	25/9/44	24/8/45	11/3/46	Sold Italy. Arrived La Spezia 11/8/59 for scrap.
Porlock Bay	K650/F650	Charles Hill and Sons, Bristol	22/11/44	14/6/45	8/3/46	Finnish Navy 1962. Discarded 1975.
St Austell Bay	K634/F634	Harland and Wolff, Belfast	30/5/44	18/11/44	29/5/45	Sold Shipbreaking Industries. Arrived Charlestown 13/2/56 for scrap.
St Brides Bay	K600/F600	Harland and Wolff, Belfast	30/5/44	16/1/45	15/6/45	Sold Shipbreaking Industries. Arrived Faslane 3/9/62 for scrapping.
Start Bay	K604/F604	Harland and Wolff, Belfast	31/8/44	15/2/45	6/9/45	Sold J. Cashmore. Arrived Newport 7/58 for scrap.
Tremadoc Bay	K605/F605	Harland and Wolff, Belfast	31/8/44	29/3/45	11/10/45	Sold Italy. Arrived Genoa 18/9/59 for scrapping.
Veryan Bay	K651/F651	Charles Hill and Sons, Bristol	8/6/44	11/11/44	13/5/45	Sold Shipbreaking Industries. Arrived Charlestown 1/7/59 for scrapping.
Whitesand Bay	K633/F633	Harland and Wolff, Belfast	8/8/44	16/12/44	30/7/45	Sold Shipbreaking Industries. Arrived Charlestown 13/2/56 for scrapping.
Widemouth Bay	K615/F615	Harland and Wolff, Belfast	26/4/44	19/10/44	13/4/45	Sold Hughes Bolckow. Arrived Blyth 23/11/57 for scrapping.
Wigtown Bay	K616/F616	Harland and Wolff, Belfast	24/10/44	26/4/45	19/1/46	Sold Shipbreaking Industries. Arrived Faslane 4/59 for scrapping.
Alert	K647/F647	Blyth Shipbuilding Co	28/7/44	10/7/45	24/10/46	Sold T. W. Ward. Arrived Inverkeithing 31/10/71 for scrapping.
Surprise	K436/F436	Smiths Dock, Middlesbrough	21/4/44	14/3/45	9/9/46	Sold P. and W. McLellan, Arrived Bo'ness for scrapping 29/6/65

Data: As completed
Displacement: 1,600 tons standard; 2,530 tons full load
Length: 307ft oa
Beam: 38½ft
Draught: 12¾ft
Guns: 4 × 4in (2 × 2) AA in Mk XVI mountings
6 × 40mm (2 × 2, 2 × 1) AA
Alert and *Surprise* had only 2 × 4in (1 × 2) and
2 × 40mm (2 × 1)

AS weapons: 1 × Hedgehog multiple spigot mortar. Depth charge throwers and rails.
Machinery: 2 × Admiralty three-drum boilers operating at 2,251lb/sq in
Four-cylinder triple expansion engines driving two shafts giving a total of 5,500ihp
Speed: 19½kt
Oil fuel: 720 tons
Complement: 157

2 The Conversions

Type 15 (Full Conversion) Frigates

At the close of World War 2, the progress shown by German submarine design had come as a shock to the Allies. The Type XXI, for example, had an underwater speed of nearly 17kt and was equipped with a variety of torpedoes including acoustic homing weapons specifically intended for use against escort vessels. The peroxide-powered Type XXVI was even faster. Against this sort of opposition, the 19kt of the standard 'Loch' class escort was hopelessly inadequate. By 1950, the Soviet Navy had absorbed the lessons of captured German technology and was embarking on a massive production programme of the 'Whisky' class submarine which was, in effect, a straight-forward copy of the German Type XXI.

With the end of hostilities in Europe, Allied naval intelligence staff were able to unfold the story of German submarine development and the Admiralty embarked on a programme designed to produce an AS vessel capable of meeting the threat posed by the new types of submarines. In the immediate postwar period the development of new weapon systems had little financial priority and consequently progress was slow. Events in the late 1940s, such as the imposition of the Churchillian-termed 'Iron Curtain', the Berlin Airlift and the start of the Korean War, led to the realisation that the world was not about to lapse into a period of utopian peace and that it was necessary to bring our armed forces up to date. Although modern frigate designs were being finalised, it would take many years before the first of these could be in service and a faster and less expensive method was needed to provide an immediate boost to our outdated AS forces.

The answer lay in the large numbers of wartime destroyers which were in service or reserve with the Royal Navy. Starting with the 'O' class, the first of which was laid down in 1940, 80 destroyers comprising the 'O', 'P', 'Q', 'R', 'S', 'T', 'U', 'V', 'W' and 'Z' classes were built to a basically standard design. Also built were a further 32 vessels of the 'Ca', 'Ch', 'Co' and 'Cr' classes to a similar standard design. There were several variations of layout, armament and equipment, but the hull and machinery was virtually identical in all classes. Although some were sunk during the war and others were sold to foreign and Commonwealth navies in the years immediately

following the cessation of hostilities, by 1951, 47 remained with the Royal Navy as well as 26 of the 'C' class vessels. Most of the remaining ships had seen relatively little war service and were consequently in very good condition.

Accordingly, plans were drawn up to convert the basic destroyer design to a fast AS frigate. The first pair of vessels to undergo reconstruction were *Relentless* at Portsmouth Dockyard and *Rocket* at Devonport starting in 1949. All superstructure, masts and armament were removed and the hull was stripped of equipment and the machinery overhauled. The forecastle deck was then extended aft to leave only a small quarterdeck. Forward of the funnel, a new superstructure was constructed across the full width of the hull and extended forward to end in a bridge with a rounded front. The new superstructure housed a spacious operations room with new radar display and communications equipment. There was also a separate sonar room and the extended forecastle deck provided much improved and more spacious accommodation for the crew. One of the problems of wartime escort vessels had been the limited and cramped accommodation which, in bad weather, seriously affected the efficiency of the crew. With the new design, strenuous efforts were made to alleviate this by giving the sailors much improved living space as well as a modern catering system. The extended forecastle deck meant that the crew could move about the ship to their duty stations without being exposed to the weather. In fact, apart from the gun crews, the ship could be operated and fought with the crew entirely under cover. This was done not only for reasons of crew comfort but also to give the ship a limited capability to operate in zones of nuclear fallout, a factor which was to play an increasingly important part in postwar warship design.

Extensive use was made of aluminium in the reconstruction of the ships; this enabled extra superstructure areas to be added without adversely affecting stability. Many postwar designs, both British and foreign, featured aluminium super-structure sections but recently a note of caution has restricted the use of this material. This followed a serious fire on the USS *Belknap* in 1975 where, following a collision, the entire upper superstructure literally disappeared as the aluminium itself burnt away. Experience in the Falklands has also led to a reappraisal of materials used in warship construction.

As befitted their new role as frigates, the ships were given a completely new armament. The main gun armament consisted of two 4in guns in a Mk XIX twin mounting which was unusually positioned aft of the main superstructure and just forward of the quarterdeck. As such, the Type 15s became the first major British warships to have an aft-mounted main armament, a feature which gave rise to lively discussion at the time! The fire of the 4in guns was controlled by a MRS-1 director positioned just forward of the gun mounting and incorporating a Type 262 centimetric gunnery radar. Above and behind the bridge a twin 40mm Mk V (Utility) mounting was carried with fire control being provided by a STD (simple tachymetric director) mounted on a raised platform just abaft of the guns. The guns were intended mainly for AA use and in this respect the Type 15s were better off than the original destroyer design despite carrying fewer guns. The reason for this was that the original destroyer armament of four 4.5in guns had only a limited elevation, whereas the 4in Mk XIX was a true high angle mounting and was provided with a proper radar-equipped fire control system.

As frigates, the main function of these vessels was to attack submarines and to this end a heavy AS armament was carried. On the quarterdeck, just below the 4in gun mounting, were two Limbo AS three-barrelled mortars. Limbo was a development of the wartime Squid, but fired its projectile over a greater range and could be reloaded, aimed and fired by remote control. After firing the mounting was tilted on to its side so that the barrels were horizontal and in line with the loading apertures of the mortar handling rooms alongside the mountings. Hydraulic rams pushed new projectiles into the barrels which were then returned to the firing position. The Limbo was aimed and fired from the new operations room in the forward superstructure. As a weapons system, Limbo was very successful and remained in operational use for over 30 years.

As part of her conversion, *Relentless* was fitted with two single torpedo tubes on trainable mountings installed on the upper deck on either beam just abaft the mainmast. These tubes were intended to fire the then new Mk 20E torpedo which was an electrically powered acoustic homing weapon intended for anti-submarine use. As the torpedo was still under development, the tubes fitted on *Relentless* were probably intended for trials use only and they were subsequently removed when the ship was refitted in 1955/56. Unlike the Limbo system, the Mk 20E torpedo was a complete failure which was mainly due to the fact

that it was too slow to catch fast-moving submarines. Despite this, several vessels in later classes of postwar frigates were equipped to fire the torpedoes and the idea finally died out around 1960 when the tubes were removed from all vessels then so fitted.

The original tripod foremast was removed and a new lattice mast was stepped to carry new radar and communication equipment. Atop this was the ANS aerial for a Type 293Q 10cm radar which provided target information for the MRS-1 fire control system. Below this, on a small platform projecting forward of the lattice structure, was the Type 974 navigation radar aerial. Forward of the foremast and mounted atop a deckhouse was the distinctively-shaped ANU aerial for the Type 277Q surface warning radar which, as its name implied, was used for the detection of surface targets including submarine snorkels or periscopes. A pole extension to the foremast carried the HF/DF aerial while both VHF and UHF communication aerials were carried on the foremast and on a short lattice mainmast stepped amidships. Several 'whip' aerials were mounted on the funnel sides and at various points around the superstructure. These aerials were to become a familiar feature of all postwar ships and replaced the previous wire aerials which were strung between the masts. They were much more resistant to blast and battle damage.

A total of 23 vessels was converted as described and, inevitably in such a large programme, there were several variations within the class. Three vessels (*Troubridge*, *Ulster*, *Zest*) were completed with a different bridge structure which was mounted a deck higher and further back than the round-faced bridge of the other vessels. The new structure did not extend the full width of the ship and featured angled sides to give better all-round visibility to the bridge staff. The new structure was almost identical to the bridge fitted to the subsequent Types 12, 14, 41, 61 and 81 frigates and for this reason became known as the 'frigate' bridge.

The new bridge displaced the twin 40mm mounting which was now positioned at the forward end of the superstructure in front of the bridge.

The type of AS weapon fitted was also subject to variation. As already related, *Relentless* and *Rocket* (the prototype conversions) were equipped with the Limbo AS mortar but the other two 'R' class converted (*Rapid* and *Roebuck*) had two Squid mortars installed in lieu. *Troubridge*, the only 'T' class to be converted to a Type 15 frigate, was Limbo-equipped as were all 'U' class conversions including *Grenville*. The nine 'V' and 'W' class vessels were given the Squid mounting and *Zest*, the only 'Z' class converted, was equipped with Limbo.

Top:
HMS *Ulysses* in 1952 before her conversion to a Type 15 frigate. She is a typical example of the 48 almost identical Emergency Programme destroyers of the 'S' to 'Z' classes laid down in 1941/42. *Real Photographs*

Centre:
First of the new Type 15 frigates, HMS *Relentless* completed her modernisation in 1951. Originally she was

fitted with AS torpedo tubes, visible amidships, but these were subsequently removed at her first refit. *Wright & Logan*

Above:
This view of HMS *Virago*, dated June 1953, clearly shows the original outline of the destroyer hull and the extent of the new superstructure. *Wright & Logan*

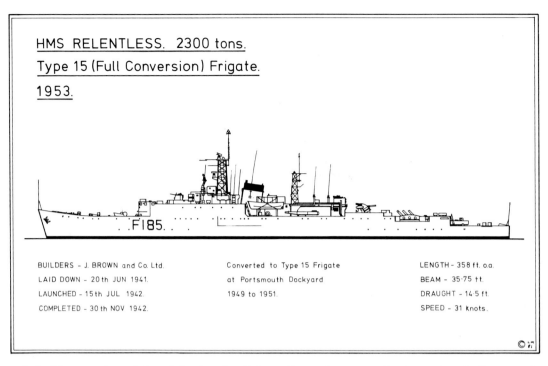

HMS RELENTLESS. 2300 tons.

Type 15 (Full Conversion) Frigate.

1953.

F185.

BUILDERS – J. BROWN and Co. Ltd.	Converted to Type 15 Frigate	LENGTH – 358 ft. o.a.
LAID DOWN – 20th JUN 1941.	at Portsmouth Dockyard	BEAM – 35·75 ft.
LAUNCHED – 15th JUL 1942.	1949 to 1951.	DRAUGHT – 14·5 ft.
COMPLETED – 30th NOV 1942.		SPEED – 31 knots.

It had been envisaged that, following the trials aboard *Relentless*, the Type 15 frigates would carry an AS torpedo armament but in the event only *Ulster* was fully equipped. Eight tubes were carried in fixed single mountings installed on each beam abreast the mainmast. Each tube was angled to fire 45° forward of the beam on each side. The tubes were removed after a while (probably 1961) when the Mk 20E torpedo was finally abandoned. The only other ship of the class to carry any AS torpedo tubes was *Undaunted*, which in 1958 carried three fixed tubes on the starboard beam but these were subsequently removed.

Undaunted was also one of two Type 15s to be fitted with a helicopter landing platform built up over the stern. The other one so fitted was *Grenville* and the work was carried out in the period 1958/59. Using these flight decks, trials were carried out with three prototype Saunders Roe P531 turbine-powered light helicopters. These operations were the first occasion when a frigate carried and operated a helicopter and, following the successful conclusion of the trials, an uprated version of the P531 was ordered in quantity for the Royal Navy. The new version became the Westland Wasp and was operated by all subsequent helicopter-equipped frigates up to and including the Type 21. *Grenville's* flightdeck was removed after a few years but *Undaunted* retained her's until the end of her career.

After conversion to Type 15 frigates, several vessels were further modified to act as training

ships and were mostly allocated to the Dartmouth Training Squadron where they were used to give sea experience to officer cadets. The modifications involved the removal of the twin 40mm mounting and the construction of an open bridge over the existing enclosed bridge. An additional deckhouse was constructed in the space previously occupied by the 40mm guns. Vessels so modified were *Venus* and *Vigilant* in 1955, followed by *Roebuck* and *Wakeful* in 1958/59. *Wakeful* subsequently had her 4in gun turret removed and extra deckhouses added aft.

Several vessels of the class were converted to act as trials and training vessels. Following the helicopter trials, *Grenville* went on to act as a trials ship for the Admiralty Surface Weapons Establishment at Portsmouth. Her 4in guns and AS mortars were removed and extra deckhouses erected aft. An extra mast was stepped in the position previously occupied by the 4in gun turret and this was used to mount experimental radio and radar equipment. Eventually the third mast was itself replaced by a massive lattice structure almost as tall as the foremast and on this was mounted the aerial of a long range surveillance radar. This was probably an early version of the Type 1022 radar now fitted to the Type 42 destroyers and to the 'Invincible' class aircraft carriers. For the trials role *Grenville* was also fitted with the enlarged open bridge over the original bridge and a glazed observation tower just in front of the foremast. *Verulam* was also used as an AS trials vessel and

Above:
HMS *Wakeful* was one of four Type 15s fitted with a raised bridge to enable them to be used for training duties with the Dartmouth Training Squadron. *IWM MH30486*

Below:
Another variation on bridge styles! The last three Type 15 conversions, including HMS *Zest* shown here, were completed with a so called 'frigate' bridge which necessitated the 40mm mounting to be moved forward. *IWM MH30485*

had her 4in guns removed and additional deckhouses added. In 1966, following a refit when her damaged stern was replaced by a section taken from *Urchin*, *Ulster* was used as a trials and training ship by ASWE. Her 40mm mounting was removed but otherwise her appearance was unaltered.

Rapid was at one time used as the seagoing training ship for HMS *Caledonia* at Rosyth. This establishment was responsible for the training of engineroom artificers and consequently her machinery was in first class order although her armament had been removed. She enjoyed a brief moment of glory when she took part in a race against HMS *Cavalier* for the title of 'Fastest Ship in the Fleet'. The race took place in July 1971 off the Firth of Forth, with the object being to cover the greatest distance in two hours. Although leading for most of the time, a boiler safety valve lifting caused a loss of boiler pressure which allowed *Cavalier* to creep ahead and win by the slenderest of margins. *Rapid* was subsequently converted to a target ship in 1974 and ended her days in this role.

Commencing in 1949, the conversion programme continued until 1957 with *Troubridge* being the last to complete. Some vessels were converted at the naval dockyards, but many were contracted out to private companies. Dates and places of conversion, together with the fate of each vessel (where known) are set out below:

Rapid converted Alex Stephens and Sons, Glasgow, 1952/53. Expended as a target 1981.

Relentless converted Portsmouth Dockyard 1949/51. Broken up T. W. Ward, Inverkeithing, 1971.

Rocket converted Devonport Dockyard, 1949/51. Sold W. H. Arnott Young; arrived Dalmuir March 1967 for scrapping.

Roebuck converted Devonport Dockyard 1952/53. Sold T. W. Ward; arrived Inverkeithing 8/8/68 for scrapping.

Troubridge converted Portsmouth Dockyard/J. Samuel White, Cowes 1955/57. Broken up J. Cashmore, Newport, 1970.

Ulster converted Chatham Dockyard 1953/56. Training hulk HMS *Raleigh*, Torpoint, 1977-80. Broken up T. W. Ward, Inverkeithing, 1980/81.

Ulysses converted Devonport Dockyard 1952/53. Broken up Plymouth, 1970.

Grenville converted private yard 1953/54. Paid off Easter 1974. Laid up Portsmouth for disposal. Broken up 1983.

Undaunted converted J. Samuel White, Cowes, 1952/54. Sunk as target off Gibraltar by combined missile and torpedo attack from HMS *Norfolk* and HMS *Swiftsure* (SSN), 1978.

Undine converted J. I. Thornycroft, Woolston,

1954. Sold J. Cashmore, Newport; arrived for scrapping 14/11/65.

Urania converted Harland and Wolff, Liverpool, 1953/54. Broken up Shipbreaking Industries, Faslane, 1971.

Urchin converted Barclay Curle 1952/54. Stern section cut off in 1966 to repair *Ulster* (qv). Sold West of Scotland Shipbreaking; arrived Troon 6/8/67 for scrapping.

Ursa converted Palmer, 1953/54. Sold J. Cashmore, Newport; arrived for scrapping September 1967.

Venus converted 1952/54 Devonport Dockyard. Broken up Briton Ferry, 1972.

Verulam converted Portsmouth Dockyard 1952. Broken up J. Cashmore, Newport, 1972.

Vigilant converted J. I. Thornycroft 1951/52. Sold Shipbreaking Industries, Faslane; arrived 4/6/65 for scrap.

Virago converted 1952/53 Chatham Dockyard. Sold Shipbreaking Industries, Faslane; arrived 4/6/65.

Volage converted J. Samuel White, Cowes, 1951/52. Broken up Portsmouth Shipbreakers, 1972.

Wakeful converted Scotts, Greenock, 1952/53. Broken up T. W. Ward, Inverkeithing, 1971.

Whirlwind converted Palmers. 1952/53. Expended as target. Sank at moorings October 1974.

Wizard converted Devonport Dockyard, 1954. Sold T. W. Ward, Inverkeithing; arrived 7/3/67 for scrapping.

Wrangler converted Harland and Wolff, Belfast 1951/52. Sold to South Africa 1957 and expended as a target, April 1976.

Zest converted Chatham Dockyard, 1954/56. Broken up W. H. Arnott Young, Dalmuir, 1970.

Several other conversions were carried out by Commonwealth navies on destroyers which had previously been transferred to them. *Quiberon*, *Quickmatch*, *Queenborough* and *Quadrant* had been transferred to the Royal Australian Navy in 1945 and were converted to Type 15 frigates in the period 1952-57. The first pair were converted at Williamstown and the other two at Cockatoo Island. The Australian conversions differed slightly from the British versions in that the bridge structure was a deck higher and set further back with the twin 40mm mounting positioned in front of it. Two conversions were carried out by the Royal Canadian Navy, which had two suitable vessels — the *Algonquin* (ex-HMS *Valentine* which transferred to the RCN on completion in 1944) and *Crescent*. Again there were minor differences from the British design: both vessels carried a twin 3in AA mounting instead of the 40mm mounting, with *Crescent* carrying the 4in mount forward and the

Above:
The Type 15s carried a Type 277Q radar abaft the bridge, a Type 293Q atop the foremast and a Type 974 navigation set lower down the mast. This is HMS *Verulam*.
Real Photographs

Below:
HMCS *Algonquin* was a 'V' class destroyer transferred on completion to the RCN in 1944. In 1954 she was converted to a fast AS frigate along the lines of the British Type 15s but there were several obvious differences. The bridge structure was considerably larger, American radar

equipment was carried on the lattice foremast and a tall funnel cap added. Armament was much heavier and comprised a twin 4in aft, a twin 3in forward and two single 40mm amidships in addition to a twin Squid installation aft. *Real Photographs*

Bottom:
HMS *Undaunted* was one of two Type 15s fitted (in 1959) with a small flightdeck aft for early trials to test the viability of operating helicopters from warships. Note the starboard Limbo mortar which is clearly visible.
Fleet Photographic Unit

3in aft. Both had enlarged bridges, two single 40mm guns and AS torpedo tubes. *Algonquin* was converted at Esquimault Dockyard in 1954 with *Crescent* following in 1956. *Crescent* was the only one of the 32 'C' class destroyers to undergo conversion to become a fast AS frigate.

As rebuilt, the new frigates were excellent AS vessels. The new design showed a thoughtful appreciation of the factors affecting AS warfare in the postwar period and they provided an effective boost for the Royal Navy's escort capability at a vital period in the Cold War of the 1950s and 1960s. There was perhaps some disappointment for traditionalists, both naval and civilian. Gone were the rakish destroyers bristling with guns and torpedo tubes, and in their place came ships looking like no other warships before them. Clean lines and few guns were the result of the changing face of naval warfare where detection and ranging equipment was almost more important than the weapons themselves. The Type 15 conversions set the scene for the development of the modern postwar frigate and subsequent designs built upon the lessons learnt with this class. The conversions represented excellent value for money and they gave a new lease of life to destroyer hulls which otherwise would probably have been discarded and scrapped much earlier. As it was, it was not until 1965 that the first of the class went to the breakers with many vessels continuing into the 1970s carrying out useful tasks as training and trials ships.

Name	No	Builder	Laid Down	Launched	Completed
Rapid	F138	Cammell Laird	16/6/41	16/7/42	20/2/43
Relentless	F185	J. Brown and Co Ltd	20/6/41	15/7/42	30/11/42
Rocket	F191	Scotts (Greenock)	14/3/41	28/10/42	4/8/42
Roebuck	F195	Scotts (Greenock)	19/6/41	10/12/42	10/6/43
Troubridge	F09	J. Brown and Co Ltd	10/11/41	23/9/42	8/3/43
Grenville	F197	Swan Hunter, Tyne	1/11/41	12/10/42	27/5/43
Ulster	F83	Swan Hunter, Tyne	12/11/41	9/11/42	30/6/43
Ulysses	F17	Cammell Laird	14/3/42	22/4/43	23/12/43
Undaunted	F53	Cammell Laird	8/9/42	19/7/43	3/3/44
Undine	F141	Thornycroft (Woolston)	10/3/42	1/6/43	23/12/43
Urania	F08	Vickers Armstrong (Barrow)	18/6/42	19/5/43	18/1/44
Urchin	F196	Vickers Armstrong (Barrow)	28/3/42	8/3/43	24/9/43
Ursa	F200	J. I. Thornycroft (Woolston)	2/5/42	22/7/43	1/3/44
Venus	F50	Fairfield (Govan)	12/1/42	23/2/43	28/8/43
Verulam	F29	Fairfield (Govan)	26/1/42	22/4/43	10/12/43
Vigilant	F93	Swan Hunter, Tyne	31/1/42	22/12/42	10/9/43
Virago	F76	Swan Hunter, Tyne	16/2/42	4/2/43	5/11/43
Volage	F41	J. Samuel White, (Cowes)	31/12/42	15/12/43	26/5/44
Wakeful	F159	Fairfield (Govan)	3/6/42	30/6/43	17/2/44
Whirlwind	F187	Hawthorn Leslie Ltd	31/7/42	30/8/43	20/7/44
Wizard	F72	Vickers Armstrong (Barrow)	14/9/42	29/9/43	30/3/44
Wrangler	F157	Vickers Armstrong (Barrow)	23/9/42	30/12/43	14/7/44
Zest	F102	J. I. Thornycroft (Woolston)	21/7/42	14/10/43	20/7/44

Data: 'R' class as destroyers
Displacement: 1,705 tons standard; 2,425 tons full load
Length: 358ft oa
Beam: 35¾ft
Draught: 13½ft (max)
Guns: 4 × 4.7in Mk IX (4 × 1) on CP XVIII mounting
1 × 2pdr quadruple pom-pom AA
6 × 20mm AA
2 × 0.303 MG
Torpedoes: 8 × 21in tubes (2 × 4)
AS weapons: 4 × depth charge throwers (4 × 1) and two stern ramps

70 depth charges carried
Machinery: 2 × Admiralty three-drum boilers working at 300lb/sq in and 630°F, driving two shafts through Parsons single reduction turbines, giving a total of 40,000shp
Speed: 36kt (32kt at full load)
Complement: 176

Data: 'R' class Type 15 conversion
Displacement: 2,300 tons standard; 2,700 tons full load
Dimensions: As originally built except full load displacement increased to 14½ft
Guns: 2 × 4in guns (1 × 2) on Mk XIX mounting

2 × 40mm AA (1 × 2) on Mk V (Utility) mounting
AS weapons: Two Limbo or Two Squid AS mortars (see text for variations)
2 × 21in torpedo tubes (2 × 1) firing Mk 20E

acoustic homing torpedoes (*Relentless* only)
Sonar: Types 170 and 174
Machinery: As originally fitted
Speed: 31kt full load
Complement: 174

Type 16 (Limited Conversion) Frigates

Following the trial conversion of *Relentless* and *Rocket* to Type 15 frigates, a major programme was put in hand in 1951 to convert a total of 44 wartime destroyers to 'Fast Anti-Submarine Frigates'. The original plan called for 24 Type 15 conversions (only 23 were actually carried out for the Royal Navy) but time and money did not permit the full reconstruction to be applied to the other 20. A scheme for a cheaper and less extensive conversion was therefore drawn up, and the ships rebuilt to this standard were designated Type 16 (Limited Conversion) frigates. In the event, only 10 destroyers were rebuilt as Type 16s. This was mainly for financial reasons as the Royal Navy was also involved at the time in a major new shipbuilding programme. In view of their limited capabilities, compared with the Type 15 frigates and new constructions, the Type 16 conversions were given a relatively low financial priority and were intended very much as a stopgap measure until more modern vessels could be brought into service.

The work involved in the reconstruction was relatively straightforward. The original destroyer main armament of 4.7in guns (4in guns in *Paladin* and *Petard*) was removed as was the mixed collection of AA guns which included 20mm, 40mm and 2pdr weapons. All ships retained their after quadruple bank of 21in torpedo tubes but the forward set, where still fitted, was removed. All depth charge rails and throwers were also removed. The tripod foremast was removed and replaced by a lattice structure to carry new radar equipment; except for *Teazer*, *Tenacious*, *Termagent* and *Terpsichore* which had been originally completed with a lattice mast.

All ships retained their standard destroyer machinery and their performance was consequently unaltered. The standard open bridge was retained on all vessels except *Teazer*, *Tumult* and *Terpsichore*, which were given a fully enclosed frigate type bridge surmounted by an open searchlight platform. The enclosed bridge, which had been a standard feature of most American wartime destroyers, only began to appear in the Royal Navy at this time and was a significant factor in increasing crew efficiency in adverse weather conditions. The only argument in favour of open bridges was the much superior visibility but this was not so important in the postwar period when radar had virtually taken over as the only significant target detection system. In those Type 16s equipped with the enclosed bridge, a small operations room was installed immediately below, but this was nowhere near as large or comprehensively equipped as in the Type 15 conversions.

Forward of the bridge, in B position, a twin 4in Mk XIX mounting was installed. Fixed rails on the side of the turret were used for carrying and firing 2in rockets which were used for target illumination purposes. A rudimentary optical director mounted above the bridge provided the fire control system (compare with the radar-equipped MRS-1 fire control system installed in the Type 15 frigates). A light AA armament of seven 40mm AA guns was carried. A Mk V twin mounting with an associated STD was installed on the superstructure island which had separated the torpedo tubes, and five Mk IX single mountings were carried, one in each bridge wing, one right aft on the quarterdeck, and two on the after steering platform just abaft the funnel.

AS armament consisted of two Squid AS mortars installed on the after superstructure in the position previously occupied by X gun. A rectangular deckhouse aft of the Squids was the mortar-handling room. Here mortar bombs were brought up by hoist from a magazine below, prepared for firing, and run out on rails to a position alongside the Squid mounting. The mounting was tilted on to its side and the mortar bomb rammed by hand into the mortar tube. This process must have been fraught with difficulty on a pitching and rolling deck in bad weather and it was for this reason that the Limbo system was developed where the loading process was carried out automatically with the handling crew under cover. The set of four 21in torpedo tubes was retained and fired the standard Mk 9 torpedoes intended for use against surface targets, although it was hoped that a suitable AS homing torpedo would be developed which could be fired from the tubes. In the event this did not happen, although in 1955/56 *Terpsichore* was fitted with two single

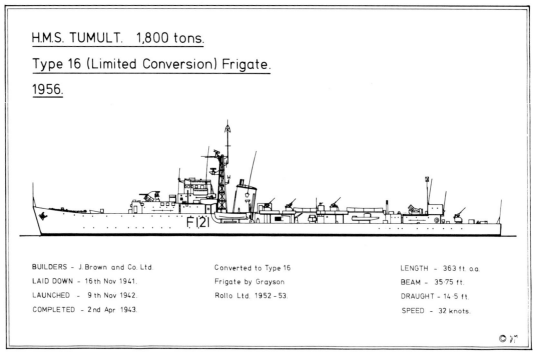

H.M.S. TUMULT. 1,800 tons.

Type 16 (Limited Conversion) Frigate.

1956.

F 121

BUILDERS - J. Brown and Co. Ltd.
LAID DOWN - 16th Nov 1941.
LAUNCHED - 9th Nov 1942.
COMPLETED - 2nd Apr 1943.

Converted to Type 16
Frigate by Grayson
Rollo Ltd. 1952 - 53.

LENGTH - 363 ft. o.a.
BEAM - 35·75 ft.
DRAUGHT - 14·5 ft.
SPEED - 32 knots.

© *n*

trainable mountings, one on either beam. These were probably for trials with the Mk 20E torpedo which was later withdrawn from service.

The radar fit was modernised with a Type 293Q surface warning radar mounted at the top of the lattice foremast and a Type 974 navigational radar on a forward projecting platform below. IFF transponder and interrogator aerials were mounted on the foremast and an air warning radar on a short polemast erected on the after deckhouse. HF/DF was carried at the top of the foremast and UHF and VHF communication aerials were mounted on the foremast cross-trees. Several communication 'whip' aerials were mounted on the funnel sides and around the bridge. A comprehensive sonar fit included Type 146B search, Type 147P depth finder, Type 162 bottom target classifier and Type 174 mortar control.

Altogether, the alterations produced a workmanlike AS vessel which was quickly and economically produced at a time when it was needed. The Type 16 was not, however, as sophisticated as the more extensively converted Type 15 and the ships had relatively short careers, being phased out of service as new construction frigates became available.

All 10 ships converted were completed in the period 1952 to 1956 with *Tuscan* being the first to commission. Details of the dates and places of the conversions together with the ships' eventual fate are listed below:

Orwell converted at Rosyth Dockyard 1952. Sold J. Cashmore and arrived Newport for scrapping 28/6/65.

Paladin converted Rosyth Dockyard 1952-54. Sold Clayton and Davie and arrived Dunston-on-Tyne 25/10/62 for scrapping.

Petard converted by Harland and Wolff, Belfast. Sold P. MacLellan, Bo'ness; arrived for scrapping June 1967.

Teazer converted by Mountstuart Dry Docks, Cardiff, 1953-54. Sold W. H. Arnott Young; arrived Dalmuir 7/8/65 for scrapping.

Tenacious converted Rosyth Dockyard 1951-52. Sold to West of Scotland Shipbreaking, Troon; arrived for scrapping 29/6/65.

Termagant converted by Grayson Rollo, Birkenhead, 1952-53. Sold W. H. Arnott Young, Dalmuir; arrived for scrapping 5/11/65.

Terpsichore converted by J. I. Thornycroft, Woolston, 1953-54. Sold to West of Scotland Shipbreaking; arrived for scrapping 17/5/66.

Tumult converted by Grayson Rollo, Birkenhead, 1953-54. Sold W. H. Arnott Young, Dalmuir; arrived for scrapping 25/10/65.

Tuscan converted by Mountstuart Dry Docks, Cardiff, 1949-50. Sold P. MacLellan, Bo'ness and arrived 26/5/66 for scrapping.

Tyrian converted Harland and Wolff, Liverpool, and Gordon Klison, Birkenhead, 1951-53. Sold West of Scotland Shipbreaking, Troon, and arrived for scrapping 9/3/65.

Below:
HMS *Rapid* was the last Type 15 in RN service, acting as a
disarmed training ship until paying off in 1974. She was
subsequently used as a target ship before being sunk
finally by torpedoes from HMS/M *Onyx* in 1981.
MoD Navy

Centre:
With the exception of HMS *Troubridge*, all the 'T' class
destroyers underwent the Type 16 Limited Conversion
refit. This is HMS *Termagant* as she appeared in 1946
prior to paying off into reserve. *Wright & Logan*

Bottom:
In addition to the 'T' class, the older destroyers *Orwell*,
Paladin and *Petard* were also converted to Type 15
frigates. The first two were subsequently adapted for use
as minelayers which entailed the removal of the torpedo
tubes and the addition of rails and discharge chutes aft.
These modifications can be seen in this view of HMS
Paladin. *Author's Collection*

Top:
HMS *Tyrian* shows the basic layout of the Type 16 with a total of seven 40mm guns as well as the twin 4in forward of the open-topped bridge. Note the torpedo tubes, and the Squid mortars on the after deckhouse.
Wright & Logan

Above:
HMS *Terpsichore* was one of three Type 16s fitted with an enclosed 'frigate' bridge (the others were *Tumult* and *Teazer*). Despite the conversion, these ships still retained the traditional destroyer outline. *Wright & Logan*

Below:
Although converted in 1952/53, HMS *Tuscan* spent most of her subsequent career laid up in reserve.
Real Photographs

Two other vessels were converted to Type 16 frigates. They were the ex-British destroyers *Onslow* and *Onslaught* which had been sold to Pakistan in 1949 and renamed *Tippu Sultan* and *Tughril* respectively. In 1957 they returned to the UK and converted to Type 16 frigates, the work being completed in 1959. Both ships were scrapped in the late 1970s.

In Royal Navy service, the ships were little altered following their reconstruction. In September 1957, *Paladin* was modified for minelaying duties with the removal of her torpedo tubes and the installation of mine-carrying rails along either side of the upper deck. In this configuration she could carry 30 mines. *Orwell* was similarly modified.

With the introduction of the Type 15 and 16 conversions, as well as the later new construction frigates, the Admiralty looked to the past to find a term to classify the various frigate types. Consequently, for a time, the larger new frigates were known as First Rate escorts; the converted frigates and the Type 14 'Blackwood' class (qv) as Second Rate escorts, and the remaining World War 2 types such as the 'Loch' class were known as Third Rate escorts. The practice of giving ships a 'Rate' stemmed from the sailing navy where the ships of the line were classified according to the number of guns carried and rated accordingly. As the older frigates and conversions passed out of service the rate classification fell into disuse.

Projected Conversions

In addition to the two conversion programmes outlined above, consideration was given to modernising some of the other remaining destroyers and a number of designs were put forward. One consistent requirement in the postwar era was for a ship capable of carrying the array of radars and associated equipment necessary to detect air attacks at long range and to direct friendly fighter forces. The ultimate result of this requirement was the Type 61 Aircraft Direction frigate described in the following chapter and in the late 1950s a number of postwar destroyers were also converted to this role. However, in 1949 work began on a project to convert up to 12 wartime destroyers including the five remaining 'M' class. Known as the Type 62 frigate, the final version featured a rebuilt superstructure along the lines of the Type 15s and an aft-mounted US-pattern twin 3in/50cal mounting with a Mk 63 director (as eventually fitted on the modernised carrier *Victorious*). An extensive radar outfit included a Type 277Q heightfinder forward, and Types 982 and 983 abaft the funnel, while additional electrical power was provided by a new 250kW turbo generator and two extra 150kW diesel generators.

Problems with stability and top weight caused by the radars led to the elimination of all except the larger 'M' class ships from the programme in 1952, while in the following year it was decided that only *Musketeer* would be converted. The whole project was finally cancelled in 1954.

The only other conversion which was seriously considered was the Type 18. This was suggested in 1950 following an appreciation of the cost of the early Type 15 conversions, one result of which had been the concept of the limited Type 16. However, the Naval Staff were unhappy with the capabilities of the latter ships and so consideration was given to mounting a double Limbo battery and associated sonar equipment instead of the double Squid. This version, the Type 18, retained the basic destroyer outline and carried one set of torpedo tubes for ASW torpedoes as well as the two Limbos. In addition a twin 40mm Bofors was mounted forward and a twin 4in aft. The bridge structure was to be rebuilt but the forecastle deck was not extended aft as in the Type 15 and a Type 277Q radar was not mounted.

The Type 18 appeared to be an attractive proposal as it had most of the operational capability of a Type 15 but would cost only £450,000 as against £600,000 for the latter and the conversion would take 15 months, three months less than a Type 15. For comparison, a Type 16 conversion was estimated to cost £260,000 and take around 10 months to complete. As the original programme called for 27 full and 18 limited conversions, considerable cost savings could be effected by the Type 18 and at one time it was envisaged that it could replace both of the other Types except for the 'O' and 'P' class destroyers which were too small for anything except the limited conversion. Initially it was planned that the five remaining 'N' class destroyers would be the first Type 18s and work was to begin in 1953/54. However, the programme was eventually cancelled when it was finally decided to run down the conversion programme and use available funds for the construction of the new ships described in the next chapter.

Type 18 Anti Submarine Frigate
Projected conversion of N class Destroyers

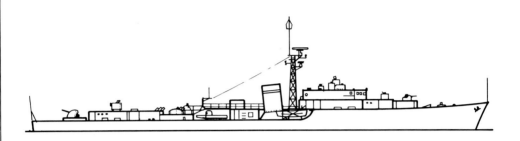

Name	No	Builder	Laid Down	Launched	Completed
Orwell	F98	J. I. Thornycroft, Woolston	16/5/40	2/4/42	7/10/42
Paladin	F169	J. Brown & Co Ltd, Clydebank	22/7/40	11/6/41	12/12/41
Petard	F56	Vickers Armstrong, Tyne	26/12/39	27/3/41	14/6/42
Teazer	F23	Cammell Laird	20/10/41	7/1/43	13/9/43
Tenacious	F44	Cammell Laird	3/12/41	24/3/43	30/10/43
Termagent	F189	W. Denny and Bros, Dumbarton	25/11/41	22/3/43	18/10/43
Terpsichore	F19	W. Denny and Bros, Dumbarton	25/11/41	17/6/43	20/1/44
Tumult	F121	J. Brown & Co, Clydebank	16/11/41	9/11/42	2/4/43
Tuscan	F156	Swan Hunter, Wallsend	9/9/41	28/5/42	11/3/43
Tyrian	F67	Swan Hunter, Wallsend	15/10/41	27/7/42	8/4/43

Data: 'T' class as destroyers
Displacement: 1,802 tons standard; 2,530 tons full load
Length: 362¾ft oa
Beam: 35¾ft
Draught: 14½ft (max)
Guns: 4 × DP 4.7in on Mk XXII mountings
2 × 40mm and 8 × 20mm AA guns (or
12 × 20mm and no 40mm)
Torpedoes: 8 × 21in tubes (2 × 4)
AS weapons: 4 × depth charge throwers and two stern racks
70 depth charges carried
Machinery: 2 × Admiralty three-drum boilers working at 300lb/sq in and 630°F, driving two shafts through Parsons single reduction turbines giving a total of 40,000shp

Speed: 36kt (32kt at full load)
Complement: 179

Data: As converted
Displacement: 1,800 tons standard; 2,300 tons full load
Dimensions: As built
Guns: 2 × 4in (1 × 2) on Mk XIX mounting
Two 40mm (1 × 2) on Mk V mounting
5 × 40mm (5 × 1) on Mk IX mountings
Torpedoes: 4 × 21in torpedo tubes (1 × 4)
AS weapons: 2 × Squid three-barrelled AS mortars
Machinery: As built
Speed: As built
Complement: 175

3 The 1951 Frigate Programme

'Salisbury' Class (Type 61) AD Frigates

The Type 15 and 16 conversions described in the last chapter were intended as a stopgap measure pending the introduction of new and purpose-built frigate designs. Work on new frigate designs had commenced as far back as 1944 when the Admiralty realised that the performance of the latest German U-boat designs would outstrip the then current frigate types. A study of the requirements for a new frigate led to the formulation of the '1945 Frigate Concept' which envisaged three separate types using a common hull and steam turbine machinery. A staff requirement called for a speed of at least 23kt at full load displacement, six months out of dry dock. It was envisaged that the ships would have to be constructed in a country possibly partly devastated by nuclear attack and therefore it was planned that the ships would be built of prefabricated sections which could be transported easily to a shipyard for assembly.

In 1947, as a result of further studies, it became apparent that provision of adequate sets of steam machinery would become problematic during wartime or emergencies. It was therefore decided to recast the designs around diesel engines as these would be easier to supply and install and also would not require such a high standard of engineroom personnel. The adoption of diesel propulsion for a large surface warship was a new departure for the Royal Navy and was probably influenced by the success of German wartime developments. They had always regarded the diesel as an eminently suitable plant for warship propulsion and by 1945 had brought it to a level of development far exceeding that of the Allies. A design existed for a German destroyer which would have achieved 37½kt together with a range of 16,000 miles at 19kt when powered by eight MAN diesels giving a power output of 76,000bhp through two shafts.

The success of the 'Loch/Bay' concept where a single hull with a standard propulsion system could be adapted for different tasks had led to the decision to attempt the same again with a more modern design. There were obvious economic benefits in this scheme which also held the advantage that production could be switched from one type to another as circumstances demanded. The three frigate types envisaged were: anti-submarine (Type 11), anti-aircraft (Type 41) and aircraft direction (Type 61). The first of these types to be laid down was a Type 61, HMS *Salisbury*, on 23 January 1951. This vessel was the first postwar design to be laid down and represented the beginning of a major programme to provide the Royal Navy with a force of ships capable of dealing with the air and underwater threats of the 'Atomic Age'. Although the other types represented a logical progression from the 'Loch/Bay' class, the Type 61 aircraft direction frigate was a new concept.

The postwar navy was structured around the complete ascendancy of air power. The aircraft carrier and its associated strike aircraft represented the main striking power of the Royal Navy: while the main threat came from land-based aircraft. The control of air battles at sea demanded powerful radar and communications equipment as well as the necessary organisation for the exploitation of such equipment. It was just not possible to fit all the electronic equipment and associated operations rooms into one warship and so the concept of a vessel whose primary function was the control and direction of aircraft was born. The concept had been tried in World War 2 using a variety of converted vessels such as tank-landing ships. Although they proved very useful they were not able to combine with major task forces as they were too slow. The new frigate design provided a suitable hull in which to mount a wide variety of radar equipment and this meant that the new type would be able to combine in a tactical sense with other vessels of an escort group. It was intended that the new aircraft direction vessels would operate mainly as part of a convoy escort or as part of a small task force which did not include larger vessels which would normally carry out the aircraft direction role — such as aircraft carriers or cruisers. It is interesting to note that the first vessel of the postwar frigate programme was of the new type and this gives some idea of the importance attached to the concept.

The all-welded hull was of a novel design, having a raised forecastle deck to improve seaworthiness and being considerably larger than previous frigate designs. Power was provided by a total of 12 Admiralty Standard Range Mk 1 diesel engines arranged in three separate enginerooms.

Top:
The Type 61 frigates illustrated the tremendous changes which had taken place in warship design following the end of World War 2. HMS *Llandaff*, shown running builders trials in 1958, carries an extensive array of radars and is armed with a Mk VI twin 4.5in mounting and a 40mm STAAG mounting aft. *Real Photographs*

Above:
A stern view of HMS *Chichester* as completed in 1958. The STAAG mounting can be seen aft, as can the exhaust trunking for the diesel engines which is enclosed in the two lattice masts. *Wright & Logan*

Below:
HMS *Lincoln* was the last of the class to be completed, in 1960, and featured a raised deckhouse aft which was intended to carry a Seacat missile system although a single 40mm gun was mounted initially.
Maritime Photo Library

Four engines were connected to each of two shafts by means of fluid drive clutches and reduction gearboxes. The remaining four ASR1 units were not connected to the propulsion system but were used for the production of electrical power, each engine driving a 360kW alternator. In *Llandaff*, one of the diesel alternators was replaced by a 500kW gas turbine-powered alternator. It was necessary to have so many separate diesel units because a diesel engine produces its optimum power and efficiency within a very narrow rpm band and consequently it is better to produce extra power when required by coupling in extra engines rather than by excessive variation of engine speed. This arrangement gave the added bonus of increased survivability in the event of battle damage due to the dispersion of the power units. *Lincoln*, the last of the class to be completed, was fitted with controllable pitch propellers in a further attempt to increase propulsion efficiency and improve control response. Another advantage of diesels was that the ship could be got under way at much shorter notice than was required for steam-powered vessels.

The diesel fuel was stored in the hull's double bottom and as it was consumed it was replaced by seawater, thereby ensuring that the ship's stability remained reasonably constant even when most of the fuel had been used and the ship would otherwise be riding light. Finally, the diesel propulsion system gave the ships higher endurance than would have been the case with an equivalent steam-powered ship. One disadvantage of the multiple diesel arrangement was the amount of internal space occupied. The machinery in the Type 61 (and Type 41) took up just over 29% of the internal deck area compared with only 20% in the contemporary Type 12 design (qv) and 18.5% in the 'Leander' class laid down 10 years later.

The *raison d'être* of this class was, of course, its radar systems, and the outfit carried was of a diversity only seen previously on capital ships. Two lattice masts were provided to carry the majority of the electronic equipment and the exhaust trunking from the diesels was carried up through them. This gave rise to the then unusual sight of a large warship with no apparent funnels. The foremast carried the VHF/UHF communication aerials, DF equipment and a Type 268 navigation radar. Forward of this, a short lattice mast carried the ANU aerial of the Type 277Q combined air/surface warning radar with a height-finding capability. Aft, a lattice mainmast supported a four-dipole aerial for the Type 960 long range (up to 150 miles) air warning radar and below this was the ANU 'cheese' aerial for the Type 293Q target designation radar. Finally, mounted atop a deckhouse aft was the distinctive 'hayrake' aerial for the Type 982 aircraft direction radar. A large operations room was provided between decks where the information from the various radars was presented to the team of aircraft and fighter controllers.

Despite the weight of electronic equipment, a

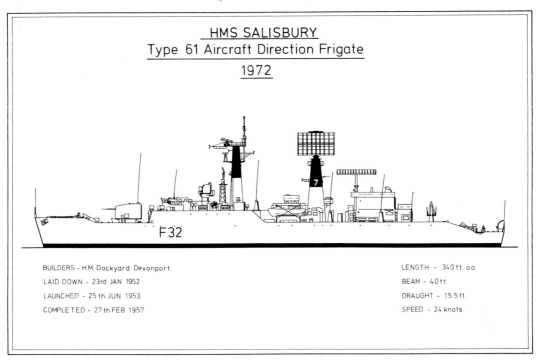

HMS SALISBURY
Type 61 Aircraft Direction Frigate
1972

F32

BUILDERS - H.M. Dockyard Devonport.	LENGTH - 340 ft. oa.
LAID DOWN - 23rd JAN 1952	BEAM - 40 ft.
LAUNCHED - 25th JUN 1953	DRAUGHT - 15.5 ft.
COMPLETED - 27th FEB 1957	SPEED - 24 knots.

normal frigate type armament was carried. This consisted of a twin Mk VI 4.5in gun turret forward and a twin 40mm STAAG mounting situated aft. Also carried was a Squid AS mortar on the quarterdeck and Types 174 and 170 sonars were fitted to provide a submarine detection and aiming system. These vessels were, therefore, able to provide a limited amount of firepower to assist in the close range defence of a convoy or task force. *Lincoln* was completed with a larger after deckhouse which was intended to carry a director for a Seacat missile system which would have replaced the 40mm AA guns. However, the Seacat system was not fitted when the ship was completed; instead a single 40mm gun was mounted in the same position as the twin 40mm STAAG of the other ships of the class.

In 1962 *Salisbury* completed a 16-month refit which included the removal of the original lattice mainmast and its replacement by a wider, plated mast or 'mack' which housed the diesel exhausts. The new mast supported a large AKE2 'bedstead' aerial for the new Type 965 long range radar which replaced the previous Type 960. The type 293Q aerial was repositioned atop the foremast on a newly constructed platform which also supported a pole topmast carrying new ESM equipment. The other ships of the class were subsequently altered to conform with this layout. In the late 1960s the whole class underwent a further major refit which involved more alterations. The foremast was plated in to match the mainmast and *Salisbury* and *Lincoln* were fitted with the Seacat missile system, *Salisbury's* after superstructure being built up to match that already on *Lincoln*. The STAAG mountings were removed from all four and, in *Llandaff* and *Chichester*, replaced by a standard Mk V twin 40mm mounting and its associated simple tachymetric director (STD). *Lincoln* and *Salisbury* were also later equipped with two single 20mm guns mounted one on either beam abreast the bridge. All four received the multiple 3in rocket launchers for the Knebworth/Corvus chaff decoy system, which were mounted abreast the foremast.

In 1973, *Chichester* was converted to act as a guardship at Hong Kong. All radars were removed except for the Type 993 (which had replaced the Type 293Q on all ships) and the navigation radar. The 4.5in main armament was retained, a single 40mm replaced the twin mounting and the single 20mm guns in the bridge wings were retained. Thus equipped she presented a sorry sight with the stump of her unused mainmast giving the ship a very unbalanced and spartan appearance. She returned to the UK in 1976 and was laid up in reserve, being scrapped at Queenborough in 1981.

Llandaff served until December 1976, when she was transferred to the Bangladesh Navy under the new name of *Oomar Farooq*. She was the first ship to be operated by this new navy and her pendant number became F16, a reversal of her original F61.

Lincoln, the only member of the class not equipped with stabilisers, was temporarily fitted with wooden bow sheathing to enable her to rough it with the gunboats of the Icelandic Navy during the 1976 Cod War but subsequently paid off into reserve and was sold off for scrapping in 1983. She had seen action in the Indonesian Confrontation of the early 1960s, the Biera patrol, and two cod wars — which demonstrates the variety of tasks carried out by frigates in the Royal Navy even in so-called peacetime.

Salisbury, the lead ship of the class, paid off into reserve in June 1978. During that year she was to be sold to Egypt and actually sailed as far as Gibraltar on her delivery voyage before the deal was cancelled and she returned to the UK. In 1980 she was designated as a static sea training ship for HMS *Raleigh* at Torpoint and continued in this role before finally being expended as a target in September 1985. It is interesting to note that, at the time of her withdrawal from service in 1978, she was the last Royal Navy ship to carry the Squid AS mortar.

The class had a long and useful career with the Royal Navy but after the first four had been laid down, the trend to general purpose designs together with the conversion of eight 'Battle' and 'Weapon' class destroyers to aircraft direction ships led to the cancellation of three further vessels of this type. The cancelled vessels would have been named *Exeter*, *Gloucester* and *Coventry*, names which were later allocated to Type 42 destroyers. The cancelled contracts were replaced with orders for other frigate types.

Name	No	Builder	Laid Down	Launched	Completed
Salisbury	F32	HM Dockyard, Devonport	23/1/52	25/6/53	27/2/57
Chichester	F59	Fairfield Shipbuilding and Engineering, Govan	26/6/53	21/4/55	16/5/58
Llandaff	F61	Hawthorn Leslie Ltd	27/8/53	30/11/55	11/4/58
Lincoln	F99	Fairfield Shipbuilding and Engineering, Govan	1/6/55	6/4/59	7/7/60

Above:
During a refit completed in 1962 HMS *Salisbury* was fitted with a new plated mainmast to carry the AKE-2 aerial for the Type 965 long range radar which replaced the original Type 960. The Type 293 was moved to the top of the foremast which was still of the original lattice construction and the twin 40mm STAAG mounting was retained.
Maritime Photo Library

Right:
HMS *Salisbury* in 1972 showing her final configuration. A tall deckhouse aft carries a GWS20 Seacat surface-to-air missile system with a quadruple launcher, the foremast has been replaced by a new plated structure, a Type 993 radar has replaced the earlier 293Q on the foremast and Corvus chaff launchers and 20mm guns are now carried in the bridge wings. *Skyfotos*

Above:
A close-up of HMS *Llandaff* in 1975 shows the disposition of the radar outfit. The Mk 6 gunnery director is equipped with Type 275 and immediately abaft of that is a short lattice mast carrying the Type 277Q. On the foremast is a Type 974 navigation set and the 'cheese' antenna of the Type 993 together with an extensive ESM outfit. The mainmast carries the Type 965 and a Type 982 is on the after deckhouse. *Llandaff* was never fitted with Seacat and a Mk V twin 40mm has replaced the original STAAG.
Wright & Logan

Above:
**HMS *Lincoln* at Malta in 1970, having been refitted with
plated masts and mounting the Seacat system aft.**
Wright & Logan

Data: As built
Displacement: 2,170 tons standard; 2,400 tons full
load
Length: 340ft oa
Beam: 40ft
Draught: 15½ft
Guns: 2×4.5in DP (1×2) in Mk IV mounting
2×40mm AA (1×2) on STAAG mounting
(1×40mm on *Lincoln*)

As weapons: 1×Squid
Sonar: Types 170, 174
Machinery: 8×Admiralty Standard Range (ASR1)
diesels driving two shafts, giving a total of
12,400shp
Speed: 24kt
Oil fuel: 230 tons
Complement: 207 (later 237)

'Leopard' Class (Type 41) AA Frigates

The genesis of this class has been described in the
previous section relating to the Type 61 frigates.
The Type 41s employed the same hull and
propulsion units and differed only in their
armament and equipment. As AA escort vessels
they were the successors of the wartime 'Bay' class
and employed the same philosophy of carrying the
heaviest gun armament possible. This consisted of
four 4.5in guns in two Mk VI turrets mounted fore
and aft. A Mk 6M director, incorporating the Type
275 gunnery radar, controlled the guns for both
surface and air target engagement. Mounted just
forward of the after 4.5in turret was a close range
blind fire director (CRBFD) which was equipped
with a Type 262 gunnery radar and this acted as a
standby director for use against aircraft if the main
director was out of action. Alternatively, the
CRBFD could be used to control the after turret
whilst the Mk 6M controlled the fore turret. Also
fitted, just abaft the mainmast was a twin 40mm
STAAG mounting again carrying the Type 262
radar. Thus equipped, the ship was capable of
firing against three separate aircraft targets

simultaneously. The heavy gun armament was on a
par with virtually all previous British destroyer
designs (except the 'Darings' which mounted six
4.5in guns) and consequently the Type 41s were
capable of carrying out several functions — such as
shore bombardment — normally performed by
destroyers. To complete the armament a Squid AS
mortar was mounted on the quarterdeck with fire
control provided by sonar Types 170 and 174, as in
the Type 61s.

Radars fitted included a Type 960 (long range air
warning) mounted atop the mainmast, and a Type
293Q target designation radar on the foremast.
HF/DF and a navigation radar were also carried.
All the ships of the class were equipped with
stabilisers which helped to maintain a steady
platform for AA gunnery. *Jaguar*, as with the Type
61 *Lincoln*, was fitted with controllable pitch
propellers.

Of the five ships laid down for the Royal Navy,
one, *Panther*, was purchased while under construction by the Indian Navy and renamed *Bramaputra*.
India subsequently ordered two more of this class

Above:
Like the 'Salisbury' class, the 'Leopard' class frigates were also diesel-powered and their exhaust trunkings were contained within the lattice masts. This early view of HMS *Puma* shows the STAAG twin 40mm mounted high up amidships to give an excellent field of fire.
Wright & Logan

Below:
HMS *Jaguar* in 1964. A single 40mm gun has replaced the troublesome STAAG mounting while the radar outfit includes a Type 960 on the mainmast and a Type 293Q on the foremast. *Maritime Photo Library*

Bottom:
In the mid-1960s all four RN ships were modernised and fitted with a new plated mainmast to carry the AKE-1 aerial for a Type 965 radar. On the foremast a Type 993 replaced the Type 293Q. This photograph shows HMS *Leopard* in 1973. *IWM MH30498*

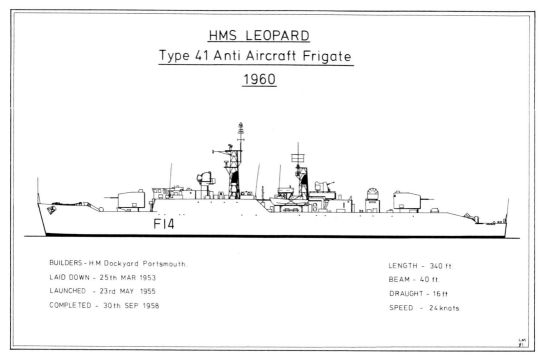

HMS LEOPARD
Type 41 Anti Aircraft Frigate
1960

F14

BUILDERS - H.M.Dockyard Portsmouth.

LAID DOWN - 25th MAR 1953

LAUNCHED - 23rd MAY 1955

COMPLETED - 30th SEP 1958

LENGTH - 340 ft.

BEAM - 40 ft.

DRAUGHT - 16 ft

SPEED - 24 knots.

and these were named *Beas* and *Betwa*. Both were completed in 1960 and differed slightly from RN vessels in that they carried a Mk V utility twin 40mm mounting instead of the more complex and less reliable STAAG mounting. Internal accommodation was also altered to suit local requirements.

When completed, the Royal Navy vessels were allocated mainly to the South American station where their impressive appearance and long range made them ideal for the traditional peacetime task of showing the flag. For this purpose they constituted the 7th Frigate Squadron and replaced the 'Bay' class frigates previously deployed to this area. Later the ships served all over the world — including participation in the 'Cod Wars' with Iceland as well as commissions in the Indian Ocean and Persian Gulf. In 1963 *Lynx* and *Puma* underwent a modernisation refit which involved the replacement of the Type 960 radar by the new Type 965. The AKE1 aerial of the type 965 was larger and heavier than the aerial of the earlier radar and so the lattice mainmast was replaced by a new plated structure. While the Type 293Q radar previously mounted on the foremast was replaced by the newer Type 993 radar. The troublesome and erratic STAAG mounting was removed and replaced by a single 40mm gun. New ESM and ECCM equipment was carried on an extended fore topmast. *Leopard* was similarly refitted between October 1964 and February 1966 with *Jaguar* following suit. It was intended that all ships of the

class would be equipped with Seacat missiles to replace the 40mm gun but this was never done, mainly for economic reasons.

By the early 1970s the lack of any missile armament made them obsolescent in their designed role. Large-scale modernisation was impracticable because of their age and the expense, and because their relatively low speed meant that they could not act as task force escorts. Consequently they were gradually withdrawn from service and laid up in reserve. *Puma*, withdrawn from service in 1974, was sold for scrap in 1976 and *Leopard* followed suit in 1978. After service with the 5th Frigate Squadron including a deployment to Iceland during the 1973 Cod War, *Jaguar* was assigned to the Standby Squadron, but, in 1976, she was recommissioned for further service in Icelandic waters. During this period she was fitted with a heavy wood sheathing to cover the bows and protect the ship from damage caused by the aggressive manoeuvring of the Icelandic gunboats. Following this she returned to reserve until sold to Bangladesh in 1978 and was renamed *Ali Hyper*. *Lynx*, last ship of the class in Royal Navy service, spent several years in reserve before also being sold to Bangladesh. She was handed over to her new owners on 12 March 1982 at Portsmouth and was renamed *Abu Baka*. She sailed for the Far East a week later, on 19 March.

In retrospect, it is unfortunate that these ships could not have been modernised with the Seacat missile system as, although their slow speed meant

Right:
With their heavy gun armament the Type 41s were almost the equal of the Navy's destroyers, although their diesels only gave a speed of 24kt. However HMS *Puma* creates a stirring sight as she builds up to full speed.
IWM MH30515

Below:
HMS *Jaguar* in 1976 after being fitted out for duties in the Icelandic Cod Wars. Note the heavy wooden sheathing intended to protect the bow and stern from damage during the dangerous close manoeuvring with the Icelandic gunboats which was a feature of this confrontation. *Skyfotos*

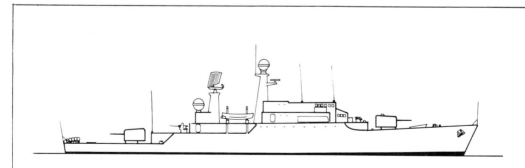

Vickers Sketch Design for a Type 41 replacement (c.1964)

they could not act as escorts for a major carrier task force, they would have been ideal for use in the recent Falklands operation where they could have provided some air defence for the merchant ships and heavy ship-to-shore bombardment firepower. Their slow speed would have been no drawback in these operations and their long range on the diesel engines would have stood them in good stead.

Name	No	Builder	Laid Down	Launched	Completed
Jaguar	F37	W. Denny and Bros	2/11/53	20/7/57	12/12/59
Leopard	F14	HM Dockyard, Portsmouth	25/3/53	23/5/55	30/9/58
Lynx	F27	J. Brown and Co Ltd	13/8/53	12/1/55	14/3/57
Puma	F34	Scotts Shipbuilding and Eng Co, Greenock	16/11/53	30/6/54	27/4/57
Panther	F31	J. Brown and Co Ltd	20/10/55	15/3/57	31/3/58

Data: As built
Displacement: 2,300 tons standard; 2,520 tons full load
Length: 340ft oa
Beam: 40ft
Draught: 16ft
Guns: 4 × 4.5in DP (2 × 2) in Mk VI mountings
2 × 40mm AA (1 × 2) on Mk V Utility mounting

AS weapons: 1 × Squid
Sonar: Types 170, 174
Machinery: 8 × Admiralty Standard Range (ASR1) diesels driving two shafts giving a total of 12,400shp
Speed: 24kt
Oil fuel: 220 tons
Complement: 205 (later 235)

'Whitby/Rothesay' Class (Type 12) AS Frigates

Although provision was made in the 1951 Frigate Programme for specialised air defence frigates (Types 41 and 61), the main thrust of the construction programme was for AS vessels. The hull and diesel propulsion system of the other types was only good for a speed of 25kt and this was not considered enough to combat submarines such as the German Type XXI (16kt underwater) and Type XXVI (22kt underwater). It was assumed that the Soviet Navy, having captured examples of these submarines at the end of the war, would have built improved versions of both. The projected AS version of the Type 41/61 was designated Type 11, but was abandoned in favour of a steam turbine-powered design which produced enough power to give a speed of 30kt. The steam plant required a larger hull than the other frigates (the extra length helping in the attainment of higher speeds) and the addition of a funnel, with the result that the final design bore little more than a passing family resemblance to the other types. The return to steam and increased dimensions meant that the new ships were considerably more expensive than the other diesel-powered vessels and were not so suitable for fast large-scale production. This apart, the Type 12 proved to be an excellent basic design with unrivalled seakeeping qualities and it emerged as the basic Royal Navy AS vessel for the next 20 years.

The hull was of a then unusual form, having a raised forecastle deck which sloped down to weather deck level just forward of the gun turret. The bow showed considerable flare and, coupled with the generally fine lines of the hull, this meant that — except in the worst conditions — spray was thrown well clear of the deck and superstructure. This was most important, especially in the North Atlantic and Arctic areas where these ships could expect to spend much of their time, as it helped to prevent an excessive build-up of ice on the ship. One of the problems encountered during World War 2 had been the difficulties caused by ice building up on the superstructure of warships. This caused weapons to become unusable, froze radar aerials solid, affected stability and in some cases put ships in danger of capsizing due to the weight of ice on the deck and upperworks. Considerable thought was directed to alleviating this problem. As well as the improved hull form already mentioned, the deck edges were radiused (instead of having the normal sharp angle between the plane of the deck and the side of the hull). This allowed water to flow more easily off the deck and the smoother surface made ice formation more difficult. The anchors were recessed into the sides of the bow which removed another cause of ice-forming spray.

The main AS weapon was the Mk 10 Limbo

mortar, which was a development of the Squid system, and two of these were carried in a sheltered well in the after quarter of the ship. From this position the mortars could be loaded and fired in any weather conditions. The three-barrelled mounting fired a 400lb streamlined projectile at ranges up to 1,000yd in any desired direction (including straight ahead when the projectiles were fired over the forward superstructure). For its time, the Limbo was an extremely effective weapon and has only recently passed from RN service, having been superseded by homing torpedoes and helicopter-launched weapons.

For submarine detection and attack information a comprehensive sonar outfit was carried. Type 174 (search) and Type 162 (bottomed target classification) sonars provided the initial detection data and a Type 170 (a pencil beam attack sonar) was carried to give the accurate bearing and depth information needed for effective use of the Limbo's capabilities. Also fitted were 12 21in torpedo tubes which were arranged on the upper deck amidships with four single fixed mountings and one twin trainable mounting on each beam. The fixed tubes were angled out at 45° to fire forward of the beam and were mounted forward of the trainable tubes. In fact not all the 'Whitby' class was so fitted on completion. *Scarborough* was the first to carry the torpedo tubes and the earlier ships were given the mountings during routine refits in the late 1950s. Although intended to fire

AS homing torpedoes rather than the standard surface torpedo, the installation was not a success because of the failure to develop an effective weapon. The Mk 20E homing torpedo used aboard these ships (and other contemporary frigates) proved to be too slow against the then current generation of high underwater speed submarines, and no suitable British replacement was developed until the Stingray lightweight homing torpedo was accepted for use in the fleet in the early 1980s. By 1963 the AS torpedo tubes had been removed from all ships of the class.

Gun armament consisted of a Mk VI twin 4.5in mounting forward and a STAAG twin 40mm AA mounting aft. The Mk VI mounting was identical to the installation in the 'Daring' class destroyers and the contemporary Type 41 and 61 frigates. A Mk 6M director, incorporating a Type 275 gunnery radar with its distinctive twin aerial dishes, provided the fire control for the dual purpose 4.5in guns. The STAAG was one of the electronic and mechanical marvels of the age. The mounting incorporated its own Type 262 gunnery radar, the aerial of which consisted of a small parabolic dish. This was rotated mechanically to give a conical scan covering an arc of 30° and when a target was detected within a range of 5,000yd, the radar would lock on to it and cause the mounting to track the target. The rate of change of the angular bearing of the target in elevation and azimuth, coupled with range information derived from the Type 262 radar, allowed an automatic computation

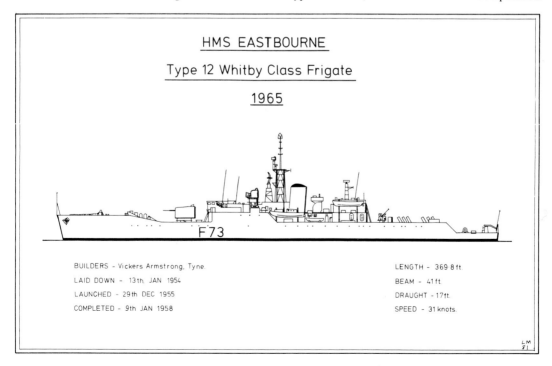

HMS EASTBOURNE

Type 12 Whitby Class Frigate

1965

F73

BUILDERS - Vickers Armstrong, Tyne.

LAID DOWN - 13th. JAN 1954

LAUNCHED - 29th DEC 1955

COMPLETED - 9th JAN 1958

LENGTH - 369·8 ft.

BEAM - 41 ft.

DRAUGHT - 17ft.

SPEED - 31 knots.

LM/81

Top:
The Type 12 AS frigate represented a great step forward in ASW capability and was undoubtedly one of the most successful designs to see service with the Royal Navy. HMS *Scarborough* illustrates the original layout of these ships with a short squat funnel, a twin 40mm STAAG mounting aft, and fixed and trainable AS torpedo tubes. *IWM MH30491*

Above:
In formulating the Type 12 design there was considerable co-ordination of effort with the RCN. The 14 ships of the

'St Laurent' and 'Restigouche' classes were contemporaries of the Type 12 and used the same hull form and machinery but differed in layout and equipment. This is HMCS *Kootenay*, completed in 1959, one of the latter class. *Real Photographs*

Below:
HMS *Whitby*, the name ship of the class, pictured in 1958. Radar outfit comprises a Type 277Q and Type 293, while the Mk 6 director was equipped with Type 275 and the STAAG mounting carried its own Type 262 centimetric radar. *Maritime Photo Library*

of the target's future position and the guns were automatically aligned with the predictor. The whole outfit (guns, radar, predictor) was carried on a fully stabilised mounting and with so many separate systems, all subject to the ravages of the weather and severe vibration when the guns fired, maintenance absorbed a disproportionate amount of time and effort. Although installed in Type 61 and 41 frigates as well as the Type 12, the difficulties associated with keeping the STAAG working eventually proved too much and it was progressively removed from all ships. In the 'Whitby' class it was replaced by a single 40mm gun.

Radar equipment included a Type 293Q, with its distinctive 'cheese' aerial carried at the top of the lattice foremast, while a Type 277Q was mounted on a short lattice structure between the gunnery director and the foremast. Other electronic equipment carried included a navigation radar and also HF/DF and ECM devices mounted on a pole extension to the foremast.

The first of the class, Whitby, was laid down in September 1952 and a further five were laid down in the following two years. The other ships of the class were Torquay, Tenby, Scarborough, Eastbourne and Blackpool. As completed, most of these ships were fitted with a rather short and upright funnel but problems with smoke and fumes, as well as boiler draughting, led to a taller raked funnel with a domed top being fitted to all ships. The later ships were completed with the new funnel design and the others modified at a later

date, although Scarborough retained her original funnel for most of her active life. As already mentioned, the deck-mounted AS torpedo tubes were removed and the extra deck space used to expand the after superstructure and increase accommodation space.

The 'Whitby' class continued in service until the early 1970s when the ship's age, and the ever-continuing defence economies, led to their gradual withdrawal. Tenby and Scarborough were sold to Pakistan in 1974, but plans to have them modernised before delivery were abandoned and they were subsequently scrapped without ever sailing under the flag of their new owners. Blackpool served with the Royal New Zealand Navy from 1966 to 1971 and on return to the UK she was placed in reserve with her 4.5in gun turret removed. Later she ended her days as a target for Rosyth-based ships before being sold to J. A. White (a Forth-based shipbreaker) in September 1980. Whitby was discarded in 1975 and was eventually broken up at Queenborough in 1979. Eastbourne was stripped of her armament in 1973 and became a seagoing training ship for engine-room trainees from HMS Caledonia, Rosyth. In 1979 she was relegated to the status of harbour training hulk and was finally scrapped in 1985. The longest lived member of the class was HMS Torquay which, since 1966, had been almost continually employed on training duties. From 1966 to 1974 she formed part of the Dartmouth Training Squadron and was then refitted to carry the first CAAIS (Computer Assisted Action

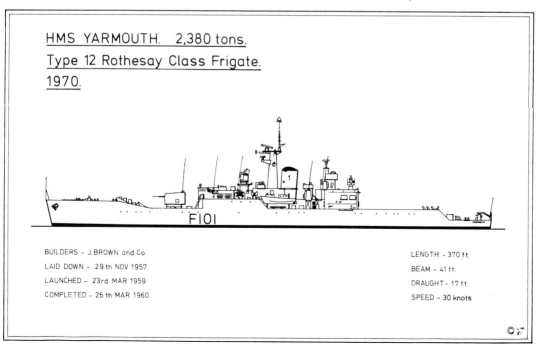

HMS YARMOUTH.   2,380 tons.
Type 12 Rothesay Class Frigate.
1970.

F101

BUILDERS - J. BROWN and Co.
LAID DOWN - 29 th NOV 1957
LAUNCHED - 23rd MAR 1959
COMPLETED - 26 th MAR 1960

LENGTH - 370 ft.
BEAM - 41 ft.
DRAUGHT - 17 ft.
SPEED - 30 knots

Information System) in a large deckhouse aft. After carrying out trials with this equipment, it was retained and used for training purposes. *Torquay* was one of the ships listed for eventual disposal in the wide-sweeping 1981 defence review but she was retained in the active fleet until paying off in March 1985. After an active career spanning 29 years she was subsequently sold off for scrapping in 1987.

Naval planning in the mid-1950s envisaged future task forces consisting of aircraft carriers protected by an inner screen of missile-armed destroyers and an outer screen of smaller fleet escorts. This outer escort was seen as a 3,000-ton vessel with a speed of 30kt or more. The guided missile destroyer requirement led eventually to the 'County' class destroyers in the mid-1960s but the smaller escort was never built. Instead, the Type 12 frigates (which had originally been designed to escort convoys and amphibious forces) were selected for the job as their speed and sea-worthiness characteristics made them suitable for such employment. In order to meet this requirement and to take advantage of improvements in armament and other equipment, the Type 12 design underwent some modification and a period of two years passed between the laying down of the last of the 'Whitby' class and the first of the altered design, HMS *Rothesay*, in November 1956.

Taking their name from the lead ship, the new group of frigates was known as the 'Rothesay' class and a total of nine was built, the last being laid down July 1958. The main external difference when compared with the previous 'Whitby' class was in the enlarged after superstructure which replaced the smaller deckhouse and twin 40mm mounting of the earlier vessels. It was intended to mount a Seacat missile launcher and its associated director in this position but, as this weapon was not available when the vessels were completing, a single 40mm gun was carried instead. The design again had provision for AS torpedo tubes but the disposition was altered. The trainable twin mounting was fitted forward of the fixed mounts which were angled to fire at 45° aft of the beam, this arrangement being the reverse of the arrangement in the 'Whitby' class.

Propulsion machinery was the same Y-100 plant as installed in the previous vessels and this gave a total of 30,000shp. Electrical power was provided by two 400kW turbo generators and two 300kW diesel generators which compared with the 350kW and 200kW output for the respective installation of the 'Whitby' class. The uptakes from the boilers were carried up to the raked funnel which had been retrospectively fitted on the other ships. Internally, improved accommodation was provided for the crew with partial bunk sleeping and air conditioning in some sections of the ship.

The performance of the Type 174 sonar and the later Type 177 (first fitted in the 'Tribal' class frigates laid down 1958-60) meant that submarine targets could be located and tracked while still outside the range of the Limbo mortars. To get over this problem the Royal Navy adopted the MATCH (MAnned Torpedo Carrying Helicopter) system and this was first introduced in the 'Tribal' class. The success of the helicopter in this role led to the decision to modify some existing vessels to carry one. Accordingly, starting with *Rothesay*, all the 'Rothesay' class was modified between 1966 and 1972. The existing after superstructure was removed as well as the forward Limbo mounting (the AS torpedo tubes had already been removed from all ships of the class), and a new structure erected which incorporated a hangar capable of housing a Wasp HAS1 helicopter and its supplies and stores. The space left by removing the Limbo was plated over to form a small flightdeck. A quadruple Seacat launcher and its associated GWS20 director was mounted atop the hangar while an MRS3 fire control system replaced the original Mk 6M director. The Type 293Q radar on the foremast was replaced by the improved Type 993 whilst the Type 277Q was made redundant by the Type 903 incorporated in the MRS3 system. Two single 20mm cannon were carried on either side of the bridge and also mounted were the multi-barrelled launchers for the chaff-carrying rockets of the Knebworth/Corvus system. These were intended to provide a passive defence against radar-guided anti-ship missiles by throwing up a group of radar decoys in the path of the missile and thus deflect it away from the target. When *Rothesay* completed her modernisation refit in 1968, she was one of the first operational ships in the fleet to carry this system. Other changes included the replacement of the lattice foremast with a taller plated structure and an increase in funnel height to carry the smoke and fumes from the boilers clear of the after superstructure and flightdeck.

Due to their extensive modernisation the 'Rothesay' class was almost comparable to the later 'Leander' class (qv) and consequently they continued in service well after the demise of the 'Whitby' class from operational duties. At the end of 1975 *Londonderry* was taken in hand for a major refit and conversion to a trials vessel and when this was completed in October 1979, she presented a radically altered profile. All armament was removed and mounted on the after superstructure was a very tall mast with another equally tall mast sprouting from the quarter deck. The after mast was in fact a portable affair and could be removed at short notice if required. Both masts were to be used for mounting aerials of equipment under trial and the ship was also used for

Top:
The later 'Whitby' class ships were completed with a raised, raked back funnel which did much to improve the appearance of these ships. HMS *Blackpool* was completed in 1958 and carries a full set of ASW torpedoes.
Wright & Logan

Above:
Following a refit completed in 1972, HMS *Torquay* was used for trials and training with CAAIS. A large deckhouse was erected aft which necessitated the removal

of the 40mm guns and one of the Limbo mortars. A plated foremast replaced the previous lattice and the funnel height was increased. The ship was the last to carry the Mk 6 director with its distinctive twin 'headlamps' for the Type 275 gunnery radar. *Skyfotos*

Below:
HMS *Tenby* pictured in the English Channel during 1970. Her funnel markings denote that she is Leader of the 5th Frigate Squadron. *Skyfotos*

Above:
During the 1960s HMS *Eastbourne* spent much of her time with the Dartmouth Training Squadron and is shown moored on the River Dart. Later, in 1972, she was stripped of all armament and continued as a training ship for artificer apprentices from HMS *Caledonia*.
Maritime Photo Library

Below:
HMS *Rothesay* was the first of the second Batch of Type 12 and is shown on completion in 1960. The after deckhouse is slightly larger than that of the 'Whitby' class and a Mk V twin 40mm is carried. A total of 12 AS torpedo tubes are mounted on the upper deck. *IWM MH30514*

Bottom:
The remainder of the 'Rothesay' class were completed with a raised after deckhouse intended to mount the Seacat missile system, although a 40mm gun was carried instead. In this 1964 view, HMS *Lowestoft* has lost her AS torpedo tubes. *Maritime Photo Library*

evaluating various items of onboard equipment such as JTIDS (Joint Tactical Information Distribution System) and various navigation aids. The ship was also fitted with what is described as a 'Pump Jet Propulsion System' although the exact nature and details of this have not been officially released. In her last commission she carried an experimental gun mounting carrying a naval version of the 30mm Rarden cannon fitted to the Army's Scorpion light tank. This gun was intended as a replacement for the 20mm and 40mm light AA guns presently carried by most RN warships, but adoption of a new light AA gun was rather overtaken by events in the Falklands and the rival BMARC/Oerlikon mounting was subsequently ordered. Following completion of her trials programme, *Londonderry* arrived in Portsmouth on 31 March 1982 for paying off. *Lowestoft*, another 'Rothesay' class ship, was also used for trials mainly in connection with sonar equipment. Other than a small structure on the quarterdeck, she showed no external variation from her sister ships.

At the beginning of 1982, several 'Rothesay' class ships had been relegated to the Standby Squadron and, following on from the 1981 defence review, were under consideration for disposal. Among these were *Berwick*, *Brighton* and *Falmouth*. In the ordinary course of events it would not have been long before the rest of the class was laid up and scrapped, as most of them had seen more than 20 years' service. The Argentine invasion of the Falkland Islands in April 1982 changed all that and one ship in particular found herself hitting the headlines in a way her crew could not possibly have foreseen. The ship concerned, HMS *Plymouth*, probably played one of the most active roles of any of the ships comprising the task force sent to recapture the islands. Sailing with the first group of Task Force ships she was involved in the operations to regain South Georgia, following which the commander of the Argentinian forces on the island, Capt Alfredo Astiz, signed the surrender documents aboard the ship. Following her success, *Plymouth* then set sail for the Falklands where she accompanied the landings at San Carlos and then acted as one of the ships providing the landings with cover against air attack. She was engaged on this duty for longer than any other ship in the task force and during this phase she fired nine Seacat missiles and claimed five enemy aircraft destroyed. On 8 June she was subjected to fierce air attack and was hit by four bombs. Luckily none of them exploded on board the ship but one of them caused depth charges to explode on the flightdeck, blowing a hole in the ship's side and starting a fire. Another bomb destroyed the Limbo AS mortar and left one of the projectiles in a dangerous state. A bomb disposal specialist was called in to defuse the mortar bomb which could have blown off the stern of the ship and in the meantime the crew was mustered on the forecastle. Once the mortar bomb was rendered safe and the fire put out, the crew was able to effect essential repairs and the ship returned to operational readiness. With the cessation of hostilities, *Plymouth* returned home, via Gibraltar, and reached Rosyth on 14 July, proudly bearing the scars of her actions. Despite the weight of metal thrown at her she suffered only five wounded and none of her crew was killed.

Plymouth was not the only 'Rothesay' class vessel to see action in the Falklands. Playing an equally important role was HMS *Yarmouth*, which had also sailed as part of the initial task force. Although not involved in the South Georgia action she was present when the *Sheffield* was hit by an Exocet missile and assisted the Type 21 frigate, HMS *Arrow*, to rescue survivors from the burning destroyer. Later, in company with *Plymouth* and other ships, she escorted the landing force into San Carlos water and for the next 10 days she took part in the fierce actions to defend the force against the relentless attacks of the Argentine Air Force. Once again she found herself engaged in the melancholy task of rescuing survivors when she assisted the *Ardent* in the last few hours before she sank after being hit by several bombs. Following her stint in 'Bomb Alley' she transferred to the naval gunfire support force, which was engaged in bombardment operations around Port Stanley, as part of the final operations to regain the Falklands. When the Argentine forces finally surrendered, *Yarmouth* was dispatched to South Thule in company with the ice patrol ship, HMS *Endurance*, to evict a party of Argentine military personnel who had been occupying the island since 1976, although their presence had been tacitly ignored at the time. Following a demonstration bombardment by *Yarmouth*, the Argentine forces surrendered without firing a shot and the island was returned to British sovereignty. *Yarmouth* was then finally able to set sail for home.

Although not directly involved in the Falklands campaign, several ships of the class were affected by events in the South Atlantic. *Falmouth* and *Berwick* were withdrawn from reserve at the start of the crisis and given rapid refits to prepare them for service. *Lowestoft*, which had been serving as a sonar trials ship, was taken in hand at Portsmouth to prepare for active service. HMS *Rhyl* was also similarly prepared and both ships were ready by mid-June when the Argentinian forces surrendered. *Lowestoft* then proceeded to Gibraltar where she was to act as guardship, replacing another ship which had been detached to the Falklands. All ships prepared for the Falklands were painted grey overall, losing the distinctive

Top:
Three Type 12s were built for South Africa including the
***President Steyn* shown here in 1963. They were similar in**
most respects to the Royal Navy ships except that they
mounted a Mk V twin 40mm aft with its own director on
the after deckhouse. *Wright & Logan*

Above:
The Limbo Mk 10 anti-submarine mortar was the
Type 12's main armament. Each ship carried two
mountings which were used in conjunction with the
Type 170 sonar to attack submarine targets up to 1,000yd
from the ship. This photograph shows the mortar barrels
rotated to the horizontal for loading through the ports on
the left. *MoD Navy*

Left:
The mortar barrels raised in the firing position.
MoD Navy

Above:
**HMS *Rothesay* after her modernisation refit in 1968. One
of the Limbo AS mortars has been removed to make way
for a hangar and flightdeck to enable the ship to operate a
Wasp helicopter. Atop the hangar is a GWS20 Seacat
missile system and a new plated mast carries a Type 993
radar as well as HF/DF and ESM equipment. The Mk 6M
director has been replaced by a MRS3 fire control system**
and Corvus chaff launchers, and 20mm guns are carried
in the bridge wings. *MoD Navy*

Below:
**An aerial view of HMS *Yarmouth* after modernisation
showing the layout of the flightdeck and the single Limbo
mortar. *MoD Navy***

Above:

HMS *Londonderry* completed a refit in 1970 during which time she was converted to act as a trials ship. Apart from being stripped of all armament, she was fitted with two additional tall plated masts intended to carry radars and other electronic equipment under test. The rear mast was intended as a temporary structure which could be removed if required. *MoD Navy*

Below:

HMS *Rhyl* was one of several Type 12s prepared for service in the Falklands war although she did not actually take part in operations. The ship has been painted grey overall and extra 20mm guns have been shipped amidships. However she was not in good condition and paid off shortly afterwards for disposal. *Mike Lennon*

Bottom:

HMS *Rothesay* and HMS *Plymouth* were the last Type 12s in commission, paying off in 1988. HMS *Plymouth*, shown here in 1986, had an extremely active war in the Falklands where she was hit by four bombs and is now preserved as a museum ship. *C&S Taylor*

black tops to the funnels and masts and having their pendant numbers painted out. The ship's name, normally carried in stainless steel letters on either side of the stern, was also removed so that the ship could not be readily identified. In some cases, extra 20mm guns were fitted.

The Falklands undoubtedly gave a new lease of life to several ships of the 'Rothesay' class although, for some, the reprieve was short-lived. *Brighton* had been laid up in 1981, was not reactivated during the war, and was later scrapped in 1985. *Londonderry* had paid off at Portsmouth in early 1982 but was brought back into service the following May for training duties and in 1983 formed part of the Dartmouth Training Squadron. She finally decommissioned in March 1984 and for several years acted as a static harbour training ship for HMS *Sultan*. She was expended as a target on 25 June 1989.

Several other 'Rothesay' class were laid up in the mid-1980s. These included *Rhyl* which paid off in 1983 and was sunk as an exercise target in 1985, and *Berwick* and *Lowestoft* which were both decommissioned in 1985 and sunk the following year. *Falmouth* paid off in 1984 and, after a period as a harbour training ship, was towed from Portsmouth to Spain for scrap on 4 May 1989. *Yarmouth*, a veteran of the Falklands, was active until April 1986 and was subsequently sunk as a target off the northwest coast of Scotland during the summer of 1987.

The last two survivors, *Plymouth* and *Rothesay*, both had very active careers in the post-Falkland era. The latter took part in the 'Orient Express' deployment to the Far East and Australia in 1983/84. This was followed by a refit, during which the ship was fitted with two new GAM-BO1 20mm guns, and deployments to the South Atlantic and service with the Dartmouth Training Squadron before finally paying off in 1988. During her 28 years of service it was calculated that she had steamed some 800,000 miles, equivalent to 40 times around the world!

HMS *Plymouth* also finished her career in 1988 and was laid up awaiting disposal. However, instead of being destined for the scrapyard it looks as if the ship will be retained for posterity. Under an agreement between the City of Plymouth and the MoD, the ship was lent to a voluntary trust for use as a museum ship in the city's Millbay Docks. Despite the success of the venture during the summer of 1988 a permanent berth could not be provided and the ship will be moved to Gosport where it will join the growing collection of preserved ships in the area. The Type 12 design was an important step in British warship development and was the Royal Navy's first 'modern' frigate, representing a complete break from the World War 2 concept of this type of ship. It is, therefore, very welcome that at least one example has been preserved and it is entirely appropriate that it should be HMS *Plymouth*, a Falklands veteran.

As with most RN frigates of the period, several Type 12 frigates were ordered by Commonwealth navies. Two 'Whitby' class were built for India and named *Talwar* and *Trishul*. They differed slightly from RN vessels in that they carried an extra two single 40mm guns. Two 'Rothesay' type were built in the UK for the Royal New Zealand Navy and these were named *Otago* and *Taranaki*. They were similar to Royal Navy vessels except for some revised crew accommodation to suit the Royal New Zealand Navy's local conditions. Both were fitted with 21in AS torpedo tubes and retained these for some years after they were removed from RN vessels. Four ships based on the Type 12 design were also built in Australia to a modified design to suit RN requirements. Finally three ships (*President Kruger*, *President Pretorious* and *President Steyn*) were completed for the South African Navy. One of these, *President Kruger*, was sunk in early 1982 following a collision with a fleet tanker while refuelling underway. Most of her crew were saved but 13 men were reported missing.

Name	No	Builder	Laid Down	Launched	Commission	Fate	Date
Whitby	F36	Cammell Laird, Birkenhead	30/9/52	2/7/54	10/7/56	Arr Queenborough for scrapping	00/01/7?
Torquay	F43	Harland and Wolff, Belfast	11/3/53	1/7/54	10/5/56	Towed ex-Portsmouth for scrapping Spain	1/7/87
Tenby	F65	Cammell Laird, Birkenhead	26/3/53	4/10/55	18/12/57	Scrapped Briton Ferry	00/00/77
Scarborough	F63	Vickers Armstrong, Tyne	11/9/53	4/4/55	10/5/57	Arr Blyth for scrapping	00/08/77
Eastbourne	F73	Vickers Armstrong, Tyne/Barrow	13/1/54	29/12/55	9/1/58	Arr Inverkeithing for scrapping	7/3/85
Blackpool	F77	Harland and Wolff, Belfast	20/12/54	14/2/57	14/8/58	Arr St David on Forth for scrapping	00/05/78
Rothesay	F107	Yarrow Shipbuilders, Clyde	6/11/56	9/12/57	23/4/60	Towed ex-Portsmouth for scraping	2/11/88

Name	No	Builder	Laid Down	Launched	Commission	Fate	Date
Londonderry	F108	J. Samuel White, Cowes	15/11/56	20/5/58	18/10/61	Expended as target	25/6/89
Brighton	F106	Yarrow Shipbuilders, Clyde	23/7/57	30/10/59	29/9/61	Arr River Medway for scrapping	16/9/85
Yarmouth	F101	J. Brown and Co, Clyde	29/11/57	23/3/59	26/3/60	Expended as exercise target	00/07/87
Falmouth	F113	Swan Hunter, Tyne	23/11/57	15/12/59	25/7/61	Towed ex-Portsmouth for scrapping in Spain	4/5/89
Rhyl	F129	HM Dockyard, Portsmouth	29/1/58	23/4/59	31/10/60	Expended as target	00/09/85
Lowestoft	F103	Alex Stephens and Sons, Clyde	19/6/58	23/6/60	26/9/61	Expended as target	16/6/86
Berwick	F115	Harland and Wolff	16/6/58	15/12/59	1/6/61	Expended as target	00/09/86
Plymouth	F126	HM Dockyard, Devonport	1/7/58	20/7/59	11/5/61	Museum ship	00/8/88

Data: As built
Displacement: 2,150 tons standard (modified 'Rothesay' 2,380); 2,560 tons full load (modified 'Rothesay' 2,800)
Length: 370ft oa
Beam: 41ft
Draught: 17.3ft
Guns: 2 × 4.5in DP (1 × 2) on Mk VI mounting 2 × 40mm (1 × 2) on STAAG mounting (1 × 40mm in 'Rothesay' class)
Torpedoes: 12 × 21in AS torpedo tubes (8 × 1 fixed, 2 × 2 trainable)
AS weapons: 2 × Limbo mortars
Sonar: Types 162, 170, 174
Machinery: 2 × Babcock and Wilcox boilers operating at 550lb/sq in and 850°F. English Electric geared turbines, two shafts giving a total of 30,000shp
Speed: 30kt
Oil fuel: 400 tons
Complement: Originally 152; later 225 (235 in modified 'Rothesay')

'Blackwood' Class (Type 14) Utility AS Frigates

Although the Type 12s ('Whitby' class) had excellent qualities as AS vessels, they were comparatively expensive to build and were not capable of rapid construction in times of emergency. The original policy of the postwar frigate programme had been to provide a single hull which could be fitted out for a variety of roles, but the Type 12 represented a departure from this policy and a further design became necessary in order to provide a cheap, easily-built and effective anti-submarine vessel. Accordingly, a new design which represented the Admiralty's idea of a minimum AS frigate was drawn up and given the designation Type 14 (Utility). To allow for rapid construction the ship was to be built up from prefabricated welded sections which could be constructed away from the main shipyard and transported by road for final assembly. This dispersion of effort was intended to allow assembly of the ships to continue in wartime even if some of the shipyards had been put out of action by enemy bombing.

Conventional steam turbines were selected as the propulsion system but, as World War 2 experience had shown that the manufacture of large numbers of turbine units was difficult in wartime conditions, it was decided that the Type 14 would be designed as a single shaft vessel to reduce demand for these vital components. A single screw, of course, meant that a vessel was more likely to be put out of action as a result of mechanical defects or by battle damage, but this was deemed acceptable as it was anticipated that the large number of such ships available in time of war would provide a degree of cover. The steam plant fitted was, in fact, half of the two-shaft installation of the Type 12 with the exception that two smaller boilers were used to provide steam for the Y-100 turbine set instead of the single larger boiler of the original installation. With an output of 15,000shp, the machinery drove the ship at a speed of almost 28kt (a considerable improvement over the wartime frigates of a similar size).

The hull was comparatively narrow for its length of 310ft and its length/beam ratio was similar to that of previous destroyer types. It featured the

Above:
Although not the first of the class, the Type 14s were known as the 'Blackwood' class after the ship of that name which is seen entering Portsmouth with a Rear Admiral's flag at the masthead. HMS *Blackwood* was one of the few Type 14s to be fitted with AS torpedo tubes which can be seen on the upper deck just below the funnel. *Fleet Photographic Unit*

Below:
HMS *Hardy* was actually the first Type 14 to be completed, in 1955, and was initially assigned to the Londonderry training flotilla. Consequently she carries the Red Hand of Ulster on her funnel badge.
Maritime Photo Library

Bottom:
HMS *Dundas* shown at speed in the English Channel during 1971. As specialised ASW ships they lacked the armament and equipment for other tasks and consequently were of limited use — a factor which contributed to their early demise. *Skyfotos*

raised forecastle deck which had characterised the other frigate designs and a raised bulwark enclosed the forward portion of this section. Although the ships were very manoeuvrable and the hull shape had excellent seagoing characteristics, it was discovered when the ships entered service that the forward hull was too lightly constructed to cope with the stresses imposed by high speeds and rough seas and the whole class was progressively strengthened in 1958-59.

The main armament, in keeping with the specialised AS role of the ships, comprised two Mk 10 Limbo mortars mounted on the quarterdeck together with their associated mortar handling rooms. Sonar Types 174, 170 and 162 provided the detection and aiming systems. This was the same outfit as carried by the 'Whitby' class and, indeed, the Type 14 design was little inferior to the larger Type 12 in terms of AS capabilities. As with the Type 12, the smaller vessels were designed to carry AS homing torpedoes to be fired from twin trainable mountings on either beam abreast the funnel. In the event, the torpedo tubes were only mounted in *Blackwood*, *Duncan*, *Exmouth*, *Malcolm* and *Palliser* but as with the other frigate designs they were removed in the early 1960s.

The only other armament consisted of three single 40mm AA guns mounted on either side of the bridge and on the quarterdeck right aft. This light gun armament was a direct result of fitting the advanced AS equipment of the larger frigates into a relatively small hull which left no room for any other significant armament. It was presumably envisaged that the Type 14s would operate in conjunction with larger ships as they would be incapable of dealing with a gun-equipped, surfaced submarine by themselves. The lack of a medium calibre gun led to much criticism of the design and certainly limited the usefulness of the class. The only radar fitted was the Type 974 which was basically a navigation set although it could provide a short range surface surveillance element.

In view of their limited capabilities, the whole class found themselves employed on the many peacetime duties which are the lot of the Royal Navy but which do not require a full size major warship. Fishery protection was one such task and *Russell*, *Palliser*, *Duncan* and *Malcolm* were allocated to the Fishery Protection Squadron in 1958-59 replacing six 'Algerine' class minesweepers. Several ships of the class were employed in the various 'Cod Wars' with Iceland where their seakeeping qualities were taxed to the utmost in the extreme weather conditions of the area. Following her service as leader of the Fishery Protection Squadron, *Duncan* was transferred to the Portland-based 2nd Training Squadron in 1965. Other Type 14s to serve with this unit included *Dundas*, *Exmouth*, *Hardy* and *Murray*. During their operational lives the ships were very little altered. As already mentioned those equipped with AS torpedo tubes had them removed while all vessels had their after 40mm gun removed. Most, with the exception of *Duncan* and

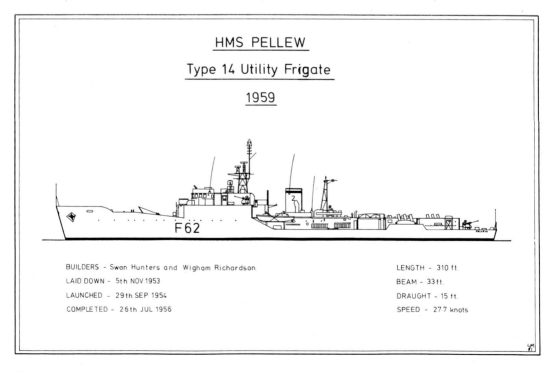

HMS PELLEW

Type 14 Utility Frigate

1959

F 62

BUILDERS - Swan Hunters and Wigham Richardson.
LAID DOWN - 5th NOV 1953
LAUNCHED - 29th SEP 1954
COMPLETED - 26th JUL 1956

LENGTH - 310 ft.
BEAM - 33 ft.
DRAUGHT - 15 ft.
SPEED - 27.7 knots

Above:
HMS *Exmouth* **was experimentally converted as the Navy's first frigate to be entirely powered by gas turbines. This midships close-up shows the arrangement of the banks of intake filters fore and aft of the funnel which houses the exhaust trunking.** *Wright & Logan*

Below:
Although the big bow enabled the Type 14s to ride well in a head sea, they were often awash amidships during rough weather and were generally thought to be extremely uncomfortable ships. HMS *Grafton* **is seen here during 1966.** *IWM MH30501*

Palliser, were equipped with the more up-to-date Type 978 navigation radar to augment the Type 974 originally fitted.

The one vessel to undergo major reconstruction was the *Exmouth* which, in 1966, was taken in hand at Chatham Dockyard where she was converted to become the Royal Navy's first major warship to be powered entirely by gas turbines. The original steam plant was removed and replaced by a 15,000shp Olympus and two Proteus (total 6,500shp) turbines. The Olympus fitted in this ship was considerably derated in order to avoid overstressing the hull which was only designed to absorb 15,000shp and was not further strengthened for higher speeds whilst being refitted for gas turbine operation. For the same reason, and for the sake of simplicity, the installation was of the COGOG type which meant that the ship could be powered by either the Olympus or the two Proteus but not both types together. The external appearance of the ship was altered by the installation of a large streamlined funnel set further aft than the original (which was removed) and by prominent intakes and filters for the gas turbines. The original armament of two Limbo mortars and two single 40mm guns was retained and the conversion was completed on 20 July 1968. She subsequently played an important part in the development of gas turbine expertise in the Royal Navy and lessons learnt in her operation were incorporated in later designs. After various tests and trials she served with the 2nd Training Squadron until being laid up in reserve in December 1976. She was subsequently sold for scrapping and arrived at Briton Ferry for breaking up in February 1979.

In a contracting navy it was not considered that any effective modernisation could be carried out on ships of this class due to their relatively small size and consequently the vessels gained the dubious distinction of being the first postwar frigates to be scrapped. *Murray* was the first to be disposed of in 1970 with *Pellew* and *Grafton* following the next year. *Blackwood* and *Malcolm* went in 1976 and 1978 respectively after being laid up for several years. *Keppel* was broken up at Sittingbourne in 1979, the same year that *Exmouth* went to the breakers. Several of the class survived as accommodation or static training ships including *Hardy* which was the last operational ship, paying off in April 1978 into reserve at Portsmouth where she was subsequently used as a stores and accommodation ship for the naval base. *Hardy* was eventually expended as a target in July 1983, but not before she had taken hits from two Exocets, Sea Skua missiles, gunfire and a torpedo – they do not build ships like that any more! *Russell* and *Palliser* were laid up at Portsmouth, the former acting as a static training ship for engineering apprentices at HMS *Sultan*, but they were scrapped in 1985 and 1983 respectively. North of the border *Dundas* was broken up at Troon during 1983 while *Duncan*, after a period as an immobile tender to the training establishment HMS *Caledonia*, was scrapped in 1985.

In retrospect it can be seen that while the Type

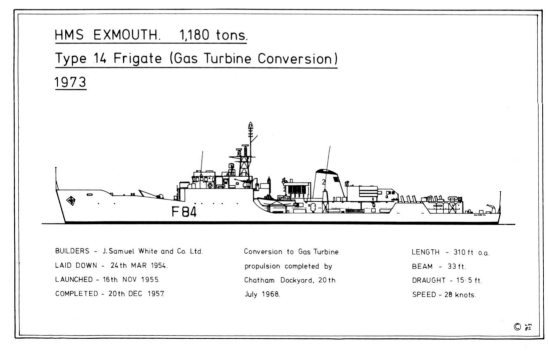

HMS EXMOUTH. 1,180 tons.

Type 14 Frigate (Gas Turbine Conversion)

1973

F 84

BUILDERS – J. Samuel White and Co. Ltd.	Conversion to Gas Turbine	LENGTH – 310 ft o.a.
LAID DOWN – 24th MAR 1954.	propulsion completed by	BEAM – 33 ft.
LAUNCHED – 16th NOV 1955.	Chatham Dockyard, 20th	DRAUGHT – 15·5 ft.
COMPLETED – 20th DEC 1957.	July 1968.	SPEED – 28 knots.

F17

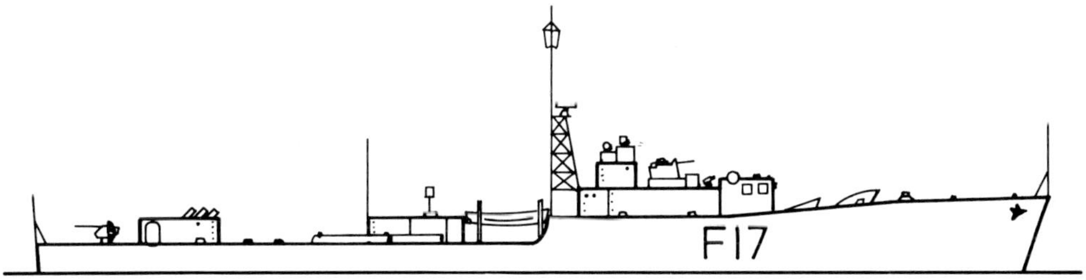

The Type 17 designation covered a variety of design studies for an AS frigate smaller than the Type 14. An AA version was tentatively designated Type 42, both projects were cancelled.

© LM 11

14 could play a useful role in a traditional World War 2 type convoy action, they were otherwise limited by their small size and specialised armament and this led to their early demise in a period when the Royal Navy was undergoing a steady decline in terms of ship numbers. An interesting comparison can be made with the contemporary French 'Le Normand' class of fast escorts which, on a similar displacement to the Type 14, mounted up to six 57mm AA guns as well as AS torpedo tubes and a Bofors AS mortar.

Ships of the Type 14 ('Blackwood') class were named after famous frigate captains of the Napoleonic period and students of warship names will be interested to note that two of the ships, *Exmouth* and *Pellew*, are named after the same man — Capt Pellew took the title of Lord Exmouth when he was raised to the peerage as a reward for his valorous escapades.

Name	No	Builders	Laid Down	Launched	Completed
Blackwood	F78	J. I. Thornycroft Co Ltd	14/9/53	4/10/55	22/8/57
Duncan	F80	J. I. Thornycroft Co Ltd	17/12/53	30/5/57	21/10/58
Dundas	F48	J. Samuel White, Cowes	17/10/52	25/19/53	9/3/56
Exmouth	F84	J. Samuel White, Cowes	24/3/54	16/11/55	20/12/57
Grafton	F51	J. Samuel White, Cowes	25/2/53	13/9/54	11/1/57
Hardy	F54	Yarrow, Scotstoun	4/2/53	25/11/53	15/12/55
Keppel	F85	Yarrow, Scotstoun	27/3/53	31/8/54	6/7/56
Malcolm	F88	Yarrow, Scotstoun	1/2/54	18/10/55	12/12/57
Murray	F91	Alex Stephens and Sons	30/11/53	25/2/55	5/6/56
Palliser	F94	Alex Stephens and Sons	15/3/55	10/5/56	13/12/57
Pellew	F62	Swan Hunter, Tyne	5/11/53	29/9/54	26/7/56
Russell	F97	Swan Hunter, Tyne	11/11/53	10/12/54	7/2/57

Data: As built
Displacement: 1,180 tons standard; 1,456 full load
Length: 310ft oa
Beam: 33ft
Draught: 15ft
Guns: 3 × 40mm (3 × 1)
Torpedoes: 4 × 21in AS (2 × 2)

AS weapons: 2 × Limbo
Machinery: 2 × Babcock and Wilcox boilers operating at 550lb/sq in and 850°F. English Electric geared turbines on one shaft giving a total of 15,000shp
Speed: 27¾kt (24½kt full load)
Complement: 112

4 General Purpose Frigates

'Tribal' Class (Type 81) GP Frigates

By 1954 the wisdom of building specialised frigate types was being questioned, particularly on cost grounds, although the operational problems of grouping the right ships together at the right time and in the right place were also an important factor. Consequently design work began in that year on a frigate which could carry out most of the specialist functions of the previous separate Types 12, 41 and 61 designs. The outcome of this work was the 'Tribal' class of general purpose frigates (designated Type 81) and the first of the new class was ordered in February 1956 although, in fact, the design was not finalised until February 1957 and the first keel not laid until January 1958.

The most interesting feature of the design was the introduction, for the first time in a major Royal Navy warship, of gas turbines as part of the main propulsion system. The system adopted was COSAG (combined steam and gas turbine) and was developed both for the Type 81 frigates and the contemporary 'County' class guided missile destroyers. The main propulsion was provided by a conventional 12,000hp steam turbine which alone could drive the ship at over 20kt while further power was available from the G-6 gas turbine (7,500shp) to boost the speed to 28kt. The advantages of this system were that the main steam turbine could be designed to give optimum fuel efficiency at normal cruising and operational speeds and the gas turbine would provide extra power on demand when required. This in turn means that less boiler capacity was required (only one boiler was installed) with appropriate savings in space and manpower. Also, in an emergency, or when the steam system was cold, the ship could be got under way and manoeuvred at only a few minutes' notice. One disadvantage of the system as installed in the 'Tribal' class, was that a second funnel was required to carry the exhaust of the gas turbine and took up deck space which would not have been lost in a conventional steam turbine installation as in the previous Type 12 design. In fact the Type 81 was the only frigate design ever to feature two prominent funnels (the Type 41/61 designs had two separate uptakes for the diesel exhausts but these were contained in the mast structures and did not appear as separate funnels). Of course the operational flexibility gained with the new system outweighed any disadvantages and

the Royal Navy was able to gain valuable experience in the operation of gas turbines in service under a wide variety of conditions. Experience was to show that the gas turbine was reliable enough to be run continuously for long periods rather than just as a boost engine. This fact was to lead to improved gas turbines being used as the sole form of propulsion in later designs (see Appendix III for details of gas turbine development).

A second major feature of the final design was the provision, for the first time in a British frigate design, of guided missiles as part of the main armament. Space was provided on each beam for a quadruple Seacat launcher and its associated GWS21 guidance and control system. The launchers were positioned abreast the foremast while the directors were mounted on platforms positioned on either side of the second funnel. Compared to later missile designs the Seacat was a relatively straightforward system. The missile was steered by radio command guidance, the signals being generated from a joystick control used by the missile aimer in the director. The target could be tracked either visually or by the Type 262 radar incorporated in the director. Due to delays in the development and procurement of the Seacat system, all the Type 81 frigates were completed with a single 40mm gun in place of each missile launcher and the GWS21 director was not fitted. The exception to this was *Zulu* which was completed with the Seacats installed as designed. The other vessels of the class were refitted with the Seacat system at a later date as the equipment became available.

A third innovation was the provision of facilities for the carriage and operation of a helicopter as an integral part of the ship's equipment. The provision of a hangar and flight deck meant that only one Limbo mortar could be carried as against the two fitted in the Type 12 and 14 designs, but this loss was more than outweighed by the greater flexibility and range of the helicopter.

Apart from the specific innovations mentioned above, the 'Tribal' class frigates differed from earlier frigates and destroyers by having a completely flush deck with considerable sheer. Forward of the midships point a superstructure block extended the full width of the ship and

Top:
HMS *Ashanti* was the first frigate to incorporate gas turbines in her machinery and heralded a new era when she entered service in 1961. This photograph was taken in 1962 and shows the ship carrying 40mm guns in place of the intended Seacat missiles, while a Saunders-Roe P531 helicopter is on the flightdeck for trial purposes pending the introduction of the Wasp into service the following year. *Wright & Logan*

Above:
The 'Tribal' class were one of the first British ships to feature full air conditioning and consequently they spent much of their time on patrol duties in the Middle East where they replaced the 'Loch' class frigates. HMS

Mohawk is seen leaving Malta en route for the Gulf during the early 1960s. Her funnel markings show that she is the Senior Officer's ship of the 9th Frigate Squadron. A Royal Marine band plays on her quarterdeck while a guard of honour parades on the flightdeck. *Wright & Logan*

Below:
The incorporation of facilities for the Wasp helicopter were an afterthought to the original design which featured two Limbo mortars amidships. One of these was deleted to provide room for a small hangar with a minimum sized flightdeck on its roof. After landing, the hangar roof acted as a lift to lower the Wasp, and the lightweight roof panels stowed on the right then covered the open hangar.
IWM MH30506

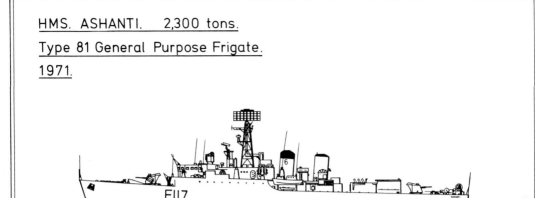

HMS. ASHANTI.   2,300 tons.

Type 81 General Purpose Frigate.

1971.

F117

BUILDERS - Yarrow and Co., Scotstoun.

LAID DOWN - 15th JAN 1958.

LAUNCHED - 9th MAR 1959.

COMPLETED - 23rd NOV 1961.

LENGTH - 360 ft. o.a.

BEAM - 42·3 ft.

DRAUGHT - 17·5 ft.

SPEED - 28 knots.

supported the bridge and mainmast. The two funnels were set well aft and raked back with the fore funnel taller than the other. Further aft was set a small superstructure which incorporated the hangar with the flightdeck on its roof.

The main gun armament comprised two single 4.5in guns in Mk V mountings positioned just forward of the bridge and on the quarterdeck. These mountings had come from scrapped 'C' group destroyers and were modified to improve the sighting and loading arrangements before being fitted. The use of these was mainly dictated by financial considerations as well as their ready availability. They fired a 25kg shell to a maximum range of 19km with a maximum rate of fire of nearly 14 rounds per minute, although the sustained rate would be nearer eight rounds per minute. The mounting allowed a maximum elevation of 50° which gave only limited effectiveness against aircraft and they were mainly intended for use against surface and shore targets. Fire control was provided by a MRS3 director mounted above and behind the bridge and incorporating a Type 903 radar for target tracking. The gun mountings featured remote power control (RPC) and were normally aimed and controlled by the director, but local fire control was possible. The forward 4.5in turret carried three 2in rocket flare launchers on either side and these were used for illuminating targets at night. This arrangement had featured on the 4in guns of the wartime frigate designs but had not appeared on other postwar designs.

The Seacat system already mentioned provided a simple and effective close range air defence system and was subsequently widely fitted to almost all British and several foreign warships. Two four-round launchers were fitted on each beam and the maximum range was approximately 4,750m.

Anti-submarine weapons consisted of a single Limbo mounting and a Wasp helicopter. The original design also included six single fixed AS torpedo tubes. These were to have been carried amidships angled out at 45°, three on each side, but were never fitted. A comprehensive outfit of sonars was carried including Types 177, 170 and 162. As these had a range well in excess of the Limbo mortar (approximately 1,000m), the Wasp helicopter was able to extend the ship's effective range considerably as an AS system by carrying depth charges and homing torpedoes to attack any detected target.

To fulfil the general purpose concept, it was necessary for the ship to carry a comprehensive radar outfit including a long range surveillance radar to enable aircraft direction tasks to be carried out. A Type 965 radar was fitted with its large AKE1 'bedstead' aerial carried on a tall lattice foremast constructed of tubular alloy to reduce weight. Forward of this a small lattice structure carried the 'cheese' aerial of a Type 993 medium range radar used for target indicating purposes. Finally a Type 978 navigation radar was carried on a small platform projecting forward from the foremast. The whole outfit of radar and other sensors and weapons was controlled from a spacious operations room immediately abaft and below the bridge. This was air conditioned and, at the time of building, incorporated some of the most up-to-date equipment available.

The helicopter hangar aft was decidedly cramped and the flightdeck was barely large enough for its purpose. After landing, the helicopter's main rotor blades were folded and the tail rotor boom also folded. The helicopter was then manoeuvred on to the lift and struck down into the hangar where the lift then formed part of the hangar floor. A folding canvas hatch cover was rigged over the lift well to provide a roof to the hangar. These arrangements were difficult to operate and consequently the helicopter was only struck below when weather conditions demanded; normally it was merely lashed down on the flightdeck, although this then restricted the field of fire of the Limbo mortar. It is possible that the ship was originally designed to carry two Limbo mortars and that later one mortar was deleted to make space for a hangar and flightdeck. In any event, later designs featured considerably improved facilities for the helicopter.

As far as the crew, these ships were a major step forward as regards comfort. They were the first frigates to be designed with cafeteria messing and bunk sleeping. Full air conditioning was provided for all accommodation, operational and working spaces which meant that the ships were suitable for employment in any climatic conditions. Previously ships had required modifications to operate in areas featuring extremes of climate such as the Persian Gulf or the Arctic. As part of the crew, a detachment of Royal Marines was carried complete with their weapons and equipment. This idea had first been tried out in HMS *Loch Killisport* and the success of the concept led to its adoption in the 'Tribal' class and later in all other frigates as well.

The class was, of course, named after the famous flotilla of 'Tribal' class destroyers which had a most distinguished war record. At the time of their inception, the destroyers represented a complete change of design philosophy when compared with previous designs and it was fitting that the Type 81 frigates, with their numerous innovations and new general purpose role, should perpetuate the famous names of their forebears. *Ashanti* was the lead ship of the class and was commissioned in late 1961, following which she was the subject of intensive trials to test the viability of her new propulsion system. Following the successful completion of these trials she was then engaged in further trials with the prototype Saunders Roe P531 helicopters to evolve suitable techniques for the operation of light helicopters from frigate flightdecks, although she did not receive her permanent Wasp helicopter until 1964.

The last vessel to complete was *Zulu* in April 1964. The whole class was employed worldwide on normal frigate duties but saw considerable service in the Middle East, Persian Gulf and West Indies where their high standards of accommodation and extensive air conditioning made them ideal for tropical service. In 1969 *Nubian* acted as a mid-Atlantic guardship for the trans-Atlantic air race organised to commemorate the 50th anniversary of the first direct aerial crossing of the ocean by Alcock and Brown. The long range of her Type 965 radar enabled her to track and control the Victor airborne tanker aircraft and steer them to a mid-ocean rendezvous with the participating military aircraft including a Royal Navy Phantom and a RAF Harrier.

Modifications were limited. In the late 1960s and early 1970s, those vessels not already equipped with Seacats were so fitted and the 40mm guns removed. At the same time, all ships were equipped with two single 20mm guns mounted on either beam just forward of the bridge. These were intended for use on peacetime police and patrol duties where the use of a larger gun or a guided missile was too expensive and inappropriate. This lesson had been learnt in the Indonesian Confrontation (1962/63) when it was found that patrolling frigates had no suitable weapons for engaging small craft such as junks and fishing boats which were being used for gun running and other anti-social activities.

Another piece of equipment to be fitted to all vessels of the class from 1970 onwards was the Knebworth/Corvus multiple rocket launcher system which was designed to provide decoys for the radar guidance system of attacking missiles. The multi-barrelled launchers were fitted on either beam abreast the bridge.

Ashanti and *Ghurka*, in 1968 and 1969 respectively, were fitted with the new Type 199 variable depth sonar (VDS). The equipment for this was installed on the quarterdeck and consisted of a winch and a controllable boom operating through a well cut in the stern.

Although a useful class for peacetime patrol and showing-the-flag duties, the relatively low speed and limited armament made the vessels unsuitable to combine with the fleet in the formation of task forces. They were employed almost exclusively on detached duties and with the introduction of new frigate types, coupled with a general rundown in naval strength, they were relegated in rapid succession first to the Standby Squadron and then listed for disposal. *Ashanti* was the first to be laid up in 1979 and the last operational ship of the class, *Tartar*, decommissioned in December 1980 when she also paid off into the Standby Squadron. Following the defence review of 1981 all seven

Top:
Ashanti and *Ghurka* were both fitted with the Type 199 Variable Depth Sonar in 1968/69. *Ashanti*, shown in this photograph, has also received her Seacat missile system and a Type 993 radar has replaced the original Type 293 abaft the bridge. *C&S Taylor*

Above:
A midships view of HMS *Eskimo* in 1979 shows the disposition of the radar outfit. A Type 965 with an AKE-1 aerial is atop the foremast and a Type 974 on the platform below while the triangular Type 993 aerial is mounted on

a separate platform abaft the bridge. Just above the bridge is an MRS3 director which carries a Type 903 gunnery radar. Abreast the second funnel are the directors for the GWS21 Seacat missile system equipped with a Type 262 centimetric tracking radar.
Wright & Logan

Below:
HMS *Zulu* was one of three 'Tribals' reactivated in the aftermath of the Falklands War. Recommissioning in August 1982, she remained active until March 1984 and was subsequently sold to Indonesia. *C&S Taylor*

vessels were listed for disposal in August 1981, although none was sold.

As a postscript, it is interesting to note a scheme proposed by Vosper Ship Repairers to modernise the ships with a view to selling them to foreign navies. The modernisation involved the removal of the two 4.5in guns and their replacement with a single automatic 76mm gun mounted forward. Aft, the Mk 10 mortar, hangar and flightdeck were to be removed and a new hangar installed serving a conventional flightdeck extending to the stern so that the ship would be capable of operating a Lynx helicopter. A large streamlined funnel replaced the previous two separate funnels and a modern lightweight fire control system was to be installed. At one time it was reported that Venezuela was interested in purchasing some of the class, but whether they would have been modernised as part of the deal was not made clear. It seems a pity that the proposed modernisation could not have been applied to the class as a whole with all ships being retained in Royal Navy service as most of them had been relegated to the disposal list well before reaching what would normally be considered the end of their useful lives.

As it happened, the Falklands crisis brought a reprieve for some of the 'Tribal' class. In order to replace losses and to cover for ships undergoing repairs and refits as a result of damage sustained, it was decided to recommission three Type 81 frigates. Following a rapid refit to bring her up to operational standard, *Tartar* was commissioned at Devonport on 17 July 1982, followed by *Ghurka* at Rosyth on 24 July and *Zulu* at Chatham on 9 August. This exercise clearly showed the value of having ships available in reserve and shows the error of selling serviceable ships as soon as they are paid off. In many cases Royal Navy ships have been withdrawn from service and sold well before the end of their useful lives, instead of being maintained as part of a reserve which could be quickly brought into service when required. It takes four or five years to build a replacement frigate, but *Zulu* was refitted and commissioned within a period of only 50 days.

None of the remaining four 'Tribals' were recommissioned and most were stripped of any serviceable equipment to keep the other three running, while *Mohawk* was already being scrapped in 1982. *Eskimo* was sunk as a target in January 1986 and *Nubian* suffered the same fate in the summer of 1987. *Ashanti*, laid up at Portsmouth for many years as an accommodation ship, was also expended as a target, being towed out for the last time on 7 September 1988.

The three ships recommissioned at the time of the Falklands War saw almost another two years' active service before paying off together at Portsmouth on 31 March 1984. They were immediately purchased by Indonesia and subsequently underwent refits at Vosper Thornycroft's Woolston yard during the following two years. *Zulu* was the first to be completed and commissioned into the Indonesian Navy on 2 May 1985, renamed *Martha Kristina Tiyahahu* (Pendant No 331). Similarly *Ghurka* recommissioned on 16 October 1985 as *Wilhelmus Zakarias Yohannes* (332) and *Tartar* as *Hasanuddin* (333) on 3 April 1986. All three remain in service today with the Indonesian Navy and, apart from a modernisation of the gunnery FCS, they remain virtually unaltered from their Royal Navy days.

Name	No	Builder	Laid Down	Launched	Commission	Fate	Date
Ashanti	F117	Yarrow Shipbuilders, Clyde	15/01/58	09/03/59	23/11/61	Expended at Target	00/09/88
Eskimo	F119	J. Samuel White, Cowes	22/10/58	20/03/60	21/02/63	Expended as target	00/01/86
Ghurka	F122	J. I. Thornycroft, Woolston	03/11/58	11/07/60	13/02/63	Sold to Indonesia	1984
Mohawk	F125	Vickers Armstrong, Barrow	23/12/60	05/04/62	29/11/63	Arr Cairnryan for scrapping	00/12/82
Nubian	F131	HM Dockyard, Portsmouth	07/09/59	06/09/60	09/10/62	Expended as target	1987
Tartar	F133	HM Dockyard, Devonport	22/10/59	19/09/60	26/02/62	Sold to Indonesia	1984
Zulu	F124	Alex Stephens and Sons, Govan	13/12/60	03/07/62	17/04/64	Sold to Indonesia	1984

Data: As built
Displacement: 2,300 tons standard; 2,700 tons full load
Length: 360ft
Beam: 42.3ft
Draught: 17.5ft
Guns: 2 × 4.5in (2 × 1) on Mk V mounting
2 × 40mm (2 × 1) AA (not *Zulu*)

Missiles: 8 × Seacat (2 × 4) with GWS21 fire control (*Zulu* only)
AS weapons: 1 × three-barrelled Limbo Mk 10
Aircraft: 1 × Westland Wasp HAS1

Machinery: COSAG. Metrovick steam turbine 12,500shp; Metrovick G6 gas turbine 7,500shp
Speed: 28kt (20kt steam turbine only)
Complement: 253

'Leander' Class (Type 12M) GP Frigates

The 1951 frigate construction programme had resulted in 26 ships of four distinct classes (six 'Whitby' class, 12 'Blackwood' class, four 'Salisbury' class, four 'Leopard' class). Follow-on orders produced the nine ships of the 'Rothesay' class and three more 'Salisbury' class. Three further 'Rothesay' class were planned although orders for these last six ships were cancelled and replaced by other contracts. Although the Royal Navy was thus given a reasonable number of escort vessels of modern design, the policy of building ships specialising in a particular role was not entirely satisfactory. From a financial point of view, it was obviously very expensive to design and build four different vessel types and the resultant lack of standardisation meant that routine operation and maintenance was more expensive than would be the case if only a single frigate type was being used. From an operational point of view there were problems in arranging suitable deployments so that the right vessels were available in the correct combinations for a particular task.

With the design and development of the 'Tribal' class, a move had been made away from the specialised types. They were, however, mainly designed for detached service on foreign stations and their speed and armament did not fit them for a role as major fleet escorts. Consequently it was decided to take the successful Type 12 design ('Whitby'/'Rothesay' class) as a basis for the development of a general purpose frigate. The basic hull and machinery of the Type 12 was retained (the Y-100 steam plant also used in the Type 14), the major difference being the elimination of the stepped quarterdeck which resulted in a completely flush deck apart from the raised forecastle section. The superstructure was completely redesigned into a single block positioned along the midships third of the hull. At the fore end of this was a new enclosed bridge giving a much improved view, especially aft. A tapered upright funnel with a domed top was mounted between two streamlined masts and a hangar for a Wasp helicopter was incorporated into the after end of the superstructure. Almost all the internal space was air conditioned which considerably improved working and living conditions although, perversely enough, many sailors preferred the

older 'Whitby' class as it still retained the scuttles which allowed natural daylight into the messdecks. Despite this, the introduction of air conditioning and the resultant elimination of many openings to the outside atmosphere meant that effective measures could be taken against nuclear fallout and chemical agents.

The new design was referred to as the Modified Type 12 and, reflecting the growing importance of the frigate type, the units were named after characters from classical mythology; names which had previously been borne by cruiser type vessels. In all, 26 ships of the class were to be built for the Royal Navy making them by far the largest class of major warships to be built in this country since the end of World War 2.

A balanced armament was carried to allow the class to carry out a wide variety of tasks. The main gun armament featured two 4.5in guns in the ubiquitous Mk VI dual purpose mounting but the Mk 6M director previously used with this gun mounting was replaced by the new MRS3 fire control system utilising the Type 903 radar. The MRS3 director, with its distinctive dish aerial, was smaller and lighter than the Mk 6M and was mounted immediately abaft the bridge. For short range air defence two single 40mm AA guns were carried on the hangar roof although the designed armament was a quadruple Seacat launcher with its associated director. The 40mm guns were only fitted on the first seven vessels (*Leander*, *Dido*, *Penelope*, *Ajax*, *Aurora*, *Galatea* and *Euryalus*) and subsequent vessels mounted the Seacats as intended. The earlier vessels were eventually refitted with the Seacats and the 40mm guns removed. In the late 1960s, those vessels carrying Seacats were equipped with two single 20mm guns mounted abreast the foremast on the upper superstructure. In the same period Knebworth/Corvus chaff dispensers were fitted abreast the mainmast as defence against air- and surface-launched anti-ship missiles. All Seacat-equipped ships mounted the GWS22 (Guided Weapon System Mk 22) director which closely resembled the MRS3 director and utilised a similar radar for target acquisition and ranging. The GWS22 director was offset to the starboard side of the hangar roof while the Seacat launcher was on the

Above:
The 'Leander' class was the largest group of frigates to be built for the Royal Navy since the end of World War 2. Although developed from the earlier 'Whitby/Rothesay' class, they were a considerable improvement on the earlier vessels and an extensive rearrangement of internal space left more room for extra equipment and improved accommodation. HMS *Ajax* was the second 'Leander' to be completed and was fitted with 40mm guns on the hangar roof. *Skyfotos*

Below:
A stern view of HMS *Aurora*, completed in 1964, showing the 40mm guns on the hangar roof, the Limbo mortar on the quarterdeck and VDS gear on the stern.
Real Photographs

Bottom:
HMS *Arethusa*, photographed in 1968, was one of the first ships to be completed with the GWS22 Seacat missile system on the hangar roof instead of the 40mm guns mounted on earlier vessels. She is also equipped with VDS gear on the stern. *Skyfotos*

port side and further aft to give a reasonable field of fire. The single exception to this arrangement was *Naiad* which was the sole example equipped with the GWS20 system. This was a much simpler system where the director was moved manually to the target bearing by matching pointers displaying information from the ship's weapon direction system. This system was fitted for the Seacat installation in the 'Rothesay' class, *Salisbury* and *Lincoln* (qv) and the assault ships *Fearless* and *Intrepid*.

Anti-submarine weapons consisted of a Mk 10 three-barrelled Limbo mortar mounted in a recessed well aft of the flightdeck and a Westland Wasp helicopter (MATCH system). With its comparatively spacious hangar and adequate flightdeck, the helicopter could be operated much more effectively than was possible with the cramped arrangement of the preceding 'Tribal' class. Maintenance could be carried out in more convenient circumstances and a greater variety of stores and spares could be carried. A wide variety of sonars was fitted including the Type 177 (or Type 184 on later vessels), Type 170B attack sonar, Type 162 bottomed target sonar, and Type 199 variable depth sonar (in some vessels only — see below). The variable depth sonar was intended to be fitted in a well situated in the extreme stern of the ship. All vessels in the class (except the last five — *Scylla, Achilles, Diomede, Apollo* and *Ariadne*) had the VDS well but only *Leander, Dido, Aurora, Naiad, Arethusa, Cleopatra, Charybdis, Hermione, Jupiter* and *Bacchante* were

actually equipped with the sonar gear. Variable depth sonar was a method of overcoming the fact that sonar rays can be refracted by layers of water of differing temperatures which meant that sonar signals from a surface vessel could be prevented from ever reaching a deep submarine. By lowering a sonar transmitter and receiver through some of the surface layers of water meant that the effective range of the sonar could be substantially increased. However, the resulting equipment was difficult to handle and operate, and was not of much use in areas of relatively shallow water such as the North Sea and British coastal waters. For these reasons the equipment was not fitted to all of the class.

The main radar was the Type 965 with an AKE1 aerial surmounted by an IFF interrogator. This was the same as that fitted to the 'Tribal' class and was used for air surveillance and aircraft direction. The aerial array was mounted on the short mainmast. For general air and surface warning a Type 993 was carried with its distinctive 'cheese' aerial mounted on a forward extension at the top of the foremast. A polelike extension to the foremast carried HF/DF and ECM equipment whilst a Type 975 or 978 navigation radar was carried on a small platform situated half-way up the foremast structure.

The resulting ships had a handsome and balanced profile and with the large number built they formed the backbone of the Royal Navy's escort force throughout the 1970s and into the 1980s. The class was actually laid down in three distinct sub-groups or batches. The first batch of 10

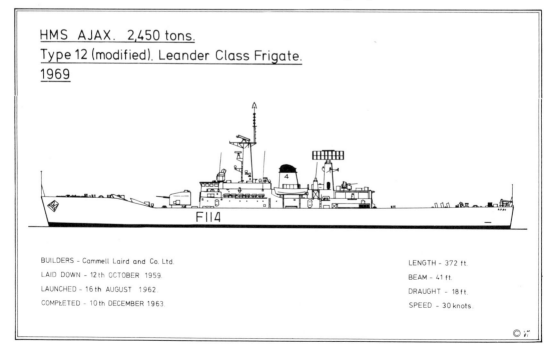

HMS AJAX. 2,450 tons.
Type 12 (modified). Leander Class Frigate.
1969

F114

BUILDERS - Cammell Laird and Co. Ltd.
LAID DOWN - 12th OCTOBER 1959.
LAUNCHED - 16th AUGUST 1962.
COMPLETED - 10th DECEMBER 1963.

LENGTH - 372 ft.
BEAM - 41 ft.
DRAUGHT - 18 ft.
SPEED - 30 knots.

© ïi

Right:
The 'Leanders' were the first RN frigates to be designed from scratch to carry a helicopter. This view of HMS *Cleopatra* in 1972 shows the flightdeck and the hangar which was integrated into the main superstructure. Note the Limbo AS mortar immediately abaft the flightdeck and the safety nets rigged for Flying Stations. *IWM MH30503*

Below:
HMS *Argonaut* as completed in 1967. Although externally similar to earlier ships, she was one of the Batch 2 ships which had the improved Y136 machinery and additional electrical generating power. *MoD Navy*

Bottom:
HMS *Juno* was one of six Batch 2 ships. A minor change in these ships was the positioning of the navigation radar which is mounted on a platform offset to port halfway up the foremast — on earlier ships the platform projected forwards. *Fleet Photographic Unit*

ships were all built to the original design whilst the second batch of six had a revised engineroom layout featuring improved machinery designated Y-136 (the first group's machinery was designated Y-100). The third group of 10 ships had their beam increased to 43ft which improved stability as well as providing extra internal volume. These were referred to as the 'Broad Beam Leanders', and again detail improvements to the propulsion machinery gave rise to a new designation, Y160. Several vessels in the first group were built instead of cancelled vessels from the earlier programmes. *Leander*, *Ajax* and *Dido* were originally laid down as 'Rothesay' class vessels where their original names would have been *Weymouth*, *Fowey* and *Hastings*. *Penelope* was originally ordered as a Type 61 named *Coventry*.

The obvious qualities of the design were not lost on foreign navies and several were built for export while others were built to the basic design in overseas yards. Two were laid down in UK yards for the Royal New Zealand Navy in 1964 and 1969, whilst a further pair were laid down in 1971 and 1972 for the Chilean Navy. The latter pair featured four Exocet launchers on the quarterdeck. The Indian, Australian and Dutch navies ordered three, two and six vessels respectively; these being built in the respective countries' own yards. The Dutch vessels carried Dutch radar equipment and had two quadruple Seacat launchers on the hangar roof.

At the beginning of the 1970s, the vessels of the first batch were approaching their mid-life refit and consideration was given to the incorporation of new weapons and electronic systems into the existing hulls. The Royal Australian Navy had developed the Ikara AS system which consisted of a rocket-propelled missile carrying a homing torpedo out to the computed position of a target submarine. The torpedo made a parachute-retarded descent into the target area and then eventually homed on to the target. The system had the great advantage of a sharply reduced reaction time as compared to the MATCH system and could also be used in all weathers. The original application of the Australian weapon system was in the Type 82 destroyers of which three were cancelled, leaving only HMS *Bristol* to complete. Subsequently it was decided to install the system in the Batch 1 'Leanders' as they became due for their major refits and *Leander*, the nameship of the class, was the first to undergo the lengthy process in the newly built Frigate Complex at Devonport Dockyard. Emerging in December 1972, her appearance was in marked contrast to the previous balanced outline of the class.

The installation of the Ikara system entailed major changes to the ships' armament and electronic systems. Forward, the 4.5in gun turret was removed and in its place a deckhouse extended forward of the bridge to a circular zareba mounted over the break in the forecastle deck. Inside the zareba was the actual missile launcher which could be covered by a folding 'pram hood' when not in use. The deckhouse contained the missile handling room where the missile could be assembled prior to being moved forward on to the launcher. The missile was in effect a small

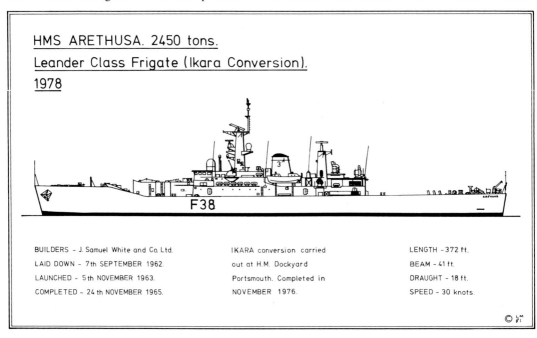

HMS ARETHUSA. 2450 tons.

Leander Class Frigate (Ikara Conversion).

1978

F38

BUILDERS – J. Samuel White and Co. Ltd.	IKARA conversion carried	LENGTH – 372 ft.
LAID DOWN – 7th SEPTEMBER 1962.	out at H.M. Dockyard	BEAM – 41 ft.
LAUNCHED – 5th NOVEMBER 1963.	Portsmouth. Completed in	DRAUGHT – 18 ft.
COMPLETED – 24th NOVEMBER 1965.	NOVEMBER 1976.	SPEED – 30 knots.

© LM 81

aeroplane with a span of 5ft (1.53m) and a length of 11ft 4in (3.43m) and was stored in the space previously occupied by the gun ammunition hoists and magazines. Whilst in store, the missile was complete with torpedo, but to save space the wings and fins were detached. When required for action the missile was moved to the missile handling room where the assembly was completed and a serviceability check carried out.

Once on the launcher, the operation of the missile was controlled by the ADAWS5 (Action Data Automation Weapon System). The ADAWS5 system fitted to the Ikara-equipped 'Leanders' was a reduced version of the ADAWS3 fitted to the Type 82, and subsequent Type 42, destroyers. Utilising a Ferranti FM1600 and a single display central equipment, the ADAWS5 provided fire control and weapon systems management. The new equipment naturally made demands on internal space and the operations room was enlarged and redesigned to provide room for two conference radar displays as well as four labelled plan displays and two tote displays showing alphanumeric information.

In place of the MRS3 director fitted to the gun-equipped 'Leanders' a missile tracking radar was mounted atop the bridge, while just abaft of the bridge there was a smaller aerial on a short pole mast. This is the aerial for the command guidance system. The firing sequence of the Ikara missile commences when a submarine target is detected and identified within range. The ADAWS5 system calculates the correct angle of firing for the missile and moves the launcher to the appropriate bearing and angle of elevation. The computer will identify the correct moment to launch and once airborne the missile is located and tracked by the tracking radar. The positions of the missile and target are continuously monitored by the computer and any necessary alterations of course are signalled to the missile by a coded radio link transmitted from the command aerial. The lightweight torpedo carried by the missile is released by radio command at a point calculated by the computer, descends into the sea by parachute, and homes acoustically on to the target. The missile body flies clear of the engagement area before ditching in the sea.

The Limbo AS mortar was retained as was the Wasp helicopter which could still be used for the dropping of homing torpedoes and other AS weapons. The converted 'Leanders' were thus equipped with no less than three separate methods of attacking submarines!

The Type 965 radar and its associated AKE1 aerial were removed as it was not required in the ships' new AS role. The internal space thus saved could be used for the installation of the new ADAWS equipment. A Cossor 1010 IFF interrog-

ator was installed with its small aerial on the mainmast. The radar fit on the foremast was basically unchanged with the Type 993 radar remaining. New additions included SCOT (satellite communications terminal) aerials mounted on platforms projecting forward to starboard and aft to port of the foremast. The HF/DF equipment previously fitted at the peak of the foremast was replaced by a small stabilised 'headlamp' aerial having an ECCM function.

At the time of their conversion, most of the Batch 1 vessels had been equipped with a Seacat launcher on the hangar roof, offset to port. The converted vessels were fitted with two quadruple launchers mounted on the after corners of the hangar. A GWS22B fire control director was mounted on an elevated platform immediately abaft the mainmast. The new arrangement increased the number of missiles available to engage aerial targets but the positioning of the director meant that it was impossible to engage targets forward of the beam. Two single 40mm on electrically powered Mk 9 mountings were installed on the upper superstructure abeam the foremast, but these were only intended to give the ship some light firepower for the peacetime policing role and were of limited effectiveness against aerial targets.

Finally all the converted ships not already so equipped, were fitted with variable depth sonar.

The sum of all these modifications was a highly specialised, but very effective, AS frigate which was totally removed from the general purpose concept which had led to the inception of the 'Leander' class. Carrying a comprehensive selection of AS weapons and sonar devices, the Ikara-equipped 'Leanders' were probably the most effective vessels of their type in the world at the time of their conversion. However, their almost total lack of any self-defence capability against air or surface attack meant that they would normally only be able to operate as part of a larger force whose composition included vessels able to provide the necessary cover.

Of the 10 vessels comprising Batch 1, all were converted to carry the Ikara system except for *Penelope* which was acting as the trials ship for the Seawolf missile system, and *Cleopatra*. Dates and place of conversion are as below:

Name	Completed	Place
Leander	December 1972	Devonport
Ajax	September 1973	Devonport
Galatea	September 1974	Devonport
Naiad	July 1975	Devonport
Euryalus	March 1976	Devonport
Aurora	March 1976	Chatham
Arethusa	April 1977	Portsmouth
Dido	October 1978	Devonport

Above:
The last 'Leander' class to be built was HMS *Ariadne*. The last 10 Batch 3 ships were known as the Broad Beam 'Leanders' due to a 2ft increase in beam. Although some were later modernised, *Ariadne* is almost unaltered in this 1984 view at Devonport. *MoD Navy*

Below:
Eight of the Batch 1 ships, including HMS *Galatea* shown here, were converted in the 1970s to specialist ASW ships carrying the Australian-developed Ikara A/S missile. *IWM MH30571*

Left:
Part of *Galatea's* operations room after modernisation showing some of the equipment associated with the ADAWS5 Action Information System. *IWM MH30509*

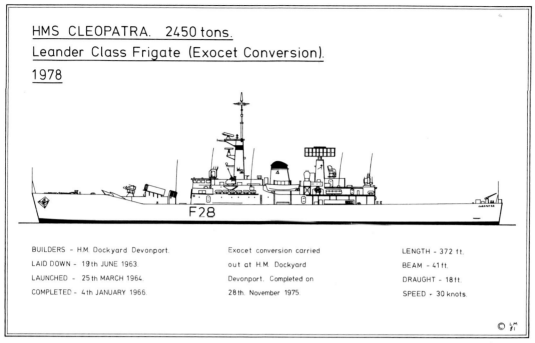

HMS CLEOPATRA. 2450 tons.
Leander Class Frigate (Exocet Conversion).
1978

F28

BUILDERS – H.M. Dockyard Devonport.
LAID DOWN – 19th JUNE 1963.
LAUNCHED – 25th MARCH 1964.
COMPLETED – 4th JANUARY 1966.

Exocet conversion carried
out at H.M. Dockyard
Devonport. Completed on
28th November 1975.

LENGTH – 372 ft.
BEAM – 41 ft.
DRAUGHT – 18 ft.
SPEED – 30 knots.

© LM 81

As the introduction of the Ikara missile to the Royal Navy led to the conversion of the earlier 'Leanders', so the introduction of the French-designed Exocet surface-to-surface missile led to the redesign and modification of the second or Batch 2 group of 'Leanders'. Exocet was a French-developed anti-ship missile powered by a two-stage solid fuel rocket motor with a maximum range of about 25 nautical miles (45km). Following successful trials aboard HMS *Norfolk* ('County' class guided missile destroyer) in May and June 1974, the missile was ordered in large quantities to be installed aboard several types of Royal Navy vessels. The demise of carrier-borne air power and the lack of large calibre guns in the fleet had meant that the Royal Navy lacked any effective method of attacking the ever-growing Russian surface fleet, and it was for this reason that some of the 'Leander' class were selected to be equipped with the new missile.

Again, fitting the new weapon system gave rise to a radical change of appearance to the well known 'Leander' class silhouette. Forward of the bridge, the twin 4.5in gun turret was removed and replaced by a low superstructure carrying four Exocet canister launchers mounted in two pairs. The Exocet launcher consists of a sealed container holding one missile. After all four missiles have been fired it is necessary to return to a shore base for the empty containers to be removed and reloads to be mounted. The container system means that the missiles are constantly ready for firing and require no maintenance while the ship is

at sea. The main drawback is the lack of reloads at sea which means that the ship's commander has to be very prudent in his use of the limited stock of missiles. One advantage of the Exocet missile is that, once it is launched, it is completely independent of the ship and requires no guidance link. This feature makes it very difficult for a potential enemy to jam or counter the missile. When a target is detected by the ship's Type 993 radar, the co-ordinates of its position are fed into the missile's inertial guidance system and constantly updated until the point of firing. Once launched, the missile speeds on its way to the computed target position skimming only a few feet above the surface of the sea (height is maintained by means of signals generated by the missile's radio altimeter). Between 12 and 15km from the target, the missile's own radar activates to provide the final guidance. The low level of approach and late activation of the radar means that effective countermeasures are difficult to mount (although British forces in the Falklands found chaff quite effective). The fact that the missile launchers were lighter than the gun turret which they replaced, coupled with the fact that no extra radar or guidance systems needed to be installed, meant that for once no topweight or stability problems were caused by the new installation. This in turn meant that a margin was available for other equipment.

The VDS well aft was plated in and the faithful Limbo system removed, the resultant gap also being plated over. These alterations provided increased accommodation below the quarterdeck and resulted in a considerable increase in the area of the flightdeck. This was to enable the ships to operate the new Lynx helicopter which in itself was a major technological advance over the previously carried Wasp. The Lynx was faster, had a greater range and endurance, and could carry a heavier load than the Wasp. In 1981, Lynx flights were equipped with the Sea Skua missile which was particularly effective against fast surface targets and replaced the previous AS12 wire-guided missiles carried by the Wasp and Lynx. To accommodate the Lynx, which was much bigger than the Wasp, the hangar was extended several feet aft.

A quadruple Seacat launcher was mounted on each after corner of the enlarged hangar with a GWS22D director on a built-up section of superstructure just abaft the mainmast. Another quadruple launcher was situated on the forecastle, just forward of the Exocet launchers, and this was controlled by a GWS22D director mounted above the bridge and replacing the MRS3 director associated with the 4.5in guns. The arrangement allowed a 360° defence against aircraft with two separate control systems, and was a great improvement on layout adopted on the Ikara conversions. The only guns carried were two Mk 9 single Bofors mountings on the upper superstructure abreast the foremast as in the earlier conversions.

Radar equipment remained basically unaltered but improved ESM and ECCM equipment was mounted on the pole foremast which was now surmounted by a distinctive 'dunce's cap' aerial. On platforms winged out port and starboard just forward of the mainmast were the bulbous covers for the SCOT aerials.

To counteract the removal of the Limbo AS mortar, the Plessey STWS-1 (Ship's Torpedo Weapon System) was fitted. This consisted of two sets of triple torpedo tubes mounted on a platform at boat deck level either side of the hangar. The tubes could be operated by remote control and fired the American Mk 44 homing torpedo. This had a diameter of 324mm (roughly 12.75in) and was the ship-launched version of the Mk 46 air-dropped torpedo which was already carried by the Wasp and Lynx helicopters.

All in all, the Exocet-equipped 'Leanders' retained more of a general purpose capability than the Ikara conversions. Their main drawback was probably the limited number of Exocets carried, but the simplicity of the installation meant that space was available to carry other equipment such as the extra Seacat launcher and the Lynx helicopter.

All the ships of Batch 2 were to be converted together with the Batch 1 ships *Cleopatra* and *Penelope*. Dates and places of conversion are as follows:

Name	Completed	Date
Cleopatra	November 1975	Devonport
Phoebe	April 1977	Devonport
Sirius	October 1977	Devonport
Minerva	March 1979	Chatham
Argonaut	March 1980	Devonport
Danae	September 1980	Devonport
Penelope	March 1981	Devonport
Juno	Conversion cancelled 1984	

It will be noticed that the majority of the extensive conversion programme involving 'Leander' class frigates was carried out at Devonport Dockyard. This was because of the specially built facilities provided by the dockyard's Frigate Complex. Here, three enormous covered dry docks were available. Each dock, housed in the largest buildings of their type in Europe, was provided with full workshop and crane facilities so that work could proceed all year round without regard to weather conditions.

Penelope, one of the Batch 1 vessels which was subsequently given the Exocet conversion, had had a chequered history. Shortly after completion in 1963 she was withdrawn from normal duties to act as a sonar trials vessel and later the Type 965 radar was removed. Following this she was selected as the trials ship for the new Seawolf and its associated GWS25 guidance and control system. After a lengthy refit, she emerged in 1973 with a considerably altered appearance. Gone was the forward gun turret, the after 40mm guns and the Limbo mortar. To house the new radar systems and the associated operators and trials staff, two large interconnected deckhouses were constructed on the flightdeck. The hangar space was also converted to provide further accommodation and no helicopter was carried. On top of the after deckhouse was the aerial of the Type 910 missile tracking radar with two dish aerials of the command link transmitters on the same mounting. The mainmast was heightened and at the top was a new cylindrical aerial housing which carried the aerials for a Type 967 L-band air surveillance radar and a Type 968 S-band surface target radar in a back-to-back arrangement. The foremast radar fit remained unaltered and the MRS3 fire control system, although redundant, was not removed. Possibly it was utilised for target tracking and ranging during the Seawolf trials. The Seawolf trials were extremely successful and the missile first went to sea on an operational ship when the first Type 22 frigate, HMS *Broadsword*, commissioned in 1979. During trials the Seawolf on one occasion demonstrated its ability to intercept a 4.5in shell in flight. The United States Navy was

Top:
HNMS *Van Speijk* was the first of six 'Leanders' built in
Holland for the Netherlands Navy. The Dutch ships
differed in the type of radar equipment installed and also
carried two Seacat launchers and directors on the hangar
roof instead of the single system on British ships.
Real Photographs

Above:
An aerial view of HMS *Leander* as modernised which
clearly shows the arrangement of the Ikara missile
launcher and handling room on the forecastle. Note also
the Limbo mortar and the VDS equipment aft.
MoD Navy

Right:
An Ikara at the point of launching. Essentially the missile
was a small torpedo-carrying aircraft which was ditched
after the Mk 46 torpedo was dropped in the vicinity of the
target. Engagement ranges were up to 10 miles from the
ship. *British Aerospace*

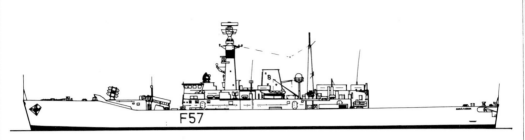

HMS ANDROMEDA. 2,600 tons.
Leander Class Frigate (Seawolf Conversion).
1981.

F57

BUILDERS - H.M. Dockyard, Portsmouth.
LAID DOWN - 25 MAY 1966.
LAUNCHED - 24 th MAY 1967.
COMPLETED - 2nd DEC 1968.

Seawolf conversion carried
out at H.M. Dockyard
Portsmouth. Completed in
April, 1981.

LENGTH - 372 ft. o.a.
BEAM - 43 ft.
DRAUGHT - 18·5 ft.
SPEED - 28 knots.

© LM 82

most impressed with the system and, at their request, *Penelope* visited America in order to demonstrate the missile to them. With her trials role completed, *Penelope* was taken in hand for conversion to an Exocet-carrying 'Leander'.

With the conversion programme for the Batch 2 vessels well under way, attention turned to the Batch 3 (broad beam) vessels. The first vessel to undergo the metamorphosis, *Andromeda*, paid off at Devonport in January 1978. When she emerged three years later her appearance was even more completely altered than had been the case with the Exocet and Ikara ships. Indeed she was barely recognisable as a 'Leander' at all! At the start of the refit all the previous main armament systems (4.5in gun turret, Seacat missiles, Limbo mortar) were removed together with their associated control systems (MRS3 and GWS22 directors). Much of the upper superstructure was lightened, particularly aft of the funnel where deckhouses around the base of the mainmast were removed as were various platforms and support structures from the hangar sides. All existing radar systems were also removed.

Mounted on a platform at the break of the forecastle was a sextuple launcher for the Seawolf missile which, as described, had previously been tested aboard HMS *Penelope*. Immediately abaft the bridge was the Type 910 tracking radar and associated command aerial dishes, the whole system comprising the GWS25 missile system. The Seawolf was a much more effective self-defence system than the Seacat carried by previous 'Leanders' and could be used against anti-ship missiles as well as aircraft.

In the well of the forecastle were four Exocet container launchers which were mounted in pairs and angled out to port and starboard — a different arrangement to the Batch 2 vessels where the launchers were aligned fore and aft. The launchers were also mounted directly on the forecastle deck rather than on a raised platform and the new arrangement meant that the Seawolf launcher had a much improved field of fire compared with the forward Seacat launcher mounted on the Batch 2 conversions.

Looking aft, the Limbo and VDS wells were plated over to provide extra accommodation and a larger flightdeck area, thus allowing room for a Lynx helicopter. To this end, the hangar was lengthened aft. The quarterdeck was cut away in the port after corner in order to provide space for the small hydraulic crane which had previously been mounted at the after end of the flightdeck where it presented something of a hazard to flying operations. It was now mounted at main deck level below the flight deck. This crane was used for streaming AS decoys, sonar listening devices and other items. On either side of the hangar on the upper deck were mounted the Plessey STWS-1 triple torpedo tubes firing AS torpedoes.

Amidships, the most striking change was to the funnel where the distinctive domed top, which was almost a 'Leander' 'trademark', was removed

Above:
HMS *Arethusa* was one of the last Batch 1 ships to be modernised. In this view an Ikara missile is on the ramp ready for launching and the single 40mm guns abreast the bridge can also be seen. Note that the Type 965 radar has been removed. *MoD Navy*

Below:
The Batch 2 Exocet conversions retained a general purpose capability and were heavily armed with no less than three quadruple Seacat launchers and two 40mm guns as well as the Exocets. HMS *Phoebe* completed her modernisation in 1977. *Fleet Photographic Unit*

leaving a rather ungraceful flat top. This was one of many moves to reduce topweight. Abaft the funnel, on the starboard side, was a platform for a Gemini inflatable craft and a small boat which had previously been carried aft on the quarterdeck. A new crane was fitted to handle the boats and the appearance of this was very similar to the cranes carried by World War 2 German light cruisers. On the port side abeam the funnel was space for a seaboat and its davits, but this was not carried by *Andromeda* when she commenced trials in April 1981, following completion of the refit.

The foremast was altered in profile to give a broad platform at the top to carry the new radar equipment. This consisted of ESM equipment mounted around a thick conical structure which carried a further circular platform on which was mounted a fully stabilised radar aerial housing. Contained in this was the back-to-back arrangement of the Type 967 and 968 radar antennae as previously fitted on HMS *Penelope*. The weight of this double system, coupled with the height at which it was mounted, meant that great efforts had to be made in other directions to reduce topweight so that stability would remain within acceptable limits and this led to the rather 'bare' look of these conversions. The usual UHF communication aerials were fitted on cross trees at the top of the foremast and a Type 975 navigation radar was mounted on a platform halfway up the mast and projecting forward and to port.

The original mainmast was removed and replaced by a taller, thinner and lighter structure surmounted by a pole aerial (possibly an improved TACAN system). Abreast the mainmast, to port and starboard, lightweight structures supported small circular platforms for the SCOT system aerials which were not fitted originally in *Andromeda* at the commencement of her post-refit trials. The 20mm guns, previously mounted just behind the enclosed bridge, were moved aft to a point abeam the foremast and lowered to boat deck level. The Knebworth/Corvus launchers remained on their platforms at boat deck level either side of the mainmast.

Not immediately obvious were alterations to the sonar and electronic equipment. The previous sonar types were replaced by the new Type 2016 which was a modern advanced capability sonar. The Seawolf GWS25 system employs two FM1600b computers and the ships are also fitted with ADAWS, probably similar to the ADAWS5 fitted to the Ikara conversions. The increased use of automation has had the effect of reducing the manning requirement and the complement of this version is only 214, which compares favourably with the 250 or more of the standard 'Leander'. Also, of course, the accommodation space for the lower number of men is improved. As converted,

the Batch 3 'Leanders' have an AS capability matched only by the later Type 22 frigates (qv) and their self-defence measures are on balance better than those of the other conversions. Including *Andromeda*, only five of the 10 broad-beamed 'Leanders' have been converted to carry the Seawolf missile system. Details of these are as follows:

Name	Completed	Place
Andromeda	December 1980	Devonport
Charybdis	August 1982	Devonport
Hermione	June 1983	Devonport
Jupiter	October 1983	Devonport
Scylla	December 1984	Devonport

Conversion of the remaining five was not undertaken on grounds of cost (£70 million for each refit) and, as a lesser consideration, to retain some ships for the NGS role.

The 'Leander' programme represented the largest class of major warships built for the Royal Navy since the end of World War 2. There were many benefits to be gained from such a long-running programme of a standard design in terms of building costs and operating economies. It is perhaps surprising that the programme was continued to the planned 26 ships in a period where continuous defence cuts and reviews were the order of the day although even so the period of construction spanned 14 years which meant that the last ships were nearing completion while the earlier ships were being extensively altered to take advantage of new weapons. The graceful outline of the 'Leander' class frigate came to be almost synonymous with the Royal Navy throughout the 1960s and 1970s. Perhaps the best known ship of the class, as far as the general public was concerned, was HMS *Phoebe* which starred in a popular TV series entitled 'Warship'. In this series about life in the modern Royal Navy she was known as HMS *Hero* although she was displaced in later series of the programme by HMS *Jupiter* which had her pendant number repainted so that the casual observer would not notice the substitution.

Of course, Royal Navy frigates have more important things to do than embark on a career in show business and, although it is not possible to trace the career of all 26 ships, it is interesting to look at the travels of one ship of the class in order to gain an insight into the work life of a typical frigate.

HMS *Bacchante* was the 20th ship of the class to be laid down and was launched in February 1968 by Lady Twiss, wife of then Second Sea Lord, Adm Sir Frank Twiss. *Bacchante* was commissioned in October 1969 and after sea trials and working up, she was allocated to the Standing

Top:
The installation of the STWS-1 AS torpedo system on the Batch 2 modernisations meant that the Limbo mortar could be removed and the flightdeck extended so that a Lynx helicopter could be carried. HMS *Sirius'* ship's flight was the first to be equipped with the Lynx, which was larger than the Wasp — requiring the hangar to be lengthened also. *Fleet Photographic Unit*

Above:
HMS *Penelope* was converted in 1973 to act as trials ship for the GWS25 Seawolf missile system. All armament was removed and the missile system installed on the flightdeck while the Type 967/968 replaced the Type 965 on the mainmast. On completion of the trials, the ship was modernised along the lines of the other Batch 2 ships, the work being completed in 1982. *C&S Taylor*

Right:
The first Batch 3 Seawolf conversion, completed in 1981, was HMS *Andromeda*. The removal of the domed top to the funnel and the general lightening of the upperworks has completely altered the character of these ships.
HMS Osprey

Naval Force Atlantic (STANAVFORLANT) which is a multi-national squadron made up of frigates and destroyers from various NATO navies. Remaining with STANAVFORLANT from April 1970 until July 1972 she then paid off into dockyard hands at Chatham for a refit during which her boilers were modified to burn diesel oil instead of the conventional heavy bunker oil. This was part of Royal Navy policy at the time of having all operational ships using the same type of fuel in order to alleviate supply and distribution problems. This refit was completed in February 1973 and later that year the ship was deployed to the West Indies as a guardship where she remained until April 1974 when she passed through the Panama Canal on her way to a showing-the-flag visit along the west coast of South America. *Bacchante* returned to Chatham for docking in June of the same year and then carried out weapon training at Portland the next month. The new year, 1975, saw her back with STANAVFORLANT for nearly two years until September 1976, after which there was a short deployment to the Middle East from which she returned in time to take part in the winter 'Cod War' with the Icelandic gunboats. Another refit commenced in January 1977 and this lasted until well into 1978 when she recommissioned for service with the 1st Frigate Squadron based at Devonport. During that year *Bacchante* had another short spell with STANAVFORLANT as well as a period in the Mediterranean and at Gibraltar. 1979 found her back in home waters until in August of that year she was assigned yet again to STANAVFORLANT (she must have been one of their most regular customers!) and travelled to the United States, Canada, Iceland and Norway. Early in 1980 *Bacchante* joined the 5th Frigate Squadron at Devonport and remained mainly in home waters carrying out fishery protection patrols and exercises as well as visiting various European ports. In March 1981 she left Plymouth to take part in the annual 'Springtrain' exercise and on completion of that she passed through the Mediterranean to the Middle East where she was assigned to the Gulf Patrol off the Straits of Hormuz at the mouth of the Persian Gulf. She returned to Plymouth in August 1981 but, in the previous month, it had been announced that as part of Mr Nott's defence review she was to be paid off into reserve along with *Achilles*, *Diomede*, *Naiad* and *Dido*. It was later announced that *Bacchante*, along with *Dido* (an Ikara conversion), was to be sold to New Zealand. She paid off at Portsmouth on 30 August 1982 and was handed over to the RNZN on 4 October 1982 and became HMNZN *Wellington*. Later in the month she sailed for her new home, reaching New Zealand on 1 December and was then laid up pending a major modernisation refit which was to

last for three-and-a-half years. The ship recommissioned on 7 July 1986 and showed a number of modifications from her previous appearance. The Mk 10 mortar aft was removed and replaced by two sets of triple A/S torpedo tubes. This has allowed the flightdeck to be extended aft for operation of a Lynx-sized helicopter although, at the moment, the RNZN still operates the Wasp. A new FCS was fitted as well as a new computerised AIO, and most of the existing radars were refurbished. Extra fuel bunkerage was incorporated to increase range by 800 miles at normal cruising speeds. *Wellington* is now one of four 'Leanders' in service with the RNZN and will eventually be replaced by a new frigate design, possibly to be built in conjunction with Australia, although progress on this is very slow.

Several 'Leander' class frigates were, as might be expected, involved in the operations to retake the Falkland Islands. The only Seawolf-equipped ship in commission at the time was *Andromeda* which returned from a deployment in the Western Atlantic on 23 April 1982, and after a quick turnround sailed for the South Atlantic where she was mainly employed as a close escort for the carrier *Invincible*. In this role her quick reaction Seawolf system was invaluable as a last-ditch defence against air and missile attack. On completion of the hostilities she was one of the ships which escorted the *Canberra* into Port Stanley harbour.

Argonaut caught the public's attention when she was hit by two bombs while stationed in San Carlos Water. One penetrated the forward magazine and the other lodged in a boiler room. Both failed to explode, otherwise the ship would most certainly have been lost. As it was it took two days to make safe and remove the bomb in the boiler room while another four days were needed to do the same to the bomb in the forward magazine. At one stage during the efforts to remove the bombs, a team of welders took cover from one of the unceasing air attacks but the heat from their equipment ignited a fire which rapidly spread and threatened to engulf the ship. Luckily the strenuous efforts of her own and other ships' crews brought the fire under control and the ship was eventually operational again. Altogether *Argonaut* was attacked 15 times and claimed at least one aircraft shot down. After effecting further repairs alongside the repair ship *Stena Seaspread* (one of the requisitioned merchant ships which formed a large part of the task force) it was a very relieved crew which set sail for Plymouth where the ship arrived on 26 June 1982.

Minerva, an Exocet-armed 'Leander', was another of the class to see action in the Falklands. After leaving Plymouth on 10 May 1982, she entered the Total Exclusion Zone on the 26th and arrived in San Carlos Water on the 29th where she

Above:
Only five of the Broad Beam 'Leanders' have been modernised by the addition of the Seawolf missile system. HMS *Scylla*, shown here, was the last to be converted and recommissioned in December 1984. Note the GAM-B01 20mm gun on the stern — a modification extended to all remaining Batch 3 ships. *MoD Navy*

Left:
A bow view of HMS *Scylla* showing the arrangement of the Seawolf and Exocet launchers on the forecastle. *MoD Navy*

Below:
HMS *Phoebe* was the first Batch 2 ship to be further modified in order to carry the Type 2031 towed array passive sonar which can be seen on the stern. Other changes include the deletion of the forward Seacat launcher and MRS3 director, and the substitution of 20mm guns for the 40mm guns previously carried abaft the bridge. *C&S Taylor*

was employed as an AA picket, relieving the battered *Argonaut*. Here she stayed for 13 days and despite being attacked many times she was not hit, although her Lynx helicopter was narrowly missed by a ground-launched Argentinian Blowpipe missile. On one occasion *Minerva* acted as controlling ship for a Sea Harrier which was vectored on to an Argentinian Air Force C-130 Hercules which it promptly shot down — the only one of its type to be lost by the Argentines. *Minerva* returned to Plymouth on 3 August in company with the Type 21 frigate, HMS *Active*.

Penelope, the ship which had carried out the trials programme for the Seawolf missile which was to prove so successful in the Falklands, was also involved in the later stages of the campaign. Sailing from Plymouth in May she arrived in time to take part in the closing stages of the operations to retake the islands. Indeed she laid claim to be the last ship to be attacked during the course of the Falklands action. Employed as an escort for forces transferring by sea from the San Carlos anchorage to other points on the islands, she was one of the ships to remain in the area after the Argentine surrender. In the period following the war the carrier *Invincible*, which had remained on station after the *Hermes* had left for home, was eventually relieved by the newly commissioned *Illustrious*. Among the ships escorting *Illustrious* was the Type 22 frigate HMS *Battleaxe* and also HMS *Danae*, an Exocet-armed 'Leander'.

In relation to their numbers, 'Leander' class frigates would not have appeared to have played a significant role in the Falklands campaign. However, it should be noted that a large proportion of the operational naval strength was dispatched to the South Atlantic, including most of the Type 21 and Type 22 frigates, so it was essential that some forces should be retained in home waters to meet the Royal Navy's NATO commitments and this was the duty that befell the majority of the 'Leander' class ships.

During the time of the Falklands War a new 'Leander' variant appeared when HMS *Phoebe*, a Batch 2 ship whose original conversion was completed in April 1977, emerged from a further refit showing a revised configuration. She was, in fact, the prototype Batch 2A conversion which was intended to act as a platform for the new Type 2031 towed array passive sonar which had been the subject of extensive trials aboard the Type 12 frigate HMS *Lowestoft* with extremely promising results. It was intended that the 2031 would be carried by the stretched Batch 2 Type 22s but, in the meantime, it was decided to modify some of the existing Leanders so that it could be deployed more quickly.

The towed array consists of a series of sensitive hydrophones, fitted within a flexible hose, towed on a long cable by the surface vessel at low speeds and at a sufficient distance to be well clear of the noise generated by the ship. Typically, the combination of such arrays and their cables can be several thousand metres long and so a large cable drum and handling equipment is necessary. Associated with the array is the sophisticated signal processing equipment necessary to make sense of the wide range of underwater sounds picked up by the hydrophones. A towed array, such as the Type 2031, is capable of detecting the sound of a moving submarine up to approximately 100 miles from the ship, although it will only provide a bearing on the contact and does not indicate range. In order to localise a contact, it is necessary to get a cross bearing from another TAS-equipped ship or else to reel in the array, make a rapid transit for several miles and then deploy the array to obtain a second bearing.

In order to accommodate the new equipment, the Batch 2A ships were considerably modified. A new platform to hold the sonar's cable drum constructed right aft on the starboard quarter, overhanging the ship's side and stern. Reflecting the ship's new role primarily as an A/S platform, the Type 965 radar was removed enabling a smaller mainmast to be stepped. The forward Seacat launcher was removed and the Exocet launchers remounted in a manner similar to the Batch 3 conversions. As with all post-Falkland refits, the seaboats were removed and replaced by inflatable craft. Finally the 40mm guns mounted high up amidships were replaced by single 20mm guns. Taken together, these changes resulted in a considerable saving of topweight in order to enhance stability.

Following *Phoebe*, three other Batch 2 ships were similarly converted – *Argonaut* (refit completed 1983), *Cleopatra* (1984) and *Sirius* (1985). In addition, one of the Batch 1 Ikara ships, *Arethusa*, has also been converted along similar lines, four Exocets replacing the Ikara missile system.

One other 'Leander', HMS *Juno*, has also been substantially modified, although in this case for a non-operational role. Originally scheduled as the last Batch 2 Exocet modernisation, this was cancelled in 1983 and the ship was later modified at Rosyth to act as a navigation training and trials ship. This involved the removal of all existing armament and the Type 965 radar. The Mk 10 mortar well was plated over to extend the flightdeck and STWS-1 torpedo system fitted, with the torpedo tubes on either beam abaft the hangar. Two single 20mm guns were mounted on the superstructure amidships. In this form the ship recommissioned in 1985 and replaced HMS *Torquay* in the training role. She has also been used as a trials ship for the Type 2050 sonar which is now

Top:
HMS *Sirius* was the fourth and last Batch 2TA ship, although HMS *Arethusa* (a Batch 1 ship) has also been converted. This view illustrates the overhang of the platform constructed to carry the sonar equipment. *HMS Osprey*

Above:
HMS *Juno* was originally scheduled for a Batch 2 Exocet refit but this was cancelled and she was modified instead to act as a navigation training ship, replacing HMS

Torquay in 1985. All the original armament has been removed as well as the Type 965 radar, although two sets of AS torpedo tubes have been installed. *MoD Navy*

Below:
HMS *Apollo* was one of the last unmodified 'Leanders' in Royal Navy service, but was sold to Pakistan in 1988. This 1986 view shows her with a Wasp helicopter embarked and a 20mm gun on the stern, but she is little changed in outline from the 'Leander' class ships completed in the early 1960s. *C&S Taylor*

being fitted in Batch 3 Type 22s and the new Type 23 frigates. In addition, the converted Batch 3 'Leanders' are having their Type 2016 sonars enhanced by the fitting of the electronics from the 2050, while retaining the original hull-mounted transducer array.

While these various modification programmes have been going forward the Royal Navy had begun to dispose of several of the 'Leanders' as a part of the seemingly relentless rundown of the fleet's destroyer and frigate strength. This response was begun as part of the provisions of the 1981 Defence White Paper and the older Batch 1 ships were the obvious candidates to start with as they were, in any case, reaching the end of their useful lives and the Ikara system was becoming obsolete. *Dido* was sold to New Zealand in 1982 and renamed *Southland*. *Ajax* was decommissioned in 1985 and subsequently laid up in the River Tamar as a static training ship for HMS *Raleigh*, the training establishment at Torpoint. Subsequently she achieved the dubious distinction of being the first 'Leander' class ship to be scrapped – at Millom in Cumbria where she arrived for breaking up in early 1988. *Galatea* paid off in 1986 and was later sunk as a target in July 1988. *Leander*, the class nameship, paid off in 1986 and was expended as a target ship in 1989 while *Naiad*, decommissioned in 1987, is currently being used in a series of explosive trials which will result in her destruction. *Aurora* also paid off in 1987 but was bought by DML (Devonport Management Ltd), the company running the now privatised Devonport Dockyard, who intend to refit the ship for sale to a foreign navy. Of the remaining Batch 1 ships, *Euryalus* and *Arethusa* were decommissioned in 1989 and are currently laid up.

At present none of the Batch 2 ships are scheduled for disposal and it can be expected that eventually the TAS-equipped ships will be the last to go. On the other hand the unconverted Batch 3 ships will soon disappear. Among the last 'Leanders' to be completed, they have plenty of life remaining and the fact that they are not equipped with expensive and sophisticated missile systems has made them attractive to many potential foreign purchasers. *Diomede* and *Apollo* were both sold to Pakistan in 1988 and *Achilles* and *Ariadne* are both scheduled to pay off in 1989. The latter ship was the last 'Leander' to operate the Wasp helicopter and it looks as if *Scylla* will be the last operational ship in the Royal Navy to be equipped with the Mk VI twin 4.5in gun mounting – originally fitted to every postwar destroyer and frigate until replaced by the automatic Mk 8 in the Type 21 frigates and subsequent ships.

The 'Leanders' have served the Royal Navy well for over 25 years and will, no doubt, continue to do so for a while yet. However, even the youngest in the fleet are almost 20 years old and consequently they are unlikely to last beyond the mid-1990s. It is interesting to look at an attempted revival of the design which occurred recently when Vosper Thornycroft announced their 'Modernised Leander' at the 1985 Royal Navy Equipment Exhibition. This was aimed at possible export orders, with particular reference to Greece which had a requirement for new frigates, and showed what could be done by the application of modern technologies to a 30-year-old design. The basic hull form was retained but was flushed-decked with a gentle sheer forward instead of the distinctive raised forecastle of the original design. Various propulsion options were offered, but the latest version has four diesels driving two shafts, supplemented by electric motors on each for slow silent running. Weapons outfit includes a single 5in gun, two Plalanx CIWS, silo-mounted VLS Nato Seasparrow SAMs, eight Harpoon SSMs and A/S torpedoes. A comprehensive radar, electronics and sonar suite is planned and the hangar and flightdeck is sized to allow operation of a Sea King or Merlin helicopter. Altogether the ship bears little external resemblance to the original 'Leander', but the design does demonstrate what is possible on a hull of this size. As frigate numbers continue to fall, the Royal Navy may well be forced to consider building ships similar to this concept in order to reduce costs and maintain the strength of the fleet.

Below:
A 1987 version of the project for a Modernised 'Leander' design put forward by Vosper Thornycroft. The change in the lines of the upper hull together with new weapon systems and a redesigned superstructure make this almost unrecognisable as a 'Leander'. Vospers hoped for an order from the Greek Navy for the design, but this was not forthcoming. *Air and Sea*

Name	No	Builder	Laid Down	Launched	Commission	Status	Date
Leander	F109	Harland and Wolff, Belfast	10/04/59	28/06/61	27/03/63	Sunk as target	00/09/89
Ajax	F114	Cammell Laird, Birkenhead	12/10/59	16/08/62	10/12/63	Arr Millom, Cumbria, for scrapping	19/02/88
Dido	F104	Yarrow Shipbuilders, Clyde	02/12/59	22/12/61	18/09/63	RNZN *Southland*	18/07/83
Penelope	F127	Vickers Armstrong, Tyne	14/03/61	17/08/62	31/10/63	Batch 2. In service 7th FS	
Aurora	F10	John Brown and Co, Clyde	01/06/61	28/11/62	09/04/64	Sold to DML. Towed ex-Portsmouth	01/08/88
Euryalus	F15	Scotts Shipbuilding and Eng Co	02/11/61	06/06/63	16/09/64	Laid up Portsmouth	00/05/89
Galatea	F18	Swan Hunter, Tyne	29/12/61	23/05/63	25/04/64	Sunk as target off Scotland	00/07/88
Arethusa	F38	J. S. White, Cowes	07/09/62	05/11/63	24/11/65	Listed for disposal	00/05/89
Naiad	F39	Yarrow Shipbuilders, Clyde	30/10/62	04/11/63	15/03/65	Expended in destructive tests	1989
Cleopatra	F28	HM Dockyard, Devonport	19/06/63	25/03/64	04/01/66	Batch 2 TA. Leader 7th FS	
Minerva	F45	Alex Stephens and Sons, Clyde	03/06/63	08/07/64	15/04/66	Batch 2. In service 7th FS	
Phoebe	F42	Vickers Armstrong, Tyne	25/07/63	19/12/64	15/05/66	Batch 2. In service 7th FS	
Sirius	F40	HM Dockyard, Portsmouth	09/08/63	22/09/64	15/06/66	Batch 2. In service 7th FS	
Juno	F52	J. Thornycroft Ltd, Woolston	16/07/64	24/11/65	18/07/66	Navigation training and trials ship	
Argonaut	F56	Hawthorn Leslie Ltd, Tyne	27/11/64	08/02/66	17/08/67	Batch 2TA. In service 7th FS	
Danae	F47	HM Dockyard, Devonport	16/12/64	31/10/65	07/09/67	Batch 2. In service 7th FS	
Hermione	F58	Alex Stephens and Sons, Clyde	06/12/65	26/04/67	11/07/69	Batch 3A. In service 8th FS	
Andromeda	F57	HM Dockyard, Portsmouth	25/05/66	24/05/67	02/12/68	Batch 3A. Leader 8th FS	
Jupiter	F60	Yarrow Shipbuilders, Clyde	03/10/66	04/09/67	09/08/69	Batch 3A. In service 8th FS	
Bacchante	F69	Vickers Armstrong, Tyne	27/10/66	29/02/68	17/10/69	RNZN *Wellington*	01/10/82
Charybdis	F75	Harland and Wolff Ltd, Belfast	27/01/67	28/02/68	02/06/69	Batch 3A. In service 8th FS	
Scylla	F71	HM Dockyard, Devonport	17/05/67	08/08/68	12/02/70	Batch 3A. In service 8th FS	
Achilles	F12	Yarrow Shipbuilders, Clyde	01/12/67	21/11/68	09/07/70	6th FS. Due to pay off	
Diomede	F16	Yarrow Shipbuilders, Clyde	30/01/68	15/04/69	02/04/71	Paid off 07/07/88. PNS *Shamshur*	15/07/88
Apollo	F70	Yarrow Shipbuilders, Clyde	01/05/69	15/10/70	28/05/72	Paid off 08/88. PNS *Zulfiquar*	14/10/88
Ariadne	F72	Yarrow Shipbuilders, Clyde	01/11/69	10/09/71	10/02/73	Leader 6th FS. Due to pay off	

Data: 'Leander' class Batch 1, HMS *Leander* (1963)
Displacement: 2,450 tons standard; 2,860 full load
Length/beam: 372ft (oa)/41ft
Draught: 18ft full load

Armament: 2×4.5in Mk 6 twin mounting, 2×40mm AA. 1×Mk 10 Limbo AS mortar
Aircraft: 1×Westland Wasp helicopter
Radar/sonar: Y100 machinery
Machinery: 2×Babcock and Wilcox boilers

operating at 550lb/sq in and 860°F. English Electric geared turbines, two shafts, 30,000shp
Speed/range: 30kt/4,500nm @ 12kt
Oil fuel: 460 tons
Complement: 251

Data: Batch 1 conversion, HMS *Naiad* (1976)
Displacement: As standard 'Leander'
Length/beam: As standard 'Leander'
Draught: As standard 'Leander'
Armament: GWS30 Ikara AS missile system. GWS22 Seacat SAM system (2×4). 2×40mm AA guns. 1×Mk 10 Limbo AS mortar
Aircraft: 1×Westland Wasp helicopter
Radar/sonar: Types 994, 1006, 903/170, 184, 162M
Machinery: As standard 'Leander'
Speed/range: As standard 'Leander'
Oil fuel: 460 tons
Complement: 257

Data: Batch 2 conversion, HMS *Danae* (1980)
Displacement: 2,650 tons standard; 3,200 tons full load
Length/beam: As standard 'Leander'
Draught: As standard 'Leander'
Armament: GWS50 Exocet 55M system (4×1). GWS22 Seacat SAM system (3×4). 2×40mm AA guns. 2×3 12.75in AS TT, STWS-1
Aircraft: 1×Westland Lynx HAS2 helicopter
Radar/sonar: Types 965, 994, 904, 1006/184, 162M
Machinery: Y136. 2×double reduction geared turbines, two shafts, 30,000shp
Speed/range: As standard 'Leander'
Oil fuel: 460 tons
Complement: 248

Data: Batch 3 conversion, HMS *Scylla* (1985)
Displacement: 2,500 tons standard; 2,962 tons full load
Length/beam: 372ft (oa)/43ft
Draught: 18ft full load
Armament: GWS25 Seawolf SAM system (1×4). GWS50 Exocet 55M. (4×1). 3×20mm guns (inc 1×GAM-BO1). 2×3 12.75in AS TT, STWS-1
Aircraft: 1×Westland Lynx HAS2 helicopter
Radar/sonar: Types 967, 968, 910, 1006/2016, 162M
Machinery: Y160. 2×double reduction geared turbines, two shafts, 30,000bhp
Speed/range: As standard 'Leander'
Oil fuel: 460 tons
Complement: 260

Data: Batch 2TA conversion, HMS *Phoebe* (1987)
Displacement: As Batch 2 'Leander'
Length/beam: As Batch 2 'Leander'
Draught: As Batch 2 'Leander'
Armament: GWS50 Exocet 55M (4×1). GWS24 Seacat SAM (2×4). 2×20mm guns. 2×3 12.75in AS TT, STWS-1
Aircraft: 1×Westland Lynx HAS2 helicopter
Radar/sonar: Types 994, 1006, 904/184, 2031, 162M
Machinery: As Batch 2 'Leander'
Speed/range: As Batch 2 'Leander'
Oil fuel: 460 tons
Complement: 250

HMS *Mermaid*

Serving only five years with the Royal Navy, this vessel had a most unusual background. She was originally ordered by the Republic of Ghana and was intended to be the flagship of their navy as well as acting as a presidential yacht for the state ruler, President Nkrumah. The ship was to be named *Black Star* and, at the time of her construction, was the largest warship to be ordered by any black African state. Her estimated cost was in the region of £5 million which was far more than this developing third world country could justifiably afford. When President Nkrumah was deposed following a coup d'état in Ghana in 1966, the new government took immediate steps to reduce the lavish expenditure of the previous ruler and the extravagant frigate being built in the United Kingdom was cancelled. The builders, Yarrow Shipbuilders and Co Ltd, were therefore left with

the problem of what to do with the partially completed ship. It was decided that the best course of action was to complete the vessel with the hope that another customer could be found. Accordingly, work continued and the vessel was launched without ceremony on 29 December 1966, and after completion in June 1968 was laid up in the Firth of Clyde to await a buyer.

The design of the ship was based upon the Royal Navy Type 41/61 hull and machinery, modified to meet the requirements of the Ghanaian Navy. The hull was flush-decked and the diesel exhausts were trunked into a streamlined single funnel. A large superstructure block housed extra accommodation including staterooms and a dining/conference room appropriate to the presidential yacht role. Armament was kept fairly simple, partly to keep the cost down, and partly because of the relatively

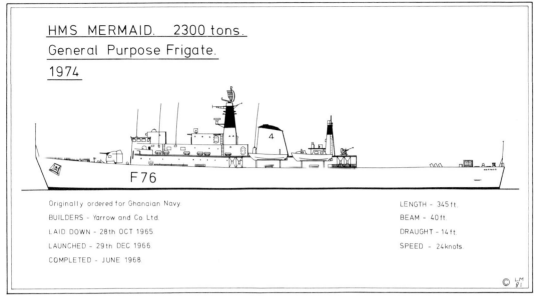

HMS MERMAID. 2300 tons.
General Purpose Frigate.
1974

F76

Originally ordered for Ghanaian Navy	LENGTH - 345 ft.
BUILDERS - Yarrow and Co Ltd.	BEAM - 40 ft.
LAID DOWN - 28th OCT 1965.	DRAUGHT - 14 ft.
LAUNCHED - 29th DEC 1966.	SPEED - 24 knots.
COMPLETED - JUNE 1968.	

© LM 81

low technical capability of the customer navy. Forward of the bridge was a Mk XIX twin 4in AA mounting while four single 40mm AA guns were mounted on the upper superstructure abreast the masts. A Squid AS mortar was situated in a well aft, similar to the arrangement of the Limbo in the 'Leander' class frigates. Sonar Types 170 and 176 were carried. The long quarterdeck could serve as a helicopter landing platform although no hangar or other facilities were provided for sustained helicopter operations. Gunnery control was provided by a simple tachymetric director mounted abaft the bridge and a Plessey AWS-1 radar on the foremast provided the necessary warning system. A navigation radar was carried on a platform projecting forward of the foremast.

After swinging at anchor for several years, the ship was eventually purchased by the British Government for use by the Royal Navy and was transferred in April 1972 to Portsmouth Dockyard and then in the following October to Chatham Dockyard. Here she was refitted to bring her up to Royal Navy standards and was finally commissioned on 16 May 1973. Her purchase from Yarrow Shipbuilders was partly politically motivated: the Conservative Government, which had been elected in 1971, saw this as a way to increase the numerical strength of the Royal Navy, while at the same time providing an indirect cash subsidy to a company which was a vital component of the country's defence industry. Having been provided with the ship by the politicians, it was left to the RN to find a use for her.

She was named *Mermaid*, a name previously carried by a 'Black Swan' class frigate, and after working up was dispatched to the Far East where she was based on Singapore. Her relatively unsophisticated armament and equipment made her unsuitable for front line duties in European waters but she could provide a useful presence in the Far East, undertaking the standard routine of patrols and visits. At times she stood in as the guardship for Hong Kong during the absences of HMS *Chichester* and she also stood by at the end of the Vietnam War in case it should become necessary to evacuate British nationals from Saigon. Returning home in 1976, she was involved in an unfortunate collision with the minesweeper HMS *Fittleton* whilst taking part in a NATO exercise. *Fittleton* sank with the loss of several lives among her RNVR crew, although the *Mermaid* was not seriously damaged. One of her last tasks in RN service was to carry out trials on a moving target indicator system which was a device enabling the radar to pick out small moving targets against the background clutter on the radar screen caused by reflections from the sea surface. When she paid off in 1977, the *Mermaid* had the distinction of being the last ship in the Royal Navy to carry the Mk XIX gun mounting which had been in service for over 30 years as the main AA armament of many types of ships before being replaced by the Mk VI twin 4.5in mounting.

In April 1977 *Mermaid* was transferred to the Malaysian Navy and was renamed *Hang Tuah*. She replaced another ex-British 'Loch' class frigate which had also been named *Hang Tuah* and following a refit by Vosper Thornycroft she sailed for Malaysia in August 1977. Retaining her RN pendant number, F76, she is still in service at the time of writing.

Name	No	Builder	Laid Down	Launched	Completed
Mermaid	F76	Yarrow Shipbuilders, Scotstoun	28/10/65	29/12/66	7/6/68

Note: Commissioned Royal Navy 16 May 1973.

Data: As built
Displacement: 2,300 tons standard; 2,520 tons full load
Length: 340ft oa
Beam: 40ft
Draught: 12ft
Guns: 2 × 4in AA (1 × 2) in Mk XIX twin mounting
4 × 40mm AA (4 × 1)

AS weapons: 1 × Squid three-barrelled mortar
Machinery: 8 × Admiralty Standard Range (ASR1) diesels driving two shafts with controllable pitch propellers giving a total of 12,400shp (16,000bhp)
Speed: 24kt
Oil fuel: 230 tons
Complement: 177 in Royal Navy service

Above:
HMS *Mermaid* in 1974, shortly after being taken over by the Royal Navy. Although a smart looking ship, her weapons and equipment did not suit her for operational deployments in the NATO area. As completed she was armed with four single 40mm guns but two of these were removed shortly after commissioning. *Wright & Logan*

Below:
Mermaid carried the last 4in DP guns in the Royal Navy. This view shows the Mk XIX mounting with left and right handed ship's crests on the gun tampions. The angled face of the bridge, a feature of most modern warships, cuts down internal reflections at night. *Author*

5 Gas Turbines and Guided Missiles

'Amazon' Class (Type 21) GP Frigates

The decision of the Labour government in 1966 to phase out the Royal Navy's aircraft carriers led not only to the cancellation of CVA-01 (a large fleet carrier of 55,000 tons), but also of three of the four planned Type 82 destroyers which were intended to escort the new carrier. At that time the smaller Type 42 destroyers, which were to replace the Type 82 design, were at a very early stage of development, as were the advanced Type 22 frigates, which were to be the follow-on replacement for the 'Leander' class. The net result was that a large gap had appeared in the Navy's shipbuilding programme and, if the Navy was to have sufficient modern fleet escorts in the 1970s a new type was needed urgently. The Royal Navy ship design departments were fully occupied with work on the Type 42 and 22 designs and so, in order to prevent an unacceptable workload on these departments, commercial companies were invited to tender suitable designs. Vosper Thornycroft offered a development of its Mk 5 and Mk 7 frigate designs which had been ordered by various foreign navies and this formed the basis of a contract for the design and development of a new frigate type for the Royal Navy. The contract for the new type, designated Type 21, was awarded to Vosper Thornycroft on 27 February 1968, and Yarrow Ltd, the Clydeside-based warship builder, was nominated to assist in the design stage and participate in the building programme.

The new Type 21 frigates turned out to be a handsome design with a sharply raked bow and streamlined modern looks which won almost universal approval. From the technical point of view, the major feature was that they were the first major warships designed from the start to be entirely propelled by gas turbines. The installation was a COGOG arrangement whose design benefited from the experience gained with HMS *Exmouth* (qv). Two Rolls-Royce Olympus gas turbines producing a total of 50,000shp provided the main propulsion giving a maximum speed of 32kt at full load. For cruising, two Rolls-Royce Tyne engines produced 8,500shp which gave a speed of 18kt. One Olympus and one Tyne were connected to each of two shafts which drove controllable pitch propellers. This arrangement

endowed the ship with an exceptional degree of flexibility and manoeuvrability. In the event of combat damage the ship could run on one shaft if necessary and each shaft could be driven by either of the engines attached to that shaft (although both engines could not be coupled simultaneously). Although main engine performance was monitored and controlled from a compartment adjacent to the enginerooms, main engine functions could be directly controlled from the bridge by aircraft style throttles. The turbine exhausts were trunked through a broad squat funnel which contributed so much to the ship's distinctive appearance. Intakes and associated filter systems were mounted either side of the superstructure just forward of the funnel.

These frigates were designed, like the 'Tribal' class, as general purpose vessels and consequently carried a mixed armament. Introduced for the first time in a frigate was the new Mk 8 automatic 4.5in gun which had first entered service aboard the Type 82 destroyer, HMS *Bristol*. This gun had been developed from the British Army's Abbot self-propelled artillery piece and, adapted for shipboard use, featured an automatic loading system which gave a sustained fire rate of 25 rounds per minute. At the base of the mounting was a 'ready use' magazine holding 15 rounds and these could be fired by remote control without the turret being manned. More sustained firing required the gun to be manned in order to maintain the supply of ammunition. The 55 calibre barrel threw a 25.5kg projectile to a range of 22km (14 miles). Maximum elevation of the barrel was 55° which meant that the gun was mainly intended for use against surface or shore targets, with a limited capability against aircraft. The only other guns fitted were the standard pair of single 20mm guns mounted on either side of the bridge.

For defence against air attack, a quadruple Seacat launcher was mounted on the roof of the helicopter hangar and was controlled by two GWS24 fire control systems mounted abaft the bridge and abaft the funnel. A pair of Knebworth/Corvus chaff dispensers was fitted forward of the bridge for ECM purposes.

No ship-mounted AS weapons were fitted

originally because the ship's Wasp helicopter was envisaged as the main weapons delivery system. Detection and ranging of submarine targets was carried out by Sonars Type 184M and Type 162M.

Compared to earlier designs, a major but less obvious advance was in the provision of advanced electronics and computers to assist in the operation and running of the ship. Computer Assisted Action Information System (CAAIS) was fitted and this was based on the Ferranti 1600B computer. Six Deccascan CA1600 display consoles with Ferranti tracker ball and keyboards were installed in the operations room. Each display is normally used for one specific task, such as ASW helicopter direction and control, but each display can accept data from any of the ship's sensor systems and can take over functions from any other display as necessary. CAAIS can be programmed to assist in target selection and recommend the best weapon to use in response. It can also be used to provide attack data for Exocet missiles (when carried) which use pre-programmed target information for the initial phase of flight, and also for helicopter-vectored attacks. The fire control section of the GWS24 Seacat system was the Ferranti WSA4 which embodied another Ferranti FM1600B computer. The WSA4 could also control the 4.5in gun, if necessary at the same time as a Seacat engagement. Two Type 912 (Italian Selenia Orion RTN10X) radars provided sensor data for the system and their aerials were mounted in front of the foremast and atop the hangar. The forward aerial is normally used for

controlling the gun whilst the after aerial is normally used in conjunction with the Seacat, for which purpose it carries a boresighted TV camera. The TV picture is displayed at the Seacat operator's position in the operations room and is used for the guidance of the missile in flight. Other radars fitted included a Type 992Q (surveillance and target indicator), a Type 978 (navigation), and a Cossor Type 1010 IFF interrogator.

Apart from the quantum increase in fighting efficiency, the fitting of extensive electronics (including electronic engine control systems) had another far-reaching effect in that the number of men required to man the ship was substantially reduced. Total complement was only 177 which compared favourably with the 250 or more required to man a 'Tribal' or 'Leander' class frigate.

In a pleasing link with the past, the ships were allocated names beginning with the letter A and most were in fact named after the 'A' class destroyers built between the wars. The original *Amazon* was a private venture design by J. I. Thornycroft, built at the request of the Admiralty in 1925 and which formed the basis of subsequent destroyer design up to the outbreak of World War 2. The new *Amazon*, first of the Type 21 frigates and nameship of the class, was launched in 1971 by HRH Princess Anne and entered service in 1974.

The design was subject to some criticism on the grounds that it was underarmed in relation to its size and cost, and several modifications were made to counter this deficiency. The major improvement

HMS ARROW. 2,750 tons.

Type 21 General Purpose Frigate.

1980.

F173

BUILDERS - Yarrow (Shipbuilders) Ltd, Glasgow.
LAID DOWN - 28th SEP 1972
LAUNCHED - 5th FEB 1974
COMPLETED - 29th JUL 1976

LENGTH - 384 ft. o.a.
BEAM - 41·8 ft.
DRAUGHT - 14·5 ft.
SPEED - 32 Knots.

Above:
HMS *Amazon*, the lead Type 21, pictured while on builder's trials in 1973. The sweeping lines of the hull and the broad funnel brought a new outline to British frigate design. Note the Type 912 radars, above the bridge and abaft the funnel, which were used in the control of gun and missile engagements. *Vosper Thornycroft*

Right:
HMS *Active* was the last of three Type 21s built by Vosper Thornycroft's Woolston yard. Shown on trials in 1977, she has provision for Exocet missile launchers before the bridge and the chaff launchers are moved to abreast the foremast. *Vosper Thornycroft*

Below:
HMS *Ambuscade* was the first Yarrow-built Type 21 and, along with *Amazon* and *Antelope*, was not initially fitted to carry Exocet missiles. *Yarrows*

was the installation of the Exocet missile system on all vessels after the first three (ie all except *Amazon*, *Antelope* and *Ambuscade*). This work was done while the vessels were completing and it was intended that the earlier vessels should be retrofitted with Exocet at their mid-life refits although *Antelope* was sunk in the Falklands before this could be done. In those ships which were completed with the missile system the installation consisted of four fixed canister launchers mounted in pairs, angled inwards, forward of the bridge. The Corvus chaff launchers previously positioned here were displaced to the upper superstructure abaft the foremast. To protect the bridge structure, blast deflectors were fitted to the forward face of the superstructure. No reloads for the missiles were carried.

It was also planned that the last four ships should be equipped with the new Seawolf missile system instead of the original Seacat installation, but this plan was dropped due to cost considerations and also to topweight and stability problems associated with the greater weight of the new missile system. As it was, all the ships of the class needed extra permanent ballast as a result of equipment fitted over and above the original design.

The first ships to complete were originally equipped with a Wasp HAS1 helicopter pending the introduction of the newer Lynx HAS2 for which the ship was designed. Successful flight trials of the Lynx were conducted aboard HMS *Amazon* in July 1977 and the first ship's flight formed in 1978 with all ships of the class being so equipped as more Lynx became available. While the Lynx much improved the AS capability of the ship because it could carry a heavier weapon load over a greater range than the Wasp, there would still be times when the ship would not be able to attack a submarine because the helicopter was unserviceable or could not operate due to weather conditions. To rectify this defect a programme was put in hand to equip the class with the Plessey STWS-1 AS torpedo system. Two triple-tubed launching systems were fitted on the weather deck either side of the hangar. *Ardent* and *Avenger* were fitted with the AS torpedo tubes while building and again it was the intention that all of the class would be so equipped as the opportunity arose.

Several items of electronic equipment have also been added during the ships' careers. The original design made provision for carrying the SCOT aerials and their protective domes on two platforms just in front of the mainmast. However, this equipment had only become available in the last few years and no ships of the class carried the aerials when completed, although all operational ships have now been so fitted. *Ardent* and *Avenger* were completed with a comprehensive ESM aerial

array carried around the top of the foremast, but below the main radar platform. Other ships of the class are being progressively modified to incorporate this equipment but both *Arrow* and *Alacrity* went through the Falklands operations without being modified.

Generally speaking, the Type 21 frigates have been very popular with their crews. Being relatively modern their accommodation and messing arrangements are of a very high standard and their rakish good looks engender a feeling of pride in the ship. They have been employed in the normal peacetime tasks of a Royal Navy frigate including training, showing the flag and security patrols. *Alacrity* was one of the first Royal Navy ships to visit China for many years when she accompanied a task force of several ships, including HMS *Coventry*, to Shanghai in the autumn of 1980. Several ships, including *Active*, *Ardent* and *Ambuscade*, were deployed to the Persian Gulf area from late 1980 in order to protect the interests of British shipping in the area following the outbreak of war between Iraq and Iran.

All this activity turned out to be but a prelude to the most intensive and dangerous naval actions since the end of World War 2. Seven of the class were involved in the operations for the recovery of the Falkland Islands following their occupation by Argentinian forces on 2 April 1982. These were *Avenger*, *Ardent*, *Antelope*, *Arrow* and *Alacrity*; while *Active* and *Ambuscade* may also have been involved in supporting operations. *Amazon* missed out on the action as she was deployed to the Middle and Far East for four months and returned to Plymouth in late June 1982.

Antelope, *Arrow* and *Alacrity* sailed in early April as part of the escort of the main task force and accompanying merchant ships including the liner *Canberra*. Operations against the Falklands commenced on 1 May with the bombing of Port Stanley but, on 4 May, HMS *Sheffield* was hit by an Exocet missile launched from an Etendard strike aircraft. Although the missile did not explode, burning fuel caused a major fire which defied all attempts to extinguish it and gradually destroyed the ship. HMS *Arrow* went alongside the *Sheffield* to assist in firefighting efforts, and, when it became apparent that the fire was uncontrollable, to embark survivors. During this period an Argentinian submarine was detected in the vicinity and a torpedo was fired at *Arrow* and *Sheffield*, although, luckily, it missed. After several hours, *Sheffield* was abandoned and *Arrow* withdrew having rescued 236 survivors from a total ship's company of approximately 300. After the landings at San Carlos on 21 May, *Arrow* was engaged for the following two weeks in providing air defence and gunfire support for the ships in the

HMS *Amazon*, nameship of the class, at speed. Note the stabilised antenna for the Type 992Q radar at the top of the foremast. *Fleet Photographic Unit*

The Type 21s were designed from the outset to carry a Lynx helicopter and the lines of the hull gave a much broader flightdeck than on earlier frigates. On this post-Falklands view of HMS *Active* can be seen the additional 20mm guns mounted on the flightdeck to improve self defence firepower. *MoD Navy*

With the exception of *Amazon*, the whole class was actively involved in the Falklands campaign. Here HMS *Arrow* is laid alongside the burning destroyer HMS *Sheffield*. Despite the valiant efforts of the crews of both ships, the destroyer was a total loss after being hit by an Exocet missile. *Fleet Photographic Unit*

area and the troops ashore. Later she was involved in bombardment operations in support of the final attacks against Port Stanley. The ship suffered no major damage and claimed three enemy aircraft shot down as well as several gun emplacements and radar sites destroyed during shore bombardments. Returning to Plymouth on 7 August, she was greeted by an enthusiastic crowd of relations and wellwishers and also by a dramatic flypast of the Royal Air Force's Red Arrows display team trailing coloured smoke over the ship. The ship and the Red Arrows had formed a happy association over the years and the RAF team were pleased to be able to welcome their adopted ship as she returned from war.

HMS *Alacrity*, after escorting the task force to the Falklands, was employed on operations in preparation for the main invasion. On at least one occasion she landed men of the Royal Marines Special Boat Squadron (SBS) to carry out reconnaissance of potential landing sites. On the night of 10 May the ship sailed through the Falklands Sound in an attempt to establish Argentinian positions and while thus engaged she came across an unidentified merchant ship which was immediately engaged with gunfire. After only a few minutes the merchant ship blew up in a sheet of flame and sank shortly afterwards. It was later established that the ship concerned was the Argentinian transport *Islas de Los Estados* which had been carrying a cargo of aviation fuel. Following the landings at San Carlos on 21 May, *Alacrity* was one of the ships escorting the *Atlantic Conveyor* just north of the Falklands when she was hit by Exocet missiles intended for the carrier *Hermes*. The missiles had been deflected by the carrier's countermeasures but had then locked on to the *Atlantic Conveyor*. Once again, an uncontrollable fire broke out and *Alacrity* went alongside to assist firefighting attempts and then to rescue survivors. Two of the ship's divers spent a considerable time in the extremely cold water and at great risk to their own lives in order to assist crew members from the *Atlantic Conveyor* who had taken to the water to escape the fires on the ship. *Alacrity* was one of the first ships to return from the Falklands, arriving back in Plymouth on 4 June and having suffered only superficial damage to her bows caused when going alongside the *Atlantic Conveyor*. She had been attacked from the air at least 10 times and on one occasion an Argentinian aircraft placed two bombs only 10ft on either side of the ship. Despite this, and a number of Exocet attacks, on her return to Plymouth the major item up for repair was the gun barrel which was worn out after firing more than 500 4.5in shells!

The third ship of the original trio, HMS *Antelope*, was not so fortunate. Escorting the landing force, which included the assault ships *Fearless* and *Intrepid* as well as the *Canberra* and other merchant ships, into Falkland Sound and San Carlos Water she survived the heavy air attacks on the first day. On Saturday, 22 May, there was a lull in the Argentinian attacks but the next day brought a renewal of the air offensive. British forces claimed six aircraft shot down plus three more probables. During this raid, a 500lb bomb hit the *Antelope* and, although it did not explode, it lodged in the engineroom. With the cessation of the air raids, the ship was moved to a quiet anchorage and almost all her crew was evacuated while efforts were made to defuse the bomb. During the night the bomb exploded, killing SSgt James Prescott of the Royal Engineers who was involved in the work on the bomb and who was awarded a posthumous Conspicuous Gallantry Medal in recognition of his bravery on this occasion. WO John Phillips, another Royal Engineer, was seriously injured in the explosion along with six others. He received a DSC for his valiant efforts to save the ship.

The explosion of the bomb, positioned as it was in the bowels of the ship, caused serious damage and started a raging fire. Although several other ships and helicopters assisted the struggle against the fire and the all-enveloping smoke, the ship was quickly gutted and on the afternoon of the following day, 24 May, she broke her back and sank. Fortunately, apart from the bomb disposal team, there were no casualties among her crew as they had all been transferred to other ships.

Unhappily, *Antelope* was not the first or only Type 21 to be sunk. On 21 May, the first day of the landings, HMS *Ardent* was detached to assist in the bombardment of the Argentinian airstrip at Goose Green. Here, in the more open waters of the Falkland Sound, she was subjected to a series of heavy air attacks by Pucaras, Skyhawks and Mirages. During these attacks a pair of Skyhawks succeeded in placing two 500lb bombs on the after section of the ship, disabling the Seacat system and causing an outbreak of fire. Damage control teams succeeded in controlling the fires but then the ship was attacked again by three more Skyhawks and two more bombs hit the side of the ship causing further damage and starting more fires. Although reduced to firing machine guns and 20mm cannon, the ship's crew fought on as the ship was subjected to further attacks. The ship's canteen manager manned a machine gun during this phase and succeeded in hitting one of the attackers. For this action, and the inspiration he provided to others, he was later awarded a DSM. Meanwhile the ship was dying as the fires took hold and the mortally damaged ship settled in the water. The ship's captain, Cdr Alan West (later to receive the DSC), reluctantly gave the order to anchor and abandon

Above:
Sadly, two Type 21s were lost during the Falklands campaign. One of these was HMS *Antelope*, hit in the engine room by a bomb which did not explode on 22 May 1982. With the hole caused by the bomb plainly visible in the ship's side, she was moved to a quiet part of the San Carlos anchorage and attempts were made to defuse the bomb, although it subsequently exploded during the night and the ship later sank. *MoD Navy*

Left:
HMS *Ardent* was also lost during the Falklands campaign, but before that she had been employed on the 'Armilla' patrol escorting British-registered merchant ships in the Gulf of Oman following the outbreak of war between Iraq and Iran. *MoD Navy*

Below:
In recent years the surviving Type 21s have suffered from severe hull cracking and this has required extensive repairs and strengthening. Visible in this 1987 view of HMS *Arrow* is the metal strip welded to the hull side at the point of maximum stress. *HMS Drake*

ship. The performance of this ship and her crew were in the finest traditions of the Royal Navy and it is sad to recall that 22 men were killed and more than 30 injured during her last fierce battle.

Fortunately, *Ardent* and *Antelope* were the only losses sustained by British frigates during the Falklands campaign. By comparison, *Ambuscade* had a fairly straightforward war. Leaving Plymouth on 9 April 1982, she proceeded to Gibraltar where she arrived on the 13th. On 3 May she left Gibraltar in company with other ships and sailed for the Falklands, stopping at Ascension Island en route in order to join up with the main invasion force. Between 21 May and 15 June she was engaged in support of the San Carlos landings and other operations. She was then detached to South Georgia carrying reliefs for the troops already ashore there, and then returned to Plymouth calling at Ascension Island on the way. By the time she docked at Devonport on 26 July, she had been at sea for 83 days, had steamed 29,226 nautical miles, fired 500 4.5in shells and her helicopter had made 377 deck landings.

A late arrival at the war was HMS *Avenger* which did not leave the UK until 10 May and arrived in the Falklands on the 25th, claiming her 15-day passage as a record for any ship involved in the task force operations. Proceeding to Falkland Sound she was a welcome replacement for the losses already suffered and she assisted in the continuing defence of the landing force against the valiant efforts of the still potent Argentine Air Force. Her divers salvaged a 20mm gun from the wreck of the *Antelope* and this was remounted on *Avenger* to increase her AA fire. Later she assisted in the final bombardments of Port Stanley and after the surrender stayed in the islands to assist in the postwar operations. On the day after the surrender she made the first landing in the West Falklands and picked up 900 Argentinian prisoners for transport to the main POW camp at Port Stanley. She eventually returned home in mid-September.

Also leaving the UK on 10 May was HMS *Active* which, in company with the other ships of the second group, arrived in the Total Exclusion Zone (TEZ) just a few hours after the sinking of HMS *Coventry*. *Active* quickly lived up to her name and during daylight hours was deployed as part of the escort screen for the main task force stationed between 150 and 180 miles east of Port Stanley. At night she was detached to escort resupply convoys to San Carlos or to carry out shore bombardments prior to the capture of Port Stanley. Inbound convoys normally departed from the edge of the TEZ at approximately 18.00 and followed set routes along the north coast of East Falkland to arrive at San Carlos by 10.00 the next day. Outbound convoys departed at 22.00 to reach

the Battle Group by 11.00. Escorts normally exchanged convoys at approximately 03.00 at a designated crossover point. Shore bombardments were normally carried out between 02.00 and 06.00 in order to deny the Argentinian forces around Stanley the maximum amount of sleep. On the night of 13/14 June, with a calm sea and a full moon, HMS *Active* and three other ships fired over 1,000 rounds on to the Moody Brook and Tumbledown Mount area. This action contributed greatly to the subsequent Argentine surrender. *Active* then remained in the Falklands area for another four weeks before finally returning to the UK on 3 August. I am indebted to Cdr P. C. B. Canter, RN (CO HMS *Active*) for the detailed information set out above.

The Type 21 frigates were probably involved in some of the fiercest fighting of the war and were certainly tested to the utmost. Several sources have criticised the design in the light of the loss of the *Antelope* and *Ardent* but, although there may be some justification for this in respect of the properties of the aluminium alloys used in the superstructure when subjected to the intense heat of the fires, on the whole the ships have proved sturdy and reliable vessels. *Ardent* in particular absorbed a tremendous amount of damage before being finally abandoned and it is doubtful if any other comparable contemporary warship type could have taken similar damage and have survived.

Following the end of hostilities the ships gradually returned to the UK although, with tension still high in the South Atlantic, several subsequently took part in the routine five-month deployments which were instituted after the war. Thus *Amazon* sailed from the UK in August 1982 as part of a force headed by the new carrier *Illustrious* while *Alacrity* was dispatched the following month. Since then the Type 21s have revisited the area on several occasions although the commitment has gradually been scaled down and at present only a single frigate is deployed to the South Atlantic at any one time.

Type 21s also continued to take part in the 'Armilla' patrol in the Gulf of Oman, a task which had been maintained by other ships including the New Zealand 'Leander' class HMNZS *Canterbury*. It was during one of these deployments that *Ambuscade* collided with the American missile destroyer USS *Dale* while exercising in the Indian Ocean. *Ambuscade* suffered major damage and was laid up in dry dock at Bombay for repairs to enable her to return to Plymouth in August 1983. With the escalation in hostilities in the Gulf area, the Type 21s were considered unsuitable for these deployments and the task was generally allocated, whenever possible, to Seawolf-armed Type 22s and 'Leanders', and to the Sea Dart-armed

Type 42 destroyers. However, shortage of suitable ships occasionally necessitated the allocation of a Type 21 to the task and, for example, *Active* was deployed to the Gulf in the summer of 1987.

Amazon was fortunate enough to be selected for a major round-the-world group deployment (Global 86) in 1986. Consisting of the ships *Beaver*, *Manchester*, *Amazon* and the submarine *Swiftsure* plus support vessels, the group sailed from the UK in April and visited South America, Panama, the US West Coast and Vancouver, Pearl Harbor, Hong Kong, the Far East and Australia before returning home in December 1986. The carrier *Illustrious* was scheduled to accompany this group but mechanical trouble prevented this until the latter stages.

More recently the Type 21s have taken part in various NATO exercises and have regularly provided the guardship for the West Indies station.

A major problem with these ships arose in 1983 with the discovery of major cracks in the hull and upper deck amidships. No doubt the arduous operations in heavy seas around the Falklands had contributed to this problem although the fact that it did not occur to older ships such as the Type 12s and 'Leanders' is an indication that the Type 21 hull was structurally weaker. The fault was first noticed on *Arrow* which underwent repairs at Devonport in 1983. The work involved the riveting of a metal strap along the hull side amidships at 1 Deck level in addition to internal strengthening. This work was progressively applied, as a matter of urgency, to other members of the class. *Amazon* suffered similar problems in May 1983 when the cracks were large enough to cause engineroom flooding. In this case the ship had to be withdrawn from service and a planned refit brought forward during which she finally received the Exocet launchers, STWS-1 torpedo tubes and EW equipment which was previously lacking. *Ambuscade* was the last Type 21 to be brought up to standard, this being done during a major £20 million refit at Devonport during 1984/85.

Other modifications which have been made since the Falklands include the addition of ballast

Above:
An artist's impression of the Type 21 Command Frigate proposed by Vosper Thornycroft for possible export orders. Featuring an increase in beam, the ship would have carried a modern weapons outfit including VLS Seawolf and Harpoon SSM missiles. *Vosper Thornycroft*

to improve stability, updating of sonar equipment and all ships have standardised on a light AA armament of four single 20mm guns — two in the bridge wings and two on the flightdeck abaft the hangar. One interesting piece of equipment fitted to *Avenger* in a major refit completed in the spring of 1988 is a hydraulically actuated trim flap mounted on the stern. Similar to, but much larger than, the trim flaps fitted to racing power boats it enables the hull to be set at the best angle to suite the power setting and sea conditions. This in turn should result in more efficient and economical operation of the engines. The fitting involves the installation of substantial vertical strengthening ribs on the transom stern to carry the hinges and actuating mechanism for the flaps. These are, presumably, fitted on a trials basis but may be extended to the other ships of the class if proved successful.

More significant are the possible improvements not made. There are no plans to fit any version of the Seawolf missile to replace the elderly Seacat, the ships have not received any of the GAM-BO1 20mm guns fitted to other active members of the fleet and the Corvus chaff launchers have not been supplemented or replaced by any of the new systems (Super RBOC or Sea Gnat) which, again, are being fitted throughout the rest of the fleet.

These omissions are partly due to the stability and strength problems experienced by the Type 21, but they also indicate that the ships will increasingly be allocated to second line duties as they reach the closing stages of their careers.

Vosper Thornycroft, joint developers of the design, were well aware of the limitations and have, over the years, offered several developed versions. As far back as 1975 a Seawolf-armed variant had been designed. This utilised a lightweight system, Seawolf/Psi, which consisted of four twin-barrelled launchers at the superstructure corners. The launchers were reloaded from below decks using a manual hoist and a Type 910 tracking radar was carried for each pair of launchers. The heavy combined Type 967/968 surveillance radars normally associated with Seawolf were replaced by a lighter antenna array using Marconi S686N and S810P radars. To accommodate this equipment, increase internal volume and restore stability margins, the hull beam was increased by 2ft. This, of course, led to the design being referred to as the Broad-Beamed Type 21. It was hoped that this version would have some export appeal even if, as happened, it was not ordered by the Royal Navy.

In the event no orders were forthcoming but the design was dusted off and updated in 1985 in response to a requirement for three modern frigates from Pakistan. The new version was known as the Type 21 Command Frigate and featured the broad-beamed hull together with the proven Olympus/Tyne COGOG machinery. Armament was considerably updated and comprised a 4.5in gun, two single 30mm guns, Goalkeeper CIWS, two quadruple Harpoon launchers and VLS Seawolf system with 24 missiles in a silo. A comprehensive radar, electronics and sonar outfit was to be carried and provision for a towed array was made. Various changes were made to the internal layout and the lessons learnt in the Falklands in respect of fire and damage control were fully incorporated.

Again no orders were obtained, but the Command Frigate showed the amount of development the basic Type 21 design was capable of. However, few of the changes could realistically have been incorporated in the Royal Navy ships as none had the broad-beamed hull which would have enabled the development versions to carry extra equipment without serious stability problems.

Name	No	Builder	Laid Down	Launched	Commission	Fate	Date
Amazon	F169	Vosper Thornycroft, Woolston	6/11/69	26/4/71	11/5/74	In service 4th FS	
Antelope	F170	Vosper Thornycroft, Woolston	23/3/71	16/3/72	19/7/75	Sank after bomb explosion, Falklands	24/5/82
Active	F171	Vosper Thornycroft, Woolston	23/7/71	23/11/72	17/6/77	In service 4th FS	
Ambuscade	F172	Yarrow Shipbuilders, Clyde	1/9/71	18/1/73	5/9/75	In service 4th FS	
Arrow	F173	Yarrow Shipbuilders, Clyde	28/9/72	5/2/74	29/7/76	In service 4th FS	
Alacrity	F174	Yarrow Shipbuilders, Clyde	5/3/73	18/9/74	2/7/77	In service 4th FS	
Ardent	F184	Yarrow Shipbuilders, Clyde	26/2/74	9/5/75	13/10/77	Sunk, air attack, Falklands	21/5/82
Avenger	F185	Yarrow Shipbuilders, Clyde	30/10/74	20/11/75	19/07/78	In service 4th FS	

Data: Type 21, HMS *Ardent* (1978)
Displacement: 2,750 tons standard; 3,250 tons full load
Length/beam: 384ft oa/41.8ft
Draught: 19.5ft full load
Armament: 1 × Mk 8 4.5in gun, 2×1 20mm guns, GWS50 Exocet SSM (4×1). GWS24 Seacat SAM system (1×4). 2×3 12.75in AS TT, STWS-1

Aircraft: 1 × Westland Lynx HAS2 helicopter
Radar/sonar: Types 992Q, 912, 1006/184M, 162M
Machinery: COGOG. 2×25,000shp Rolls-Royce Olympus gas turbines, 2×4,250shp Rolls-Royce RM1A Tyne gas turbines
Speed/range: 32kt/4,000 miles at 17kt
Oil fuel: ?
Complement: 177

'Broadsword' Class (Type 22) GP Frigates

The development of a successor to the excellent 'Leander' class frigates proved to be a long-drawn-out affair. Initial design efforts in the early 1960s centred on an enlarged 'Leander' carrying the Sea Dart AA missile which was under development at the time. The resulting general purpose escort vessel eventually grew in size and capability and finally became the Type 82 fleet escort destroyer which was designed to act as an escort to the new fast aircraft carrier (CVA-01). With the cancellation of the carrier in the February Defence White Paper, 1966, plans to build four Type 82 vessels were cancelled and only one, HMS *Bristol*, was completed. The loss of CVA-01 and the subsequent decision to phase out the rest of the aircraft carriers meant that by the mid-1970s the RN would have no effective defence against air attack and as a result top priority was given to the design and development of an air defence escort vessel which would be equipped with the Sea Dart system. The outcome of this effort was the Type 42 destroyer and the first example, HMS *Sheffield*, was commissioned in February 1975. A total of 14 ships have been ordered and they now carry the main responsibility for the air defence of the fleet.

With the priority accorded to the Type 42, work on the 'Leander' replacement proceeded slowly and, as already related, the privately designed Type 21 was produced as a stopgap measure. By the early 1970s the new design, now designated Type 22, was more or less complete but the first vessel of the class was not laid down until February 1975, with others being laid down at approximately yearly intervals.

The specification for the Type 22 called for a vessel capable of sustained AS operations, but with a general purpose capability also. An early decision was made that the class would be gas turbine powered and in fact the machinery installation was identical to that of the Type 42 destroyers which produced beneficial operating economies for the Navy and meant that a common spares holding could be utilised.

Although it is likely that consideration was given to the installation of the Ikara system, the main AS weapon finally selected was the Lynx helicopter. The Lynx's development started in 1967 and the first army version flew in March 1971 — the first naval version flying in May 1972. It represented a great improvement over the Wasp and could carry a greater load of weapons and sensors over greater distances. Also, being twin-engined, it could return to its parent vessel in the event of a single engine failure. All previous helicopter-equipped Royal Navy frigates had carried only one helicopter which meant that if the helicopter was unserviceable or was being refuelled or rearmed then the ship was bereft of its main AS weapon. Consequently it was decided that the Type 22 would carry two Lynx helicopters in a double hangar. A normal flightdeck was positioned over the stern and was large enough to allow one Lynx to land or take off. The second Lynx, if aboard, had to be stowed in the hangar to allow flightdeck operations to proceed.

The Type 22 was also designed to carry the Plessey STWS-1 triple AS torpedo launchers which were positioned on either beam abaft the funnel. Originally intended to fire the standard 12.75in

homing torpedo, the system is also able to fire the new Stingray lightweight torpedo. The Lynx helicopters will also be able to carry the Stingray and the two systems together give the Type 22 an outstanding AS capability.

Detection and tracking of submarine targets is carried out by a Type 2016 multi-frequency panoramic sonar. Other sonars are carried to give the precise information required for the attack phase using the helicopters or the ship-launched torpedoes.

The ability to maintain high speeds in a rough sea is a major requirement for modern AS vessels and to achieve this the hull of the Type 22 closely follows the lines of the 'Leander' class which was renowned for its seakeeping qualities. The hull is basically flush-decked with the characteristic raised forecastle as in the 'Leanders'. A superstructure deck, extending the full width of the ship, stretches from the break of the forecastle to the hangar aft. This has provided a considerable volume of internal space for the extensive computers, weapon control systems and improved accommodation which are all features of any modern warship. The upper superstructure, masts and funnel have been kept as clean as possible with only essential weapon launchers, aerials and deck fittings being mounted outside the main superstructure blocks. This makes the ship easier to clean down if affected by nuclear fallout and also provides less radar reflective surfaces for missile guidance systems to lock on to.

To carry out the general purpose requirements of the design the ship is equipped with two missile systems. For use against surface targets four Exocet container launchers, angled inward in pairs, are carried on the forecastle deck. Two sextuple launchers for the Seawolf missile are carried, one on the hangar roof and the other forward of the bridge. Together with their tracking and guidance radars and control system, the Seawolf missiles constitute the GWS25 missile system and provide the ship with a most effective defence against aircraft and missiles.

Other weapons carried include two Mk 9 40mm Bofors mountings carried abreast the foremast and the standard multiple rocket launchers of the Knebworth/Corvus decoy system. At the time of their inception, the Type 22 frigates were the first major warships in the Royal Navy to dispense with the gun as part of their main armament; the 40mm guns were really only intended for peacetime patrol duties although they also represented a last-ditch defence against missiles. In the field of engineering the class were also of interest in that they were the first British warships designed to metric standards instead of the old Imperial measures.

As is only to be expected these days, the Type 22

carries an extensive range of radar and electronic equipment. At the top of the foremast is the combined aerial for the Type 967/968 radar carried on a fully stabilised mounting. This equipment was first tested aboard HMS *Penelope* and is now also fitted to those 'Leander' class ships converted to carry the Seawolf missile. The 967/968 acts as an air and surface surveillance system and provides target information for the Seawolf tracking radars and also for the Exocet guidance system. As has been mentioned previously, the Exocet missile is provided with an updated target position before it is launched and flies most of the distance to the target using this pre-programmed information before switching on its own radar for final positioning. In this context it is interesting to note that current Royal Navy experience has shown that the Lynx helicopters, equipped as they are with the excellent Ferranti Seaspray radar, have proved most useful in providing targeting data for the Exocet; either giving information on targets over the radar horizon or else providing target information on normal targets so that the parent

vessel does not need to betray its position by transmitting with its own radar. Coupled with the fact that the Lynx is now being equipped with the Sea Skua air-to-surface missile, the Type 22 now displays an anti-ship capacity not equalled by previous frigates.

For Seawolf guidance, the Type 910 guidance and tracking radar systems are carried, one atop the bridge structure and the other on the hangar structure aft. Below the main radar platform on the foremast are the sensors for a comprehensive ESM outfit while the mainmast carries HF/DF equipment at the mast top as well as more ESM equipment. Flying platforms are provided just forward of the funnel to carry the SCOT aerials although these were not always fitted on completion. The whole sensor and weapons fit is controlled by the ship's computerised Action Information System (AIO) which is a further development of the Computer Assisted Action Information System (CAAIS) fitted in earlier frigates. One other radar is carried; a Type 1006 navigation and short range surveillance radar with

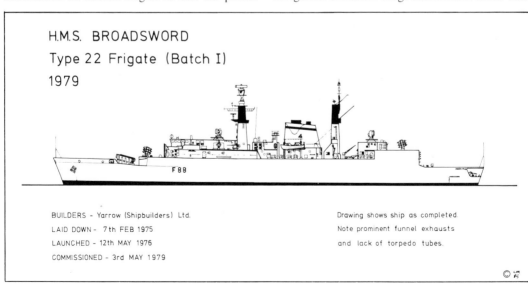

H.M.S. BROADSWORD
Type 22 Frigate (Batch I)
1979

F 88

BUILDERS - Yarrow (Shipbuilders) Ltd.
LAID DOWN - 7th FEB 1975
LAUNCHED - 12th MAY 1976
COMMISSIONED - 3rd MAY 1979

Drawing shows ship as completed.
Note prominent funnel exhausts
and lack of torpedo tubes.

Left:
The Type 22 represented a great leap in the size and capability of the modern frigate. HMS *Broadsword* was the first of the class and was completed in 1979. *C&S Taylor*

Right:
A feature of the first pair of ships was the wide spacing of the funnel exhaust trunking and this is shown in this bow view of HMS *Broadsword* running trials. Both ships are scheduled to be refitted with the slimmer funnel featured on later ships. *Yarrows*

Below:
The length of the Batch 1 Type 22s was determined by the size of the drydocks in the Devonport Dockyard frigate complex where ships can be repaired and refitted under cover. The docks were later enlarged to take the lengthened Batch 2 ships. *MoD Navy*

its aerial mounted on a small platform projecting forward and to port of the foremast.

The ship is powered by a COGOG arrangement of two Rolls-Royce Olympus marine turbines coupled with two Rolls-Royce Tyne gas turbines for cruising power. The installation gives the ship a cruising speed of 18kt using the Tynes, while maximum speed with the Olympus engines is 30kt. Great care has been taken in the design of the ship to ensure that the engine units can be easily removed and replaced so that a policy of 'upkeep by exchange' can be implemented. Four diesel-powered one-megawatt generators are carried, two forward of the main engines and two aft of them, to ensure a reliable supply of electrical power (440V, three-phase, 60Hz). The electrical supply system is duplicated and either system can be driven by any two generators to meet the full load requirement of the ship. In this way the ship's electrical power system can be maintained despite considerable battle damage: a vital factor considering a modern warship's absolute dependence on electronic systems.

The extensive use of electronics and computers has meant that the manning complement required for the ship is considerably less than would previously have been expected for a ship of this size and complexity. In fact the total of 250 men is about the same as the original complement of the early 'Leander' class, despite the fact that the Type 22 is nearly twice the displacement and carries a much more sophisticated armament. All internal space is air conditioned and a high standard of accommodation is provided for all crew members. Extensive use is made of modular furniture constructed from aluminium and GRP, and modern fireproof laminates provided a light and airy decor to the messdecks, although some would say that the result gives a cold and clinical appearance.

The lead ship of the class, *Broadsword*, was handed over to the RN at Plymouth in April 1979 just over three years after she was laid down. This represented a very creditable performance by the

Above left:
HMS *Brilliant* was completed with a revised funnel design. With her sister ship, *Broadsword*, she played an important part in the Falklands war and was involved in the operations to recover South Georgia. Later she was the first ship to fire Seawolfs in anger and shot down three aircraft out of an attacking wave of four — an unprecedented successful combat debut for any weapon system! *Fleet Photographic Unit*

Left:
The Batch 2 ships were instantly recognisable by a 41ft increase in hull length amidships and a sharply raked bow. Armament was identical to the earlier ships and comprised a double-ended GWS25 Seawolf system, two 40mm guns and AS torpedoes. A major addition was the Type 2031 towed array sonar housed below the flightdeck. *PRO, Flag Officer, Plymouth*

Top:
Part of HMS *Boxer's* operations room showing some of the display consoles associated with the ship's Computer Assisted Command System (CACS). Tactical situations can be shown on the large display screens using information derived from the radars, sonars and data links while tabular information is shown on the small rectangular screens. *Plessey Naval Systems*

Above:
HMS *Brave* was the first to have the extended flightdeck and enlarged hangar necessary to operate a Sea King or Merlin helicopter. She also introduced the Type 911 tracking radar on her Seawolf directors and was the first Royal Navy ship to use Rolls-Royce Spey gas turbines as part of her propulsion machinery. *C&S Taylor*

builders, Yarrow Shipbuilders, considering the complexity of the design and the inevitable problems connected with the construction of the first ship of a new class. The second vessel, *Battleaxe*, was also completed in just over three years and commissioned in March 1980, but the next two took nearer four years to complete. In service, the main role of the Type 22 is to act as leader of an AS task force for which its excellent communication facilities make it ideally suited. They can also combine with the larger ASW cruisers ('Invincible' class) to form a powerful ASW force which would be tasked with the closing off of the Greenland-Iceland-UK gap to the passage of Soviet submarines positioning to attack vital trans-Atlantic convoys.

In 1980 it was announced that the fifth and subsequent members of the class would be lengthened to provide additional internal space which would be mainly occupied by additional sonar equipment, both active and passive. *Boxer*, the first of the Batch II variant, was laid down in 1979 and launched in 1981, entering service at the end of 1983. Externally the obvious difference from the preceding ships was the hull, which was lengthened amidships by 41ft forward of the machinery spaces, and the addition of a sharply raked bow. This latter feature is normally associated with a bow sonar but none of the Batch II ships have been so fitted to date, although the new Ferranti Type 2050 may be installed at a later date. Below the flightdeck aft was the large drum and cable handling equipment associated with the Type 2031 towed array passive sonar.

Internal changes included additional accommodation, a larger operations room and an increase in bunker capacity. However, the most important change was the introduction of a Computer Assisted Command System (CACS-1) to replace the CAAIS fitted in the first four ships. This equipment was intended to be considerably more capable and faster in operation than its predecessor with, for instance, the ability to handle up to 500 target tracks instead of the 60 in CAAIS. However, the CACS-1 fitted to *Boxer* was the first example of its type, there being no shore-based development rig, and when the ship commenced trials in 1984 it became apparent that the equipment was not living up to expectations. Consequently the ship has spent a considerable amount of time on further trials in an effort to iron out the bugs. Although the CACS-1 is now working, after a fashion, the results of the trials have entailed a complete review of the CACS systems which were to be fitted to later ships and a completely new system is now under development.

It was originally intended to build a significant number of Type 22 frigates but the Defence White Paper introduced by Defence Minister John Nott in July 1981 appeared to spell the end of plans to continue building the class as they were deemed too expensive. It was announced that one more Type 22 would be ordered in addition to the six already approved at the time of the White Paper, but no more would be subsequently built. Even the seventh one ordered was really little more than a sop to the Navy to make up for the decision to sell the carrier *Invincible*. However, the die was cast and it had been decided in government circles that it could no longer afford to construct large and sophisticated ships in any significant numbers and that subsequent frigates would be of a much simpler, and therefore cheaper, design. Already, as an economy measure, those Type 22 frigates in

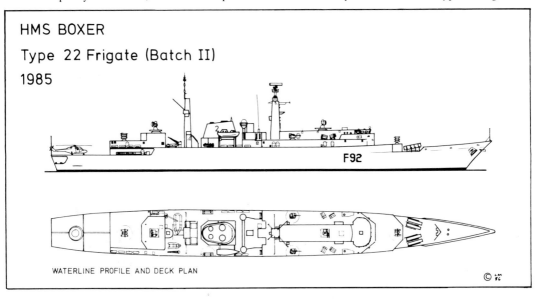

HMS BOXER

Type 22 Frigate (Batch II)

1985

F92

WATERLINE PROFILE AND DECK PLAN

© *tc*

Above:
HMS *Sheffield* was one of two Type 22s named in
commemoration of the Type 42 destroyers, *Sheffield* and
Coventry, lost in the Falklands and was completed in 1988.
Visible in this photograph are the dual antenna on the
Type 911 tracking radar and the Sea Gnat decoy system
launchers in the bridge wings.   *HMS Osprey*

Below:
A Sea King helicopter aboard HMS *London* during trials
to check the operation of large helicopters from the
extended flightdeck. The use of such large helicopters
considerably enhances the ship's effective radius as an
ASW platform. Note the large fairlead on the port side of
the transom through which the towed array sonar is
deployed.   *HMS Osprey*

service were only equipped with one Lynx helicopter instead of the planned two, although it was planned to embark the extra helicopter in wartime. As it happened, the Type 22 went to war much earlier than anybody expected.

When the Falklands were invaded in early April 1982, *Brilliant* and *Broadsword* were among the first ships of the task force to sail, acting as close escorts to the two carriers *Hermes* and *Invincible*. *Brilliant* was soon in action. Equipped now with two Lynx helicopters she took part in the operations to recapture South Georgia and her two helicopters took part in the attack on the Argentinian submarine *Santa Fe*. Leaving South Georgia she proceeded to rejoin the main body of the task force and resume her duties as part of the defence screen of the two carriers. On 12 May, while engaged on this task, she was attacked by a wave of Argentinian Skyhawks and her Seawolf missiles shot down two of them while a third was observed crashing into the sea as it tried to avoid another Seawolf. This action was a significant milestone in warship development as it was the first operational use of the Seawolf missile and the success rate fully justified the effort and expense involved in this rapid reaction system. The Seawolf system is automatic in action, detecting and identifying targets, training and launching missiles to counter perceived threats without the intervention of human operators. So good did the system prove itself to be in combat conditions that it was said, with more than a grain of truth, that on

many occasions the first warning of impending attack was the 'whoosh' as a Seawolf left its launcher.

Just before the main invasion at San Carlos, *Brilliant* was involved in the rescue of survivors from the Sea King helicopter which crashed in the sea while transferring SAS personnel between ships as part of the preparations for the main landings. On the day of the landings her aircraft direction team were responsible for vectoring Sea Harriers on many successful interceptions of Argentinian Skyhawks and Mirages. During the next few days she assisted in the defence of the beachhead and although near-missed by several bombs and hit by aircraft cannon fire she suffered no serious damage and only three minor casualties. On 25 May, *Brilliant* was on hand when the *Atlantic Conveyor* was hit and sunk by an Exocet missile and once again was involved in rescuing survivors, 25 of whom were brought on board. In the closing days of the campaign in mid-June she acted as escort to the merchant ships *St Edmund*, *Container Bezant* and *Europic Ferry*, which were carrying vitally-needed Chinook helicopters. While *Brilliant* stood by, the Chinooks were assembled and distributed among the ships before flying off together to the Falklands. Following her exploits in the South Atlantic, *Brilliant* set sail for home and arrived at her home port of Plymouth to a rapturous welcome on 13 August 1982.

Broadsword was on her way to the Middle East to take part in Gulf patrol necessitated by the

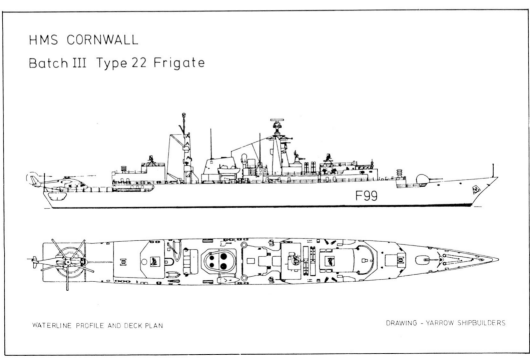

HMS CORNWALL

Batch III Type 22 Frigate

F99

WATERLINE PROFILE AND DECK PLAN

DRAWING - YARROW SHIPBUILDERS

Above:
The Batch 3 ships have a considerably uprated weapons outfit which includes the 4.5in gun forward, Harpoon missiles abaft the bridge and a Goalkeeper CIWS in front of the foremast. HMS *Cornwall* was the first of the class to be completed, joining the fleet in 1988. *HMS Osprey*

Below:
The Dutch Goalkeeper CIWS was purchased as a result of experience in the Falklands and is a highly effective self-defence system. The GAU-8/A gatling gun fires 4,200 rounds/min and the mounting carries its own search and target tracking radars. Goalkeeper will be fitted to the new Type 23 frigates as well as the existing Type 22s.
Hollandse Signaalapparaten

Iran-Iraq war when she was redirected to accompany the task force south to the Falklands. Although not involved in the South Georgia operations, she nevertheless had a very active war. While attacked several times from the air in the days immediately following the San Carlos landings, her luck held out until 25 May when she was operating in close company with the Type 42 destroyer *Coventry*. Several waves of Skyhawks attacked both ships and one bomb ricocheted off the sea and ripped through the stern and flight deck, destroying a Lynx helicopter parked there. Fortunately the bomb did not explode and the damage was later repaired with the ship remaining operational in the meantime. The *Coventry* did not fare so well and several bombs hit her on the port side causing her quickly to heel over and sink. *Broadsword* immediately moved in and was able to rescue most of the survivors. During the Falkland operations, *Broadsword* claimed at least three enemy aircraft destroyed and despite being attacked more than a dozen times she sustained only 12 minor casualties. She arrived back in Plymouth on 23 August to the by then traditional welcome by thousands of well-wishers and a flotilla of small craft following the ship to her berth.

Although *Battleaxe* was with other ships taking part in Exercise 'Springtrain 82' and entered Gibraltar on 24 March 1982, she was not sent to the South Atlantic as part of the task force. Retained in home waters until August 1982, she then sailed south as part of the force escorting the carrier *Illustrious* which was to relieve HMS *Invincible*. Just after the close of hostilities the fourth ship of the class, HMS *Brazen*, was commissioned for service on 2 July 1982. Her completion had been brought forward as a result of a splendid effort by Yarrow Shipbuilders in case she should be needed in the Falklands. After completing trials and operational training, she deployed to the South Atlantic in the following October in company with the frigates *Phoebe* and *Sirius*.

The Type 22 frigate emerged from the Falkland campaign with an excellent reputation. The Seawolf system was now combat-proven and the ships had stood up well to the dual test of enemy action and heavy weather. Already, in February 1982, Mr Nott had announced that it had been decided to order an eighth ship of the class as a result of an offer by Yarrow to cut the price of the ship by £6 million. Following the success of the other ships in the Falklands, it was further announced by the Minister in parliament that it had been decided to order another (the ninth) Type 22 as a move towards replacing the war losses.

In the Government White Paper published in December 1982, entitled *The Falklands Campaign: The Lessons*, it was announced that a total of five

new Type 22 frigates would be built to replace the losses in the Falklands. This included the ninth ship already ordered and brought total procurement up to 12 ships. Also announced in the same document was the information that three of the five ships would be of a new Batch 3 version which would differ from the earlier versions in that it would carry the Mk 8 automatic 4.5in gun. In fact, as will be seen, the Batch 3 ships ultimately incorporated other significant changes which were ultimately to make them the most powerful surface warships, excluding aircraft carriers, in the Royal Navy.

It was expected that these would definitely be the final orders for the Type 22s, especially as work was now under way on the succeeding Type 23, the first of which was ordered in October 1984. However, in view of the delays with that programme and due to some competitive tendering by the shipyards involved, orders for another two Batch 3 ships were placed with Swan Hunter and Cammell Laird. Details of previous orders were altered so that, ultimately, six Batch 2 and four Batch 3 ships, in addition to the original four Batch I, were finally completed.

The first eight ships (four Batch 1 and four Batch 2) were all built by Yarrow Shipbuilders Ltd at their Clydeside yard. Following representations from the City of London the eighth ship, which was to have been HMS *Bloodhound*, became HMS *London*. The remaining Batch 2 orders went to Swan Hunters and were named *Sheffield* and *Coventry* in perpetuation of the names of the gallant Type 42 destroyers lost in the Falklands War. Of the Batch 3 ships, the first two orders went to Yarrows with the final two going to the other yards mentioned above. As these ships differed considerably from the earlier batches, a new set of names beginning with the letter 'C' were allocated (*Cornwall*, *Cumberland*, *Campbeltown* and *Chatham*).

The new Batch 2 ships were basically identical to *Boxer* and *Beaver* with the exception that the last four ships (from *Brave* onwards) featured an enlarged hangar and flightdeck to house an EH101 Merlin or Sea King helicopter. The use of a larger helicopter will give these ships the ability to prosecute submarine targets detected at very long range (possibly up to 100 miles) by the towed array sonar. Trials with this had proved extremely successful and the US Navy was, reportedly, most impressed when HMS *Beaver* demonstrated the equipment during Exercise 'RIMPAC 86' in the Pacific.

A further feature introduced in these ships was the new Type 911 tracking radar for use with the Seawolf GWS25 system. It had been found in the Falklands that the earlier Type 910 radars had difficulty in tracking targets very close to the sea

Right:
A model of HMS *Chatham* showing the bow sonar housing fitted to the Batch 3 ships. *Air and Sea*

Below:
HMS *Cumberland* makes a dashing sight as she carries out full speed trials. The addition of the 4.5in guns forward gives these ships a much more aggressive profile. Note the overhanging bow anchor which is designed to pass clear of the bow sonar dome when lowered. *Yarrows*

Bottom:
HMS *Campbeltown* is the latest Batch 3 to join the fleet, commissioning in May 1989. In this photograph she is still running trials and lacks some equipment and armament including the Harpoon missile launchers and the twin GSA8 electro-optical directors. *Rolls-Royce*

due to 'second path' reflections via the sea's surface. In the 911 radar, developed from that used in the land-based Rapier missile system, this problem was reduced by the use of higher frequencies ('K' band) allowing narrow and more accurate beams.

HMS *Brave* was also unique in that two Rolls-Royce Spey SM1 gas turbines replaced the Olympus units in the standard COGOG arrangement. The Spey unit was smaller and lighter than the Olympus (56,130lb as compared with 68,000lb) and offered considerable savings in fuel consumption. However, power output was only 18,774hp compared with 28,000 for the Olympus so that the ship's maximum speed was slightly reduced. The main reason for this installation was to get the Spey to sea in an operational environment so that it could be fully assessed before being fitted to the new Type 23 frigates. The remaining Batch 2 ships (*London*, *Sheffield* and *Coventry*) reverted to the standard Olympus/Tyne arrangement.

However, the Spey reappeared in the Batch 3 ships which used a COGAG arrangement instead of the COGOG layout used in *Brave*. The significance of this was that both the Spey and Tyne engines could be coupled to each shaft simultaneously (instead of either one or the other in the COGOG system) and this combined output went some way to making up for the lower power rating of the Spey. A major impact is in the cruising range of the ships as the Batch 3s can cover 7,500 miles at 17kt as opposed to only 4,500 miles for the original Batch 1 ships.

Apart from the new machinery, the Batch 3 design featured several significant improvements to the weapons outfit. As already mentioned, one of the major additions was the mounting of a 4.5in gun on the forecastle. To make room for this the Exocet launchers were removed and replaced by two quadruple launchers for the US Harpoon missile mounted abaft the bridge. Although the double-ended Seawolf GWS25 system was retained, a Goalkeeper CIWS was mounted high up amidships and provision is made for two single LSE 30mm guns. Goalkeeper is one of the current crop of CIWS and is manufactured in the Netherlands although the gun is a General Electric GAU-8/A multi-barrelled 30mm with the staggering rate of fire of 4,200rounds/min. The mounting carries its own search and tracking radars, is completely automatic in operation, and is designed to engage targets from 1,500m down to a minimum range of 350m. Coupled with the Seawolf missile, the CIWS gives the Batch 3 ships an exceptionally strong defence against air and missile attack. The ship also carries the STWS-2 A/S torpedo system which can fire the sophisticated Stingray torpedo. Finally, a Sea King helicopter will be embarked pending the availability of the EH101 Merlin in

around 1993.

Fire control systems for the ship's gun and missile armament are improved by the addition of two GSA-8 Sea Archer 30 series Electro-Optical directors. These are fitted on either beam atop the bridge and offer a means of tracking and ranging targets in a passive mode using infra-red thermal imaging and television cameras, together with a laser rangefinder. The advantage of this system is that, in suitable conditions, it makes radar emissions unnecessary and the target may thus be unaware that it is being tracked.

Internally the Batch 2 ships are fitted with a version of the Computer Assisted Command System (CACS-5 in this case) first installed in HMS *Boxer*. However, it must be assumed that this has suffered from the problems associated with the early CACS-1 and the CACS-4 destined for the Type 23 frigates, and may be some time before any defects are completely eradicated. Despite this problem, the Batch 3 Type 22s are the most heavily armed ships in the Royal Navy today and demonstrate the amazing growth in the size, cost and sophistication of the modern frigate. With the trend now towards smaller and cheaper ships, it may be that they will be the largest and most powerful frigates ever to see service with the Royal Navy.

As befits their capabilities, all versions of the Type 22 have taken part in important deployments since the end of the Falklands War. With their double Seawolf missile systems they were much in demand in areas where air or missile attack was a possibility and so, for example, most of the Batch 1 ships have spent some time as part of the patrols covering the Falklands after the end of hostilities. However, this commitment has now been scaled down and normally only one of the older frigates is on deployment in the South Atlantic.

The 'Armilla' patrol in the Gulf of Oman has frequently been undertaken by various ships of the class including HMS *Boxer* in 1988, finally fully operational after spending much of her early career on trials with the CACS-1 system and the Type 2031 towed array sonar.

The ships ordered in the wake of the Falklands War have only recently been completed. Three (*Sheffield*, *Coventry* and *Cornwall*) commissioned in 1988 and the remaining three (*Cumberland*, *Campbeltown* and *Chatham*) during 1989. There will be a gap of several years before the Type 23 comes on stream in substantial numbers and this will leave the 14 Type 22s as the backbone of the Royal Navy's anti-submarine forces until well into the 1990s. In retrospect, the Navy must consider itself lucky to have secured so many of these fine ships although it is unfortunate that it took a war in the South Atlantic to provide the incentive to build them.

Name	No	Builder	Laid Down	Launched	Commission	Fate	Date
Broadsword	F88	Yarrow Shipbuilders, Clyde	7/2/75	12/5/76	3/5/79	In service 2nd FS	
Battleaxe	F89	Yarrow Shipbuilders, Clyde	4/2/76	18/5/77	28/3/80	In service 2nd FS	
Brilliant	F90	Yarrow Shipbuilders, Clyde	25/3/77	15/12/78	15/5/81	In service 2nd FS	
Brazen	F91	Yarrow Shipbuilders, Clyde	18/8/78	4/3/80	2/7/82	In service 2nd FS	
Boxer	F92	Yarrow Shipbuilders, Clyde	1/11/79	17/6/81	21/12/83	In service 1st FS	
Beaver	F93	Yarrow Shipbuilders, Clyde	20/6/80	8/5/82	13/12/84	In service 1st FS	
Brave	F94	Yarrow Shipbuilders, Clyde	24/5/82	19/11/83	4/7/86	In service 1st FS	
London	F95	Yarrow Shipbuilders, Clyde	7/2/83	27/10/84	5/6/87	In service 1st FS	
Sheffield	F96	Swan Hunter, Tyne	29/3/84	26/3/86	26/7/88	In service 1st FS	
Coventry	F98	Swan Hunter, Tyne	29/3/84	8/4/86	14/10/88	In service 1st FS	
Cornwall	F99	Yarrow Shipbuilders, Clyde	12/9/83	14/10/85	19/4/88	In service 8th FS	
Cumberland	F85	Yarrow Shipbuilders, Clyde	12/10/84	21/6/86	10/06/89	In service 8th FS	
Campbeltown	F86	Cammell Laird, Birkenhead	4/12/85	07/10/87	00/05/89	In service 8th FS	
Chatham	F87	Swan Hunter, Tyne	12/5/86	20/1/88	00/00/90	Handed over	16/11/89

Data: Type 22, Batch 1, HMS *Brilliant* (1981)
Displacement: 3,500 tons standard; 4,000 tons full load
Length/beam: 430ft (oa)/48.5ft
Draught: 19.9ft full load
Armament: GWS25 Seawolf SAM system (2×6). GWS50 Exocet SSM system (4×1). 2×1 40mm guns. 2×3 ASTT, STWS-2
Aircraft: 2×Lynx HAS2 helicopters
Radar/sonar: Types 967, 968, 910, 1006/2016, 162M
Machinery: COGOG. 2×Rolls-Royce TM3B Olympus gas turbines (25,000shp each), 2×Rolls-Royce RM1A Tyne gas turbines
Speed/range: 30kt/4,500nm, at 18kt
Oil fuel: 600 tons
Complement: 235

Data: Type 22, Batch 2, HMS *Beaver* (1985)
Displacement: 4,100 tons standard; 4,800 tons full load
Length/beam: 485.55ft (oa)/48.35ft
Draught: 21ft full load
Armament: As Batch 1
Aircraft: As Batch 1. EH101/Sea King in last four
Radar/sonar: Types 967, 968, 911, 1007/2016, 2031Z, 162M
Machinery: As Batch 1 except *Brave* which has 2×Rolls-Royce SM1A Spey gas turbines in place of the two Olympus
Speed/range: 30kt/—
Oil fuel: 900 tons
Complement: 273

Data: Type 22, Batch 3, HMS *Cornwall* (1988)
Displacement: 4,200 tons standard; 5,250 tons full load
Length/beam: As Batch 2
Draught: As Batch 2
Armament: GWS25 Seawolf SAM system (2×6). 8×Harpoon SSM, 1×Mk 8 4.5in gun, 2×30mm guns, Goalkeeper CIWS, STWS-2 AS torpedo system (2×3)
Aircraft: 1×EH101/Sea King helicopter
Radar/sonar: Types 967, 968, 911, 1007/2050, 2031Z, 162M
Machinery: COGAG. 2×Rolls-Royce Spey SM1A gas turbines (18,770shp each), 2×Rolls-Royce RM1A Tyne gas turbines (4,250shp each)
Speed/range: 29kt/7,500nm, at 17kt
Oil fuel: 900 tons
Complement: 286

6 Into the Nineties

The Type 22 frigates described in the previous chapter are undoubtedly among the most successful warships built for the Royal Navy since 1945, but their continued evolution has led to a ship which can perhaps more realistically be regarded as a cruiser rather than a simple frigate. The considerable anti-ship capability of the Batch III version is a manifestation of the concept of a general purpose frigate, but the scale and range of these weapons lifts the ship almost into the cruiser or destroyer category. The size and performance of the later Type 22s does not come cheaply and they are almost certainly destined to be the largest and most expensive – in real terms – frigates ever likely to be built for the Royal Navy.

Although there have been problems with some of the sophisticated electronic equipment, the Navy has been pleased with the performance of the Type 22s, particularly with the Seawolf missile and the 2016 and later 2031 sonars while the Lynx/Sea Skua helicopter/missile combination was well proved in the Falklands. Many of the problems highlighted in the latter conflict have been resolved in the more recently completed ships although the two Type 22s in the Falklands were fortunate that their ability to absorb major battle damage was not severely tested.

However, the Type 22s were not alone in proving themselves in the difficult and dangerous South Atlantic actions and perhaps the most remarkable exploits were those of the two Type 12 frigates *Plymouth* and *Yarmouth*. Although the basic design was over 30 years old, and the ships themselves had seen over 20 years' service, both showed themselves almost the equal of later designs when in action. This highlighted a trend in Royal Navy thinking which had begun to gain ground at the beginning of the decade and which was considering whether the interests of the Royal Navy would be better served by a frigate type which was smaller, simpler and cheaper than the existing Type 22.

By late 1978 the only major warships under construction for the Royal Navy were the 'Invincible' class carriers, Type 42 destroyers, Type 22 frigates and nuclear-powered hunter-killer submarines. Although all of these were fine ships of their type, only a limited number could be built with the funds available from a sorely pressed defence budget. Strangely enough many of the ships ordered or under construction at the time had been provided for by a Labour government which saw a naval shipbuilding programme as a way of keeping unemployment in areas of traditional industries where much of their voting support came from. The Royal Navy was also faced with policies which required the dispatch of ships outside the European theatre to meet commitments such as the 'Armilla' patrol in the Gulf of Oman. This was to be a long-term commitment which continues even today. To maintain two ships on station for such patrol duties requires the services of at least six ships if refits and time spent on passage is taken into account. Consequently it was felt that a cheaper and simpler design was required to back up the Type 22 and to provide the Royal Navy with the numerical strength which it needed. Preliminary design efforts were started in conjunction with British Shipbuilders under the designation Type 23.

The shipbuilding industry welcomed the idea of a return to more moderate dimensions as it was being found that, despite the obvious excellence of the Type 22 design, it was too expensive and specialised to be a viable proposition in terms of sales to foreign navies. In contrast to earlier designs of the 'fifties and 'sixties, neither the Type 21 'Amazon' class nor the Type 22s attracted any foreign sales despite the high hopes of the builders, Yarrows and Vosper Thornycroft (it should be mentioned that the latter company achieved some success with an order of six 'Niteroi' class frigates for the Brazilian Navy, the design of these owing much to the Type 21). However, in an increasingly competitive world, British builders were losing out to foreign builders, particularly the Italians with the 'Lupo' class frigates and the Germans with the various 'MEKO' types. In many cases these orders were being gained from countries which had previously bought British ships.

Yarrow Shipbuilders had a design study, designated Type 24, which was suitable for export and which the company hoped the Royal Navy would buy in order to increase its export prospects. A model of this design revealed in 1980 showed a flush-decked hull, larger than a 'Leander', with a flightdeck and hangar for two Lynx helicopters aft. Armament comprised a single 4.5in gun forward, two single 30mm amidships, A/S torpedoes and fixed surface-to-surface missile launchers abreast the funnel. Four twin launchers for an unspecified short range surface-to-air missile were carried at the fore and aft corners of the superstructure.

Propulsion could have been either diesel or gas turbine, and hull-mounted sonar was carried. With the announcement of the Type 23 programme, work on the Type 24 ceased without any orders being secured.

The Conservative government, elected in 1979, came to power promising a real increase in defence spending. However, even they fell prey to the desire to equip our armed forces with what could be afforded instead of what was actually required. By July 1981 Sir John Knott, the Defence Minister, was ready to present his now notorious White Paper which, as well as proposing sweeping cuts in the strength of the active fleet, also announced the end of the Type 22 building programme. The future of British frigate construction was to rest on the projected Type 23 design which appealed to the government due to its low unit cost – quoted as being £70 million as against £130 million of the Type 22 at 1981 prices. As we have seen, the events in the South Atlantic in the

following year had the effect of brushing aside this ill-devised programme and the Type 22 frigates continued to be built, some as replacements for Falklands losses. However, the Type 23 programme was now firmly established and it was expected the first of the class would enter service around 1988.

In retrospect the Falklands can be seen as a watershed in the design of RN ships and there were to be several effects on the frigate building programme in the following years. As already covered, the Type 22s received a new lease of life and several fundamental design changes were incorporated. The Type 23 programme was reviewed and the basic concept changed out of all recognition while many British shipbuilders produced a variety of designs to take advantage of the lessons of the conflict. The Type 23 and later projects are described in detail in the following pages.

'Duke' Class (Type 23) GP Frigates

As originally envisaged, the Type 23 was mainly intended as a platform for the newly developed towed array sonars which were becoming a practical proposition at that time. The ship would carry a lightweight missile system for self defence against air attack and would also have landing and refuelling facilities for a helicopter, although no hangar would be fitted. It was envisaged that each group of Type 23 frigates would be accompanied by a new design of fleet auxiliaries which would provide hangar and repair facilities for the frigate's helicopters. Although intended to keep down the cost of individual frigates, it is doubtful if the programme as a whole would have been any cheaper as the large auxiliaries would be expensive to build and would become prime targets in their own right, necessitating the installation of complex and expensive self-defence weapon systems. In any case the tactical problems associated with such a method of operation would have placed a severe constraint on the deployment of each individual frigate.

However, such measures were necessary if the unit cost was to be kept as low as the £70 million which was the target figure. In many respects the philosophy of the design resembled that which had produced the limited capability Type 14 frigates of the 1950s. One of the prime requirements for successful operation of towed array sonars was the achievement of the lowest possible acoustic signature from the hull and machinery. Apart from

detailed research into suitable hull forms, this also led to the Type 23 introducing a completely novel propulstion system – CODLAG.

CODLAG, or Combined Diesel Electric And Gas Turbine to give its full designation, has three separate elements – gas turbines for cruising and high speeds, and diesel generating sets driving electric motors for low speeds and quiet running. An incidental benefit of this system is that fixed-pitch propellers optimised for quiet running can be used, as power for going astern is provided simply by reversing the polarity of the electric motors. Each of the two shafts can be driven by either its own gas turbine through a reduction gearbox or by the shaft-mounted electric motor fed by power from the diesel generator sets.

The choice of gas turbine rested between the Olympus which had already been proven in the earlier Type 21 and 23 ships or the new Rolls-Royce SM1A Spey. The latter was smaller and lighter than the Olympus but power output was only 18,775shp compared to 28,000shp in the TM3 version of the Olympus. As high speed was not a prime consideration and great efforts were being made to keep the hull length down to 100m (390ft) and displacement to 2,500 tonnes, the Spey was finally chosen. In fact at one stage it was proposed that only one Spey would be fitted, driving the twin shafts through a combined gearbox, and giving a speed of only 25kt.

By mid-1981 the characteristics of the Type 23

had been defined as above with armament consisting of an OTO Melera 76mm gun, Exocet MM40 surface-to-surface missiles and two STWS-2 triple AS torpedo tubes. Helicopter landing and refuelling facilities were incorporated and the ship carried hull and towed array sonars. This represented a minimum frigate and, although it might have been built for something approaching the target price, it would have been severely restricted in its operational applications.

By the end of 1981, even before the Falklands conflict, the design had been recast to improve its export appeal and operational capabilities. The hull was lengthened by 15m and a hangar was added to allow operation of a Sea King or EH101 Merlin helicopter. In view of the air threat to ships deployed in the North Atlantic, self-defence capability was improved by the addition of a Seawolf surface-to-air guided missile system forward and light automatic guns amidships. The torpedo tubes were to be incorporated into the hangar structure to improve reloading procedures which could now be carried out under cover. By May 1982 the second Spey gas turbine had been reinstated and a second Seawolf tracking radar was added to give full 360° coverage.

The ship was now approaching the previous Type 22 in terms of complexity and cost, which was now estimated at around £90 million as opposed to £120 million for the Type 22. In the 12 months following the Falklands War further changes were made to build on experience gained in the conflict. In particular, modifications were made to the damage control arrangements and the ship was divided into five self-contained fire zones, each with its own fire-fighting arrangements, escape routes and electrical power supply. New fireproof or non-toxic materials were incorporated and sensitive areas such as the operations room and machinery control room, as well as some cable and pipe runs, were armoured against splinter and shrapnel damage.

More obvious external changes include the substitution of the Vickers 4.5in automatic gun for the original OTO 76mm to give heavier firepower for the NGS role, and the adoption of the vertical launch GWS26 Seawolf missile system instead of the GWS25 system with the six-round launcher as fitted in previous ships. Two additional fixed torpedo tubes were added at the fore end of the hangar and the hull-mounted Type 2016 sonar was replaced by a bow-mounted Type 2050 sonar. These changes necessitated a further increase in hull length to 123m between perpendiculars and 133m (436ft 4in) overall while standard displacement rose to 3,100 tonnes at full load.

In this form Yarrow Shipbuilders were given a £16 million contract to commence detailed design and development in August 1983. In fact this proved to be the start of several major political battles of the final choice of equipment for the ship. The first of these concerned the tracking radar for the Seawolf missile system. As originally proposed, the ship would have carried a lightweight system utilising a twin launcher and the Hollandse Signaalapparaten VM40 tracking radar. The use of a Dutch radar at a time of high unemployment in the UK gave rise to a major

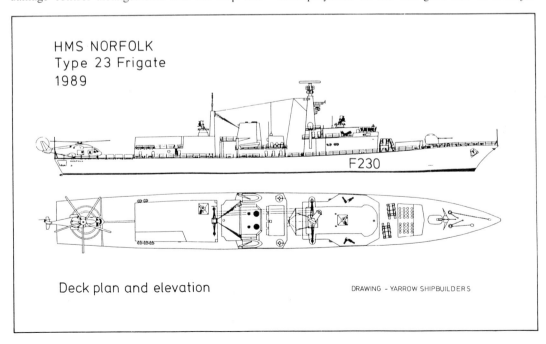

HMS NORFOLK
Type 23 Frigate
1989

F230

Deck plan and elevation

DRAWING - YARROW SHIPBUILDERS

political storm as the government insisted that all defence equipment would only be ordered after competitive tendering on an international basis. In the end, GEC/Marconi was the successful bidder with its I-band 805SW radar developed from that used by the land-based Rapier missile system. When, in mid-1983, the decision to utilise the vertical launch GWS26 system was made, the Marconi radar was retained and in the final design two 805s (Type 911 in Royal Navy parlance) are mounted, one abaft the bridge and the other on the hangar roof.

The GWS26 Seawolf system utilised a silo, containing 32 missiles stowed in vertical containers, positioned on the forecastle immediately abaft the 4.5mm gun mounting. Compared to the standard Seawolf, the vertical launch system (VLS) missile incorporates a number of improvements and modifications. The most obvious of these is the addition of a jettisonable tandem boost motor which has integral thrust vector control so that after launch the missile can be turned over to a horizontal trajectory on the target bearing. The missile itself is 2m long and weighs around 80kg, while the total weight of the missile, booster and canister is only 200kg. One problem encountered with the VLS was the dispersion of the booster motor exhaust gases and the design of the launch canister is such that these are turned through 180° and vented vertically upwards as the missile is launched.

VLS does away with the need for separate missile magazines, complex handling systems and launchers. In addition it provides 360° coverage and the missile can be assigned to either of the Type 911 tracker radars, thus giving greater flexibility in response against threats.

The choice of the Vickers-built 4.5in gun was a fairly straightforward decision as the Italian OTO Melera 76mm weapon was too light for the NGS role. However, the next battle was to secure the contract to supply a surface-to-air missile system and here, too, the Italians were one of four contenders with their Otomat missile. The other weapons considered were the French MM40 improved Exocet, the American Harpoon built by McDonnell Douglas, and the British Aerospace Sea Eagle. The Exocet and Otomat were eliminated in the early stages and the eventual winner was the Harpoon, despite considerable political pressure to purchase the British-built Sea Eagle which had been ordered by the Royal Navy and RAF in its air-launched version. The Block 1C version of the Harpoon, ordered in April 1984 for both the Type 23 and the Batch III version of the Type 22, features a 12,000lb thrust rocket booster for launching and a Teledyne CAE J402-CA-400 turbojet with a thrust of 300kg (660lb) for the cruising phase. This combination gives the missile

a range of around 90 miles at a speed of Mach 0.85 and a 500lb warhead is carried. The advanced Block 1C model has improvements to its guidance system which enables it to carry out complex evasive action during the approach to the target and to pull up for a final diving attack on to the target to improve penetration. Before launch the target's co-ordinates are fed to the missile's inertial guidance system and an onboard radar, designed to be resistant to enemy electronic counter-measures, is switched on for guidance in the final stages of attack. The Type 23 carries a total of eight Harpoons in two groups of four fixed canister launchers. Originally these were to have been mounted amidships between the superstructure blocks but have now been moved forward to the forecastle between the Seawolf vertical launch silo and the bridge.

Other weapon systems include four fixed anti-submarine torpedo tubes mounted within the fore part of the hangar superstructure. These can fire either Mk 46 or Stingray homing torpedoes and form part of the Magazine Torpedo Launch System (MTLS) which uses a mechanised handling and loading system in contrast to the clumsy manual loading required by the STWS trainable launchers installed in earlier ships. Finally, there are two single Oerlikon KCB 30mm guns on LS30B mountings carried abreast the funnel. Rate of fire for these weapons is 650 rounds/min and the mounting can be fired under local control using a joystick and gyro-stabilised optical sights, or by remote control from the operations room.

Apart from the torpedoes and the 30mm guns, the rest of the armament is concentrated on the forecastle while the after part of the ship is taken up with the hangar and a large flightdeck. This arrangement does raise the possibility of the ship losing almost all its offensive capability by damage forward where the 4.5mm gun, Seawolf and Harpoon missiles could all be put out of action simultaneously.

As far as helicopters are concerned, it is planned that the first ships of the class to be completed will initially operate Sea Kings, already being introduced aboard the later Type 22s, as the naval version of the EH101 Merlin will not enter service until around 1996. However, the latter will offer a substantial improvement in the ship's AS capability as its endurance of up to 5hr with a full weapons load will enable submarine contacts to be pursued and attacked up to 100 miles from the ship. This is necessary to take full advantage of the performance of the ship's sonars, particularly the Type 2031 passive towed array sonar. The bow-mounted Type 2050 sonar, produced by Ferranti, can operate in both active and passive modes, as well as being used as an attack sonar in conjuction with the ship launched AS torpedoes.

Radar equipment includes the latest Plessey Type 966 mounted atop the foremast. The 966 is a multiple-purpose radar with a height-finding capability and, as well as being used as a general surveillance and warning radar, is also used as a target indicator for the GWS26 missile system and the 4.5in gun FCS. In these roles it replaces the Type 992Q and combined Type 967/968 radars carried on earlier frigates. Fore and aft are the Type 911 tracking radars, which can also be used for directing the 4.5in gun, and a Kelvin Hughes Type 1007 navigation radar is mounted halfway up the foremast.

Also mounted on the foremast is the sensor module for the GSA8 (Sea Archer 30) electro/optical fire control system. Using infra-red and optical tracking techniques, this system is primarily intended for use in conjunction with the ship's gun armament, but it is also capable of acting as a target tracker for the Seawolf missile system.

As part of the ship's electronic warfare outfit a UAF-1 ESM system, based on the Racal Cutlass system, is mounted atop the mainmast above the hangar. This operates over a wide frequency spectrum and received signals are compared with a computerised library of over 2,000 known radar and emission signals. This enables emitting targets to be accurately and quickly identified while the equipment can also determine and track target bearing. The ESM system display consoles can store data on up to 150 intercepts and display the current 30 main threats at any one time. Information from this system can be utilised to direct the ship's fire control systems on to a target which may then be unaware that it has been detected, identified and is being tracked until such time as it is illuminated by the Type 911 tracking radar immediately before a Seawolf is launched.

Other electronic equipment includes the Marconi ICS3 communications handling system which links all radio equipment (MF, HF, VHF and UHF), satellite communications equipment (SCOT 1D), VLF underwater communications and ships internal phones and speech circuits. The ICS3, assisted by a fully automatic message distribution system (DIMPS) can thus handle the complicated web of ship-to-ship, ship-to-air and ship-to-shore communications.

It will be apparent from the foregoing that there is a considerable interdependence between the various sensors and weapon systems and a considerable amount of data is continuously generated. This data must be sorted, verified, transmitted and acted upon by the various computers, weapon systems and human operators situated throughout the ship. To facilitate the transfer of data there are three interchangeable data highways, one along the keel and the other on either beam, which connect the various weapon systems and sensors to the ship's Action Information System. All this was intended to be incorporated in, and controlled by, a Computer Assisted Command System. Originally contracted to Ferranti, the CACS-4 system planned for the Type 23 was to be an improved version of the CACS-1 fitted to HMS *Boxer* and later Type 22s.

However, the sorry history of the CACS system led to another of the major political rows which seem to have become a routine part of the Type 23 programme. Trials with the CACS-1 aboard HMS *Boxer* revealed that it was not capable of performing to the required standard, in particular the sheer volume of data being generated was overwhelming the capacity of the system and leading to major breakdowns. The problems became so acute that it was realised that the CACS-4 for the Type 23 would not be capable of carrying out the tasks required of it. Consequently, in 1987, the government announced the cancellation of the CACS programme and announced that tenders would be invited for New Command System (NCS) to be fitted to the Type 23. In the event the new contract was awarded to Dowty SENA, a British consortium which also includes the Ferranti Co.

The NCS will be based on the new FM2400 computers, which Ferranti have developed to replace the earlier FM1600 range installed in Type 21 and 22 frigates, and utilise a range of autonomous display consoles developed by Plessey. However, the result of cancelling the CACS-4 in favour of a completely new system means that most of the Type 23s currently on order will enter service without any Computer Command System at all. This will severely restrict their operational effectiveness and limit their usefulness in potentially hazardous areas of operation such as the Gulf. It will be a matter of the highest priority to rectify this unfortunate turn of events which has done little to enhance the reputation of the British electronics industry.

In the final Type 23 design the propulsion system was fixed as two Spey SM1 gas turbines driving two shafts through reduction gearboxes. Also on each shaft is a GEC 1.5MW/660V electric motor rated at 1,750shp fed via a thyristor converter with power from up to four diesel generators. These are Paxman Valenta 12RP200CZ 1,900bhp diesels driving Brush 1,300kW alternators and can also be used to provide additional direct electrical power for the ship's services if disconnected from the power train. Normal electrical power for the weapon systems and other services is provided by two separate motor generators producing 440V on a 60Hz 3-phase supply.

The propulsion system is housed amidships in four separate compartments. In the centre is the gas turbine room with the two Speys and aft of that

Above:
This impression of the Type 23 shows the basic outline of the design. A particular feature is the concentration of the main armament (4.5in gun, Seawolf VLS silo, Harpoon SSMs) on the forecastle, while the after part of the ship is taken up with the hangar and flightdeck for a Merlin or Sea King helicopter. The superstructure is carefully designed to reduce the radar signature of the ship and this accounts for the sloping sides of the hangar, bridge and funnel. *Yarrows*

Below:
HMS *Norfolk*, the first Type 23, at sea during trials. Evident in this view is the grouping of the main armament well forward and the seaworthy lines of the hull. Note the UAF-1 ESM array just below the top of the foremast. *Yarrow Shipbuilders*

Bottom:
HMS *Norfolk*, the lead Type 23, fitting out at Yarrows' Scotstoun yard on the River Clyde. At the masthead is the antenna for the Plessey Type 996 radar which will gradually replace the Types 967/968 and 992Q throughout the fleet. *Rolls-Royce*

is the motor/gear room housing the reduction gears and electric motors. Forward of the gas turbines is the forward auxiliary machinery room housing two diesel generators, while the remaining two are housed in an upper auxiliary machinery room. All the diesels are raft-mounted on resilient mounts and hooded to reduce the noise signature to a minimum.

Compared to the previous Type 22 this machinery layout offers considerable savings in space, weight and cost. The two Speys effectively replace the two Olympus and two Tynes while the earlier design still required four 1MW diesel generators. There are some drawbacks. Maximum available shaft horsepower is around 37,500shp compared with 56,000shp in the Type 22, resulting in lower maximum and cruising speeds, although the Speys will use considerably less fuel in most circumstances. The introduction of the electric drive introduces flexibility of operation but it should be noted that when it is required to operate at full power on the electric motors, the four generators can only just meet the full power demand of the ship and its services. In other words, if only one generator set is out of action for any reason then there will be a shortfall in the power available, resulting in a reduction of power to the shafts or the shutting down of some of the ship's services. However, the system – although complex – is designed to offer considerable flexibility in operation with many options in the event of battle damage.

A high degree of automation in the running of the ship, its weapon systems and machinery has resulted in a relatively small crew. Normal complement will be around 150, typically 15 officers, 50 senior ratings and 85 junior ratings. Accommodation is provided for a total complement of up to 180 which will allow for training and special circumstances. It is interesting to compare these figures with that for the later Type 22s where the complement is around 270 and the smaller and much less capable Type 21 which requires 177 men. This reduction assists in reducing the overall running costs of the ship although it is a trend which is causing problems throughout the Navy: insufficient men are available for routine tasks such as cleaning ship and forming damage control parties.

Following completion of the detailed design work by Yarrows, it was natural that they should also be successful in tendering for the contract to build the lead Type 23 and this was awarded on 24 October 1984, although the ship was not formally laid down until December 1985. Despite the importance of the Type 23 programme to the Royal Navy, the government was slow to place orders, causing considerable apprehension among the shipyards looking for work and to the political lobby which looked for signs of a commitment to maintain a fleet of around 50 frigates and destroyers. To do this required an ordering rate of

Above left:
The Type 23 is unique in using CODLAG machinery — a combination of gas turbines and diesel electric propulsion systems. This view shows the two Rolls-Royce SM1A gas turbine modules installed in HMS *Norfolk's* main engine room. *Rolls-Royce*

Above:
HMS *Marlborough* on the slipway at Swan Hunter's Tyne yard immediately prior to launching on 21 January 1989. Note the offset position of the plinth for the after Type 911 tracking radar on the hangar roof. *Air and Sea*

Right:
A stern view of HMS *Marlborough* showing the shafts for the two propellers, the large fairlead on the transom for the towed array sonar, and the width of the angled funnel casing. *Air and Sea*

Below:
HMS *Marlborough* fitting out. The lines of the hull appear to be optimised for the low and medium speeds at which the towed array will be deployed, rather than for maximum speed.

three ships per year but in fact the next orders were not announced until August 1986 when a further pair were ordered from Yarrows and a third ship from Swan Hunter on the Tyne. These ships were not laid down until the following year and it was not until August 1988 that another three orders were forthcoming, this time all from Yarrows.

It was assumed that the Type 23s would perpetuate the alphabetical system of naming frigates which, with a few exceptions, had been perpetuated with the Type 21s and various batches of the Type 22s. With 'D' as the next letter in sequence, it was originally expected that at least some of the names of the 'Daring' class destroyers of the 1950s and '60s would be revived and for a while the Type 23 was unofficially referred to as the 'Daring' class. However, the Navy obviously felt restricted in its choice of names by such a system and when the first order was placed it was announced that the Type 23 would be officially known as the 'Duke' class, the lead ship being named HMS *Norfolk*. The next three ships were named *Marlborough*, *Argyll* and *Lancaster*, while the latest ships are to be *Iron Duke*, *Monmouth* and *Montrose*. These are mostly cruiser names from the WW1 era and make a pleasing change to recent practice. With the dramatic reduction in the number of major surface ships manned by the Royal Navy, the choice of warship names has assumed greater significance and, inevitably, it is impossible to please all interested parties.

In September 1987, Vice-Adm Sir Derek Reffell, Controller of the Royal Navy, stated that at least 20 Type 23s would be required by the Royal Navy and it was anticipated that the first 12 would be completed to the same basic design although later ships would be built to a modified Batch II design. No details of such a variant have yet been released.

The lead ship, HMS *Norfolk*, will commission during 1989 but the second and third, *Argyll* and *Marlborough*, are unlikely to be completed before 1991. Thereafter delivery rates should become more regular as building times for the latest ships can be expected to reduce. Long lead items for an eighth ship have already been ordered and so it is likely that at least one other ship will be ordered in 1989.

At one time the Royal Navy was in danger of losing HMS *Argyll* as the ship was offered to Pakistan in an effort to obtain an export order for a total of three ships. A second ship would be built by Yarrows and the third constructed in Karachi with British technical assistance. By offering one of the Royal Navy's ships already under construction as part of the order, an early delivery could be guaranteed and it was hoped that this would help to clinch the contract, but in the event the deal fell through.

Despite the various technical and political problems which have dogged the Type 23 from its inception, the end result is a well-armed and balanced design which makes the most of current technology and should be unrivalled as an anti-submarine platform. The major problem, which must be corrected as a matter of the highest priority, is the lack of a fully operational Control and Command System. The other concern is that the ships will not be built in sufficient numbers to satisfy the Royal Navy's requirements. With the Type 22 programme complete, the 'Duke' class is the only major surface combat ship currently under construction. Despite the rate at which the older frigates, particularly the remaining 'Leander' class, are being retired, new ships are not coming forward in the numbers required to sustain the fleet at its present size. For example, in 1988 only three new frigates were commissioned while no less than eight were sold, scrapped or sunk as targets. The next year or two will show if the government genuinely intends to maintain the destroyer and frigate force at its current levels or whether it will be permitted to decrease still further.

Name	No	Builder	Laid Down	Launched	Commission	Status	Date
Norfolk	F230	Yarrow Shipbuilders, Clyde	19/12/85	10/07/87	28/11/89	Trials	1990
Argyll	F231	Swan Hunter, Tyne	22/10/87	21/01/89		Fitting out	1990
Lancaster	F232	Yarrow Shipbuilders, Clyde	20/03/87			Fitting out	1990
Marlborough	F233	Yarrow Shipbuilders, Clyde	18/12/87			Building	1990
Iron Duke	F234	Yarrow Shipbuilders, Clyde				Ordered	11/07/88
Monmouth	F235	Yarrow Shipbuilders, Clyde				Ordered	11/07/88
Montrose	F236	Yarrow Shipbuilders, Clyde				Ordered	11/07/88

Northumberland, *Richmond* and *Westminster* ordered 19/12/89 from Swan Hunter, Tyne.

Data: Type 23, HMS *Norfolk* (1989)
Displacement: 3,500 tons standard; 3,850 tons full load
Length/beam: 436.35ft (oa)/49.21ft
Draught: 18ft full load
Armament: GWS26 VLS Seawolf SAM (1×32), 8×Harpoon SSM. 1×Mk 8 4.5in gun. 2×30mm guns.

Aircraft: 1×EH101/Sea King helicopter
Radar/sonar: Types 966, 911, 1007/2050, 2031
Machinery: CODLAG. 2×18,770shp Rolls-Royce SM1A gas turbines. 4×7,000hp Paxman Valenta diesel generators. 2×GEC electric motors
Speed/range: 28kt/7,800nm at 15kt
Oil fuel: –
Complement: 157

Frigate Designs in the Post-Falkland Era

Although the Type 23 programme is now firmly established and the design has benefited from experience in the Falklands, it is not the only design which has been projected or considered in recent years. With Yarrow Shipbuilders acting as lead yard for the Type 23 and obtaining the majority of the subsequent orders, other shipbuilders produced a variety of designs which they hoped might interest the Royal Navy or provide a basis for much sought-after export orders. Foremost amongst these is a series of designs for a light frigate evolved by Vosper Thornycroft. Despite its involvement in the Type 21 programme, most of the orders went to Yarrow, and Vospers did not obtain any Type 22 contracts (although they were awarded orders for three Type 42 destroyers). Consequently the company has produced a number of designs which it hoped would fill the gaps on the slipways. Some of these were modern versions of existing ships, such as the Modified 'Leander' and the Type 21 'Command Frigate' described in previous chapters, but in addition a range of so-called 'Light Frigates' was introduced. These drew heavily on Vosper Thornycroft's previous experience with the Type 21 and also several frigate designs which had been built for export. These latter included the large Mk 10 frigates built for Brazil in the 1970s and the smaller Mk 5 and Mk 7 ordered by Iran and Libya respectively. In the 1980s a new series of frigate designs was produced including the Mk 15, 16 and 17, the latter being a ship of around 1,700 tons with a speed of 35kt and capable of carrying a Lynx helicopter. In addition to a medium calibre gun and a twin 40mm mounting, the design also featured surface-to-surface and anti-submarine missiles in boxed containers instead of complex launcher systems.

With the benefit of experience gained in the Falklands the Mk 17 was updated in 1983 to become the Mk 18, the hull of which was 108m long and based on the Type 21, while displacement rose to 1,900 tonnes. Great attention was paid to damage control and the ship was divided into four major fire zones each with its own air conditioning, diesel generator, fire main bypass and self-contained fire-fighting arrangements. Special attention was given to reducing the profile of the ship to reduce radar detection range. This was partly achieved by attention to the superstructure design but also by the concept of a below-decks hangar reached by a flightdeck lift. Machinery was CODOG with two diesels and a gas turbine. Armament comprised a 4.5in automatic gun, Otomat Mk II surface-to-surface missiles, Seaguard CIWS with the option of a short range surface-to-air missile system, while a boxed version of the Ikara missile could replace some of the Otomats if required.

Vosper Thornycroft further modified its Mk 18 design in 1985 and it became known as the 98m Light Frigate. Although reduced in size, it retained a similar layout including the below-decks hangar and the CODOG propulsion system comprising one Rolls-Royce Spey gas turbine and two diesels. These could be supplemented by electric motor drive for silent running, as in the Type 23. Armament consisted of an Oto Melera 76/62 Super Rapid gun, two LSE 30mm guns, Goalkeeper CIWS, four Harpoon SSMs in fixed launchers and four Stingray AS torpedoes also in fixed container launchers. A Lynx helicopter was carried and both hull-mounted and towed array sonars were projected, as was a full radar and EW outfit. In many respects this design was an austere version of the Type 23 with scaled-down capabilities. Apart from being smaller, it also had a complement of only 84 men – half that of a Type 23 – and consequently would have been very economic in overall running costs.

By the mid-1980s it was apparent that the Royal Navy was committed to the Type 23 to follow on from the Type 22 but it was also obvious that, as the older and smaller frigates such as the Leanders and Type 21s were retired, that a gap would appear in the fleet's inventory. While the Type 22 and 23 were excellent examples of their kind, they were large and expensive and a decline in the numerical strength of the surface fleet appeared inevitable. In addition, for the larger ships to earn their keep, it was desirable that they should be deployed on tasks which would utilise their extensive capabilities. There appeared, therefore, to be a requirement for a smaller and less sophisticated frigate which could be used for a number of secondary duties including extended offshore patrol deployments. An ocean-going capability was required which meant a minimum displacement of around 1,600 tonnes and a useful weapons outfit including an effective self defence against air attack was desirable. It was hoped that the Royal Navy could be persuaded to buy such a design in order to maintain its numerical strength and to give a boost to the export orders which would undoubtedly follow the selection of the successful contender.

For offshore patrol duties the Royal Navy originally ordered the 'Isles' class ships based on commercial trawler designs and designated OPV (Ocean Patrol Vessel). These were followed by two 1,400-tonne 'Castle' class OPV Mk 2 and, despite their relatively small size, both ships deployed to the Falklands during the war. The requirement for a larger ship for worldwide patrol duties led to the designation OPV-3 and several designs were prepared to meet this specification.

Vosper Thornycroft came up with its 85m Mk 19 OPV which was similar to the 'Castle' class in outline with a 76mm gun forward and a flightdeck, and below-decks hangar for a Lynx helicopter aft. Other companies also pursued this prize and produced some quite sophisticated designs which went beyond the OPV role and entered into the light frigate category.

Foremost among these was Hall Russell Ltd of Aberdeen which had been responsible for the design of the 'Castle' class OPVs. Although armed versions of the 'Castle' class were offered for the OPV-3 specification, a consortium was formed with British Aerospace, Plessey and CAP to develop a new design named Skeandhu. Offered in two versions, the larger displaced 1,850 tons and would make 26kt on diesel engines with a total output of 20,800bhp. Various armament options were offered but the most complete outfit consisted of a 76mm Oto Melera gun, two 30mm guns, Harpoon or Exocet SSMs in fixed launchers, lightweight Seawolf with a quadruple launcher, Stingray torpedoes and a Lynx helicopter housed in a conventional hangar. Towed array sonar could be fitted and the obligatory radar and EW outfit was carried, subject to a number of options. Complement was 77 as a result of extensive automation of weapon systems and machinery.

In 1987 the design was enlarged and updated to become known as the 'Loch' class – a reference to the earlier class of wartime frigates and to the company's Scottish connections. The 'Loch' class Light Frigate displaced 2,500 tonnes and overall length was 107.8m. A novel propulsion system known as CODAL (Combined Diesel And Electric) was proposed in which the main power was provided by two Pielstick 7,940kW diesels, one on each shaft, and these could be supplemented by two electric motors drawing power from two 2,270kW Pielstick diesel generating sets. Alternatively the ship could be driven on the electric motors alone for slow or silent running. Four 350kW Paxman diesel generators provide electrical power for the ship's services. Choice of weapons outfit was left to the customer but provision was made for a medium calibre gun (up to 5in), a CIWS, a PDMS such as the GWS26 VLS Seawolf, surface-to-surface missiles, ship-launched AS torpedoes and a helicopter. Accommodation was provided for up to 152 men which included a proportion under training. Again this design showed much use of the technology which was being applied to the contemporary Type 23, particularly the use of diesel electric propulsion for slow silent running in conjunction with towed array sonars. Unfortunately Hall Russell was unsuccess-

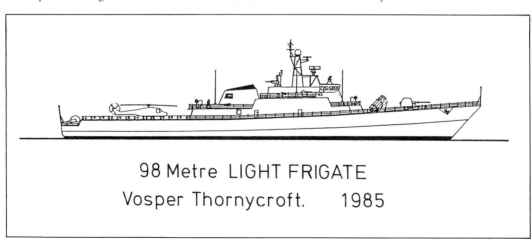

98 Metre LIGHT FRIGATE
Vosper Thornycroft.   1985

Above:
Vosper Thornycroft's projected Mk 18 Frigate design incorporated experience from the Falklands conflict. The hangar for the Lynx helicopter was situated below the flightdeck and accessed by a lift. This reduced the size of the superstructure which, in turn, reduced the ship's radar signature. *Vosper Thornycroft*

Below:
Refinement of the Mk 18 project led to the 98M Light Frigate design of 1985. On the stern are boxed container launchers for Stingray torpedoes and a Goalkeeper CIWS is mounted high up abaft the mast. Propulsion machinery consisted of a Spey gas turbine and two diesels, with electric motors for silent running. *Vosper Thornycroft*

Bottom:
A model of Hall Russell's 'Loch' class Light Frigate design displayed at the 1987 Royal Navy Equipment Exhibition. The twin funnels are an unusual feature. *Air and Sea*

ful in obtaining orders for any of these designs and in 1988 the yard was forced to close down due to lack of work.

A company which has managed to survive on a trickle of orders from the Royal Navy is Swan Hunters on the River Tyne. Having built a few Type 22s, work is currently concentrated on completing the sole Type 23 order (HMS *Marlborough*) which was not won by Yarrows. Swan Hunter has developed a range of offshore patrol ships and light frigates which are being marketed under the name 'Spearfish' although, as yet, no orders have been secured.

Yarrows has succeeded in gaining the lion's share of Royal Navy frigate orders in recent years and their slipways are fully occupied. However, the company has taken advantage of its experience with the Type 23 programme to produce a range of frigates which have an obvious family connection. Designated Ocean Patrol Ships, there are three

versions of which the smallest displaces 1,800 tonnes and is diesel powered. The two larger variants displace 2,500 tonnes and differ mainly in the machinery outfit. OPS2 has a CODLAD (Combined Diesel Electric and Diesel) system giving a maximum speed of 24kt or 11kt on electric motors, while the OPS3 has a straightforward CODOG arrangement to give 31kt. All three mount a 4.5in gun, Harpoon SSMs, onboard torpedoes and a Lynx-sized helicopter. In addition the larger OPS2/3 are equipped with the VLS Seawolf system as used on the Type 23 although in this case the launch silos are mounted in the hangar superstructure. These designs are obviously aimed at the export market and are unlikely to be purchased by the Royal Navy.

In fact the whole concept of the OPV3-type vessel was abandoned, almost entirely because the necessary funding could not be made available. One result of this, already mentioned, was the

Loch Class LIGHT FRIGATE

Hall Russell Limited.   1987

Below:
A concept for a future frigate design by CAP, a British defence software company. Utilising a very high degree of automation would enable the ship to function with a complement of only 50 while the clean lines and small superstructure block would reduce the ship's radar signature. *Air and Sea*

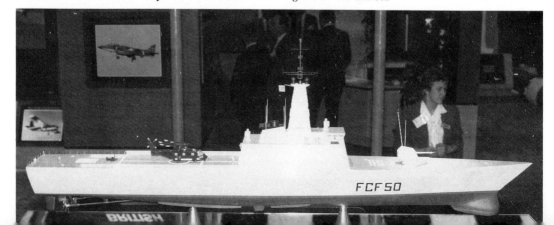

closure of the Hall Russell yard, while Vosper Thornycroft has virtually ceased to market its frigate-sized designs and is concentrating on its successful range of fast attack craft and corvettes up to 65m. This reduction in the scope of the British warship building industry must be viewed with dismay while the virtual concentration of frigate building in one yard, while making some economic sense, cannot be a sound industrial strategy.

This review of British frigate designs in the post-Falklands era would not be complete without mention of the controversy surrounding proposals for a radically different approach to such ships. In the early 1980s a private design bureau, Morgan Giles Associates based on the Isle of Wight, suggested that a wide-beam hull could offer significant advantages over the conventional warship's slim hull with a typical length to beam ratio of 10:1. Based on this concept, the S90 frigate design displaced 3,000 tonnes on a hull 91.5m long and 19m beam – a length/beam ratio of around 4.8:1. Briefly, the advantages of this design were given as improved stability, better buoyancy and stability margins for damage control, more deck space for weapon systems and cheaper first costs. These proposals were strongly pushed as an alternative to the more conventional Type 23 design and the matter achieved notorious proportions with considerable press interest and political involvement. Unfortunately this tended to override a purely technical appreciation of these factors and the affair became seen as a battle between the Establishment (in the form of the Royal Navy's Ship Department at Bath which was responsible for the conventional Type 23 concept) and Private Enterprise (represented as being innovative and imaginative). The argument raged on even after the Type 23 design was frozen and orders had been placed. An independent commission of enquiry was set up to look into the matter and to consider allegations that the government had deliberately ignored data which proved the S90 concept was superior to the Type 23 design. This commission reported that there was no clear technical advantage in the 'short fat' hull form and that the conventional hull selected for the Type 23 met the operational requirements of the Royal Navy. Despite accusations of bias by the committee, it would appear that the debate is closed although, no doubt, it will be renewed when new frigate designs are being considered in the future.

As a postscript it is interesting to note that the French Navy has recently (1988) ordered a class of six 2,600-tonne patrol frigates which feature a fin-stabilising hull with an overall length of 93.5m and a beam of 14m, giving a length/beam ratio of 6.68:1. Preliminary sketches show a design similar in concept to the S90 and with facilities for operating a Super Puma helicopter. No doubt the various protagonists in the saga recounted above will be keeping a close eye on the progress of these ships.

NFR 90 Project

Despite the Royal Navy's involvement in the South Atlantic, the 'Armilla' patrol in the Gulf of Oman and various worldwide deployments, its main operational commitment is in European waters and the North Atlantic as part of the NATO forces. In conjuction with the US and Canadian navies, most of the European navies are committed to the defence of Europe and the maintenance of the vital North Atlantic sea lanes. Taken together, these navies can field a formidable fleet but one which would still be stretched to contain the Soviet submarine menace. One of the problems which has beset NATO from its earliest days is the standardisation of weapons and equipment and it is among the naval forces that some of the greatest disparities exist. Although most NATO frigates are intended for ASW in the North Atlantic, each of the major countries has produced its own designs in relatively small numbers. Thus the British have the Type 22 and 23, the Dutch have the 'Koortenaer' class and the smaller 'M' class, the Germans have the F122 and 124 designs and the Canadian Navy is building the CPF (Canadian Patrol Frigate).

These programmes all reflect the desire of each country to maintain its own shipbuilding industry and to demonstrate a design capacity which improves chances of export orders. Although it has often been suggested since NATO was formed that a standard design could be evolved for use by all member navies, it is only now, because of the relentless rise in the cost of modern warships, that some member states are seriously looking at a project for a new frigate design which will meet the requirements of the alliance as a whole. The resulting economics of scale in such a programme will, it is hoped, result in a proportionately lower first cost as well as reducing running expenses.

Currently, eight nations are involved in the project which is designated NFR90. Apart from the United Kingdom, the others are Canada, France, Germany, Italy, the Netherlands, Spain

Above:
A model showing the principal features of the NFR90 project. Armament of this version appears to consist of a 5in automatic gun, a VLS surface-to-air missile silo, two Goalkeeper CIWS, Harpoon SSMs and A/S torpedoes. A large hangar is capable of housing possibly two Merlin-sized aircraft and a bow sonar housing is plainly visible. *Supermarine Consortium*

and the United States. In addition Greece, Turkey and Belgium have expressed an interest and are monitoring developments. As is to be expected in a programme of this nature, progress has seemed slow and bureaucratic. Feasibility studies completed at the end of 1985 showed that it was possible for such a collaborative project to succeed and that significant cost savings could be achieved, while at the same time it would be possible to apply national variations in equipment without prejudicing the whole programme. Following on from this an official NATO Staff Requirement was drawn up and presented to the member countries' governments in mid-1987. There then followed a period of consideration by each state before a formal Memorandum of Understanding was signed to proceed with the Project Definition Stage. At this stage there was a strong possibility that the British government would pull out of the project on grounds of cost and non-compatibility with Royal Navy Staff Requirements. A major argument against withdrawal was that British companies would then almost certainly be excluded from bidding for contracts to supply equipment for the ships. Consequently it was announced in January 1988 that the United Kingdom would participate in the Project Definition Stage at a cost of £100 million and at the same time Adm Geoffrey Marsh RN was appointed as Project Manager.

On the industrial side a consortium of British companies including British Aerospace, Vosper Thornycroft and several equipment and electronics manufacturers have formed the Supermarine Consortium Ltd to participate in the NFR90 project.

All this does not guarantee that the final NFR90 design will ever be built or, even if it is, that any will be ordered by the Royal Navy. Strangely enough, if it is ordered by the United Kingdom, initially it will be as a replacement for the Type 42 destroyers which will begin reaching the end of their useful lives at the end of the 1990s. In this event it will be the AAW version of the NFR90 which will be ordered but the problem here is that, as yet, no suitable medium/long range surface-to-air missile system is available to replace the Sea Dart. Currently the Royal Navy is keeping its options open by continuing low-key work on a possible national Type 42 replacement.

As far as frigates are concerned, the Type 23 will continue to be ordered well into the 1990s and the NFR90 will perhaps follow on at the turn of the century. The most optimistic guess for a projected timescale would see the first NFR90 ship completed in 1996, but follow-on orders could keep the production programme going until 2020. Current production plans call for a total of 48 ships of which the largest order will be for 18 ships for the US Navy while the Royal Navy will order 12 as replacements for the Type 42s. However, it has already been shown what effects politics can have on a national programme such as the Type 22 or 23 and the problems in co-ordinating the political and financial concerns of eight countries are proportionately greater. Once a common design has been agreed, the greatest problems will arise from the desire of each country to have what it sees as an equitable part in the building programme, particularly in respect of the supply of weapon systems, electronics and machinery.

The NFR90 project offered a great opportunity to European industry and could have provided a great symbol of allied unity of purpose. Unfortunately it was announced towards the end of 1989 that the United Kingdom was withdrawing from the programme on cost grounds and because the project timescale did not match with RN requirements. Instead, work is now progressing on a national design for an air defence frigate to replace the Type 42 destroyers at the end of the 1990s. These new ships will be armed with FAMS (Future Air Defence Missile System) which is being developed jointly by British Aerospace and the French Aerospace Industry. No other details of the project have been released but it is unfortunate that the UK will not participate in the NFR90 project which is still going ahead on a reduced scale.

Appendices

1 RN Warship Type Designations

With the introduction of new frigate designs in the postwar period, the Royal Navy adopted a system of type numbers to designate the various designs The type number allocated depended on the main function of the ship concerned and the sequence of numbers were as follows:

0 to 40   Anti-submarine escorts.
41 to 60   Anti-aircraft escorts.
61 to 80   Aircraft direction escorts.
81 to 99   General purpose escorts.

Originally the type numbers were intended to be applied to frigate designs but, with the lessening distinction between frigates and destroyers, some numbers were also allocated to destroyers. The following list gives all known type numbers allocated to date including those allocated to destroyers.

Type 11   Diesel-powered design for an AS frigate to complement Type 41 and 61. Abandoned in favour of the Type 12.
Type 12   Steam-powered fast AS frigate. 'Whitby' and 'Rothesay' classes.
Improved Type 12   'Leander' class general purpose frigates developed from basic Type 12 design.
Type 14   'Blackwood' class utility AS frigate.
Type 15   Full conversion of wartime destroyers to fast AS frigates.
Type 16   Limited conversion of wartime destroyers to fast AS frigates.
Type 17   Designation applied to design for a third-rate AS vessel smaller and slower than the Type 14. Armed with one Limbo and a single 40mm gun. Designation later applied to another study for a very large AS frigate. No details available.
Type 18   Projected conversion of emergency programme destroyers to be armed with two Limbo, torpedo tubes for AS torpedoes, twin

4in and twin 40mm guns. Intended to provide the capabilities of the Type 15 while requiring less extensive alterations and hence reducing cost. No such conversions were carried out, although the five remaining 'N' class destroyers were earmarked for this programme.
Type 19   Projected high speed escort with a similar armament to the 'Whitby' class, but with a speed of 43kt. Presumably meant to combat the high underwater speed of nuclear powered submarines but the introduction of torpedo-carrying helicopters aboard frigates made high surface speeds unnecessary.
Type 21   'Amazon' class gas turbine-powered patrol frigates.
Type 22   'Broadsword' class gas turbine-powered AS frigate. 'Leander' replacement.
Type 23   'Duke' class general purpose frigates. First ship, HMS *Norfolk*, due to commission in 1989.
Type 24   Commercial design by Yarrow, intended mainly for export. Not built.
Type 41   'Jaguar' class AA frigates.
Type 42   'Sheffield' class air defence guided missile destroyers. Designation also applied to a design in 1954 for a steam-powered escort armed with three single automatic 4in guns. Intended mainly for North Sea and coastal duties.
Type 43   Large guided missile destroyer armed with Seadart and Seawolf. Not built.
Type 44   AA escort vessel. No details available.
Type 61   'Salisbury' class aircraft direction frigates.
Type 62   Projected conversion of 'M' class destroyers, presumably along the lines of the later 'Weapon' and 'Battle' class destroyers converted to radar picket ships.
Type 81   'Tribal' class general purpose frigates.
Type 82   Projected class of four general purpose fleet escorts. Only one, HMS *Bristol*, built.

2 Frigate Pendant Numbers

At the end of World War 2 all Royal Navy escort vessels were carrying pendant numbers with flags K (frigates and corvettes), L ('Hunt' class escort destroyers) and U (sloops) superior. In 1947/48 all these groups of vessels were reclassified as frigates and given a pendant number with flag F superior. In most cases this merely involved a change of prefix letter whilst the ship retained its original number. For example, the frigate *Loch Craggie* changed from K609 to F609. Where such a straightforward change would have resulted in two ships carrying the same number, a multiple of 100 was added or subtracted to one ship's number in order to prevent the double allocation. Thus the 'Hunt' class destroyer *Whaddon*, previously L45, became F145 while the sloop *Wild Goose* changed from U45 to F45. The following list gives all frigate pendant numbers allocated since the introduction of the present system in 1948. Where the same number has been allocated to more than one ship, the ships are listed in order of allocation. The class of each frigate is also given in brackets except where this is obvious from the name (eg 'Loch' or 'Castle' classes).

F02	*Liddesdale* (Hunt)	F44	*Tenacious* (Type 16)	F79	*Brissenden* (Hunt)
F05	*Atherstone* (Hunt)	F45	*Wild Goose* (Black Swan)	F80	*Duncan* (Type 14)
F06	*Bigbury Bay*		*Minerva* (Leander)	F81	*Stork* (Black Swan)
F07	*Acteon* (Black Swan)	F47	*Fleetwood* (Sloop)	F82	*Magpie* (Black Swan)
F08	*Exmoor* (Hunt)		*Danae* (Leander)	F83	*Ulster* (Type 15)
	Urania (Type 15)	F48	*Dundas* (Type 14)	F84	*Exmouth* (Type 14)
F09	*Easton* (Hunt)	F49	*Pheasant* (Black Swan)	F85	*Arabis* (Flower)
	Troubridge (Type 15)	F50	*Rochester* (Sloop)		*Keppel* (Type 14)
F10	*Aurora* (Leander)		*Venus* (Type 15)		*Cumberland* (Type 22)
F12	*Bamborough Castle*	F51	*Grafton* (Type 14)	F86	*Pelican* (Sloop)
	Achilles (Leander)	F52	*Juno* (Leander)		*Campbeltown* (Type 22)
F14	*Beaufort* (Hunt)	F53	*Undaunted* (Type 15)	F87	*Eglinton* (Hunt)
	Leopard (Type 41)	F54	*Hardy* (Type 14)		*Chatham* (Type 22)
F15	*Eggesford* (Hunt)	F55	*Silverton* (Hunt)	F88	*Lamerton* (Hunt)
	Euryalus (Leander)	F56	*Test* (River)		*Malcolm* (Type 14)
F16	*Stevenstone* (Hunt)		*Petard* (Type 16)		*Broadsword* (Type 22)
	Diomede (Leander)		*Argonaut* (Leander)	F89	*Allington Castle*
F17	*Ulysses* (Type 15)	F57	*Black Swan*		*Battleaxe* (Type 22)
F18	*Flamingo* (Black Swan)		*Andromeda* (Leander)	F90	*Woodcock* (Black Swan)
	Galatea (Leander)	F58	*Hart* (Black Swan)		*Brilliant* (Type 22)
F19	*Terpsichore* (Type 16)		*Hermione* (Leander)	F91	*Murray* (Type 14)
F20	*Snipe* (Black Swan)	F59	*Zetland* (Hunt)		*Brazen* (Type 22)
F21	*Dart* (River)		*Chichester* (Type 61)	F92	*Exe* (River)
F22	*Wheatland* (Hunt)	F60	*Alacrity* (Black Swan)		*Boxer* (Type 22)
F23	*Teazer* (Type 16)		*Jupiter* (Leander)	F93	*Vigilant* (Type 15)
F25	*Southdown* (Hunt)	F61	*Llandaff* (Type 61)		*Beaver* (Type 22)
F27	*Lynx* (Type 41)	F62	*Pellew* (Type 14)	F94	*Palliser* (Type 14)
F28	*Wren* (Black Swan)	F63	*Scarborough* (Type 12)		*Brave* (Type 22)
	Cleopatra (Leander)	F64	*Nereide* (Black Swan)	F96	*Peacock* (Black Swan)
F29	*Whimbrel* (Black Swan)	F65	*Tenby* (Type 12)		*Sheffield* (Type 22)
	Verulam (Type 15)	F66	*Starling* (Black Swan)	F97	*Russell* (Type 14)
F30	*Mermaid* (Black Swan)	F67	*Tyrian* (Type 16)	F98	*Orwell* (Type 16)
F31	*Panther* (Type 41)	F69	*Redpole* (Black Swan)		*Coventry* (Type 22)
F32	*Salisbury* (Type 61)		*Bacchante* (Leander)	F99	*Lincoln* (Type 61)
F33	*Opossum* (Black Swan)	F70	*Farndale* (Hunt)		*Cornwall* (Type 22)
F34	*Puma* (Type 41)		*Apollo* (Leander)	F101	*Yarmouth* (Type 12)
F35	*Enard Bay*	F71	*Sparrow* (Black Swan)	F102	*Zest* (Type 15)
F36	*Whitby* (Type 12)		*Scylla* (Leander)	F103	*Arbutus* (Flower)
F37	*Jaguar* (Type 41)	F72	*Wizard* (Type 15)		*Lowestoft* (Type 12)
F38	*Cygnet* (Black Swan)		*Ariadne* (Leander)	F104	*Dido* (Leander)
	Arethusa (Leander)	F73	*Eastbourne* (Type 12)	F105	*Alnwick Castle*
F39	*Hind* (Black Swan)	F75	*Haydon* (Hunt)	F106	*Brighton* (Type 12)
	Naiad (Leander)		*Charybdis* (Leander)	F107	*Rothesay* (Type 12)
F40	*Sirius* (Leander)	F76	*Virago* (Type 15)	F108	*Londonderry* (Type 12)
F41	*Volage* (Type 15)		*Mermaid* (1973)	F109	*Leander* (Leander)
F42	*Modeste* (Black Swan)	F77	*Blackpool* (Type 12)	F112	*Albrighton* (Hunt)
	Phoebe (Leander)	F78	*Cottesmore* (Hunt)	F113	*Falmouth* (Type 12)
F43	*Torquay* (Type 12)		*Blackwood* (Type 14)	F114	*Ajax* (Leander)

F115	Berwick (Type 12)	F195	Roebuck (Type 15)	F391	Loch Killin
F116	Amethyst (Black Swan)	F196	Cowslip (Flower)	F397	Launceston Castle
F117	Ashanti (Tribal)		Urchin (Type 15)	F399	Tintagel Castle
F118	Tallybont (Hunt)	F197	Grenville (Type 15)	F413	Farnham Castle
F119	Eskimo (Tribal)	F198	Oakley (Hunt)	F417	Halladale (River)
F120	Garth (Hunt)	F199	Tetcott (Hunt)	F420	Kenilworth Castle
F121	Tumult (Type 16)	F200	Ursa (Type 15)	F421	Loch Shin
F122	Ghurka (Tribal)	F206	Avondale (Hunt)	F422	Loch Eck
F123	Crane (Black Swan)	F215	Nith (River)	F423	Largo Bay
F124	Zulu (Tribal)	F217	Swale (River)	F424	Loch Achanalt
F125	Mohawk (Tribal)	F219	Ness (River)	F425	Loch Dunvegan
F126	Bedale (Hunt)	F221	Chelmer (River)	F426	Loch Achray
	Plymouth (Type 12)	F222	Tevlot (River)	F428	Loch Alvie
F127	Penelope (Leander)	F224	Rother (River)	F429	Loch Fyne
F128	Wilton (Hunt)	F230	Wear (River)	F431	Loch Tarbert
F129	Rhyl (Type 12)		Norfolk (Type 23)	F433	Loch Insh
F130	Blankney (Hunt)	F231	Argyll (Type 23)	F434	Loch Quioch
F131	Chiddingfold (Hunt)	F232	Tay (River)	F436	Surprise (Bay)
	Nubian (Tribal)		Lancaster (Type 23)	F437	Loch Lomond
F132	Belvoir (Hunt)	F233	Marlborough (Type 23)	F449	Pevensey Castle
F133	Tartar (Tribal)	F234	Iron Duke (Type 23)	F517	Loch Morlich
F134	Bicester (Hunt)	F235	Jed (River)	F523	Dovey (River)
F135	Cattistock (Hunt)		Monmouth (Type 23)	F525	Ribble (River)
F137	Hambledon (Hunt)	F236	Montrose (Type 23)	F530	Oakham Castle
F138	Rapid (Type 15)	F241	Kale (River)	F600	St Brides Bay
F141	Undine (Type 15)	F246	Spey (River)	F603	Loch Arkaig
F142	Brocklesby (Hunt)	F248	Waveney (River)	F604	Start Bay
F143	Blackmore (Hunt)	F252	Helford (River)	F605	Tremadoc Bay
F145	Whaddon (Hunt)	F253	Helmsdale (River)	F608	Padstow Bay
F146	Cleveland (Hunt)	F254	Ettrick (River)	F609	Loch Craggie
F148	Holderness (Hunt)	F257	Derg (River)	F615	Widemouth Bay
F150	Bleasdale (Hunt)	F269	Meon (River)	F616	Wigtown Bay
F152	Cowdray (Hunt)	F270	Nene (River)	F619	Loch Glendhu
F154	Cotswold (Hunt)	F271	Plym (River)	F620	Loch Gorm
F155	Ballinderry (River)	F272	Tavy (River)	F622	Burghead Bay
F156	Tuscan (Type 16)	F286	Amberley Castle	F624	Morecambe Bay
F157	Wrangler (Type 15)	F293	Tees (River)	F625	Loch Katrine
F158	Quantock (Hunt)	F294	Towey (River)	F627	Mounts Bay
F159	Wakeful (Type 15)	F295	Usk (River)	F628	Loch Killisport
F162	Croome (Hunt)	F331	Awe (River)	F630	Cardigan Bay
F169	Paladin (Type 16)	F332	Avon (River)	F633	Whitsand Bay
	Amazon (Type 21)	F355	Hadleigh Castle	F634	St Austell Bay
F170	Antelope (Type 21)	F356	Odzani (River)	F636	Carnarvon Bay
F171	Calpe (Hunt)	F362	Portchester Castle	F639	Loch More
	Active (Type 21)	F365	Lochy (River)	F644	Cawsand Bay
F172	Ambuscade (Type 21)	F367	Taff (River)	F645	Loch Ruthven
F173	Arrow (Type 21)	F371	Wye (River)	F647	Alert (Bay)
F174	Middleton (Hunt)	F372	Rushen Castle	F648	Loch Scavaig
	Alacrity (Type 21)	F379	Carisbrooke Castle	F650	Porlock Bay
F176	Brecon (Hunt)	F383	Flint Castle	F651	Veryan Bay
F182	Meynell (Hunt)	F384	Leeds Castle	F655	Loch Tralaig
F184	Ardent (Type 21)	F386	Hedingham Castle	F658	Loch Veyatie
F185	Relentless (Type 15)	F387	Berkeley Castle	F690	Caistor Castle
	Avenger (Type 21)	F388	Dumbarton Castle	F691	Lancaster Castle
F187	Whirlwind (Type 15)	F389	Knaresborough Castle	F692	Oxford Castle
F189	Termagent (Type 16)	F390	Loch Fada	F693	Morpeth Castle
F190	Ledbury (Hunt)				
F191	Rocket (Type 15)				
F192	Pytchley (Hunt)				

Notes: Only Royal Navy vessels are listed above. Ships of Commonwealth navies were also allocated new numbers with Flag 'F' superior, but these are not included.

3 RN Gas Turbine Development

One of the major technical developments of World War 2 was the evolution of the gas turbine as a practical power plant for aircraft, either as a pure turbojet or as a turboprop. The Royal Navy was quick to perceive the possibilities of this new powerplant in the field of warship propulsion and shortly after the end of the war it was decided to convert a motor gunboat (MGB2009) to gas turbine propulsion in order to test the practicality of such an installation. The engine used was an aircraft powerplant modified for marine use; the Metropolitan-Vickers Gatric. This engine was of axial flow design, with a nine-stage compressor and a four-stage turbine driving the gearbox. MGB2009 ran for four years and provided much useful data on the operation of gas turbines at sea.

In 1948, a successor to the Gatric was ordered. This was an adaptation of the Metropolitan-Vickers Beryl, another axial flow aircraft engine which was also the powerplant for the Saunders-Roe twin jet flying boat fighter which was under development at the same time. This engine drove a separate power turbine and produced 4,800bhp on a shore test rig. Two G2s were installed in the two 'Bold' class fast patrol boats (*Bold Pioneer*, *Bold Pathfinder*) which were completed in 1951/52 but the results were not very satisfactory as numerous serious teething problems were encountered. However, this is the price of progress and numerous useful lessons were learnt from the operation of these vessels.

Capitalising on the experience gained with the previous vessels, designs were drawn up in the mid-1950s for a new class of fast patrol boat using Bristol Siddeley Proteus gas turbines. These were again aircraft engines and powered the Britannia airliner which in service was probably one of the most fuel-efficient aircraft of its time although it was eclipsed in performance by the contemporary pure jet airliners. The new boats, the 'Brave' class, employed three Proteus engines of 3,500hp each giving a maximum speed of over 50kt and a cruising speed of 44kt. Only two vessels were completed for the Royal Navy, *Brave Swordsman* and *Brave Borderer*, but their spectacular performance led to export orders from several countries for similar craft. Several of the foreign orders specified auxiliary diesel engines for cruising to overcome the relatively low endurance of the purely gas turbine-powered vessels. This arrangement was known as CODOG (combined diesel or gas turbine).

All the foregoing designs employed aircraft engines which had a low specific weight (ie high power-to-weight ratio) but were expensive on fuel. In 1946, Rolls-Royce was contracted to design and develop a gas turbine plant specifically designed for marine use and suitable for powering a 200-ton gunboat. The outcome of this contract was the RM60 powerplant which probably had one of the most complex cycles ever evolved for a gas turbine. Commencing with a low pressure axial compressor, the air was led through an intercooler, a first stage centrifugal compressor, another intercooler, a second stage centrifugal compressor, heat exchanger, combustion chamber, three single-stage turbines (one for each compressor stage), and a two-stage power turbine. The result must have been a thermodynamacist's nightmare! The object of all this complexity was to achieve a flat fuel consumption curve (ie an even increase in fuel consumption with increasing power settings). Two RM60 units were installed in HMS *Grey Goose*, a war-built steam gunboat which commissioned in 1955 for trials. In service the RM60 proved to be an excellent powerplant, particularly in respect of fuel consumption but the complexity of the design led to high development costs and no further work on the design was carried out following completion of the trials aboard *Grey Goose*.

While development of the RM60 continued, a contract was placed with English Electric for a gas turbine unit designated EL60A. This was a much more straightforward unit than the RM60 and was intended for installation in the frigate *Hotham* which was an American-built vessel of the 'Captain' class. *Hotham*'s normal powerplant was a two-shaft turbo-electric system and the intention was to replace one of the steam turbines in order that a direct comparison of the steam and gas turbine plants could be made. Although the *Hotham* was taken in hand for conversion, development of the EL60 was abandoned in 1952 after shore trials showed that the plant was overweight and not flexible enough in operation. The *Hotham* was returned to the United States and scrapped.

In 1954 design work commenced on the Type 81 general purpose frigates and it was decided to incorporate a mixed steam and gas turbine plant which was also under development for a destroyer design which eventually became the 'County' class guided missile destroyers. The new plant envisaged a 12,500shp steam turbine for normal and cruising purposes and a 7,500shp gas turbine as a boost engine for maximum speed and emergency manoeuvring. This arrangement was known as COSAG (combined steam and gas turbine). The gas turbine was a development by AEI (amalgamated with English Electric) and designated G6. In operational use the system was highly successful

Above:
HMS *Bold Pioneer* was one of two gas turbine-powered experimental fast patrol boats. She is armed with a lightweight 4.5in gun adapted from an army design for a lightweight howitzer. The G2 gas turbine proved troublesome and both vessels saw only limited service. *Bold Pioneer* was scrapped in 1958 but her sister ship, *Bold Pathfinder* was not listed for disposal until 1962. *Wright & Logan*

Below:
The Type 81 was the first frigate design to incorporate a gas turbine and this accounted for the two funnels. The turbine exhausted through the after funnel while the steam boiler uptakes were contained in the fore funnel. This photograph shows HMS *Ghurka* as completed in 1963. *Fleet Photographic Unit*

Bottom:
The first all-gas turbine frigate in any navy was the Type 21, exemplified here by HMS *Avenger*, the last of the class to be completed. Her engines were all adaptations of well proven aviation turbine engines. *Yarrows*

and the G6 proved capable of more extended periods of running than was envisaged in the original concept of a boost engine.

As a result of the success of the installation in the 'County' and 'Tribal' class vessels, thoughts turned to the possibility of all-gas turbine-powered vessels and to test this concept it was decided to convert a Type 14 frigate. Development of gas turbines purely for marine use had proved very expensive so it was decided to revert to the practice of modifying existing aero engines for warship use. The most powerful aircraft engine available was the Olympus which powered the Vulcan heavy bomber and in later versions the supersonic TSR2. With the addition of a power turbine stage, and modified for marine use, an Olympus powerplant was installed in HMS *Exmouth* (Type 14 frigate). Also installed were two Proteus gas turbines rated at 3,250shp each for cruising power. The Olympus was derated to 15,000shp as the hull of the Type 14 was not capable of absorbing more. The installation was completed in 1968 and the ship was subsequently employed on trials to test the viability of the concept. However, even before the *Exmouth* commenced her trials, the Royal Navy was already convinced of the advantages of gas turbine propulsion and in 1967 decided that all major warships would be gas turbine-powered.

The first vessel to be designed from the start for all-gas turbine propulsion was the Type 21 frigates designed by Thornycroft to naval requirements. This class of vessel employed the Olympus for high speed work and two marine versions of the Rolls-Royce Tyne turboprop, another aircraft engine which powered the Vanguard airliner among others. The two Tynes, rated at 4,250shp each, gave the ship a cruising speed of 18kt while the Olympus, now rated at 25,000shp, allowed a maximum speed of 32kt.

The Tyne/Olympus combination proved reliable and efficient in operation and was specified for all subsequent designs including the Type 22 frigate and Type 42 destroyer, while the through-deck cruisers ordered in the early 1970s were to be powered by four Olympus engines. Thus in 25 years the gas turbine progressed from an experimental curiosity to the main means of propulsion of a modern warship.

The advantages of the gas turbine as a warship propulsion plant are numerous. They are slightly more economic on fuel than an equivalent steam plant and are easier to control, replying almost simultaneously to changes of power settings. This in turn leads to less engineroom staff required on watch, a factor which is also helped by the fact that the complete engine module can be easily removed and replaced which means that on-board maintenance is reduced. The fact that major repairs and overhauls can be carried out ashore while another engine is installed in the ship means that the amount of time a ship needs to spend in dockyard hands is sharply reduced. In fact, as was shown in the Falkland Islands, large ships such as the carrier *Invincible* can actually carry out an engine change while at sea. Of course this is not possible in a smaller ship such as a frigate but it does illustrate the advantages of the modular concept of the gas turbine. The Type 42 destroyer HMS *Southampton* changed one of her Tyne units while at anchor alongside the repair ship *Stena Seaspread* in the relative calm of San Carlos Water, showing that with limited facilities this sort of work can be carried out when required.

Another advantage lies in the fact that most marine gas turbines are modified versions of existing aero engine designs which means that the cost of initial design and development has already been absorbed by the aerospace industry, thus reducing the total cost of the engine programme as far as the Navy is concerned. Additionally the necessary industrial base for the production of engines and spares is guaranteed.

There are some disadvantages which cannot be ignored, especially by the warship designer. Gas turbines are very sensitive to the environment in which they operate and consequently extensive air ducting and filters are necessary for both the intake and the exhaust gases. This ducting can take up a lot of internal space amidships and experience has shown that this also leads to problems in containing fires caused by battle damage as the large open ducts can provide considerable draughting for such fires. This may have been a factor in the loss of the *Antelope* – although it must be said that a bomb exploding deep in the engineroom of a ship is bound to cause considerable damage.

Exhausts from gas turbines are considerably hotter than in a steam turbine installation and so provision has to be made to keep masts and aerials away from the exhaust. Also the flow of hot gases aft could seriously affect helicopter operations from the flightdeck and careful design of funnel and superstructure is needed to avoid problems. One solution to this problem was the 'Loxton bends' or 'elephant ears' which were fitted to the funnel of HMS *Sheffield*. However, in this particular case they were found not to be necessary and were not fitted to subsequent Type 42 ships. Another point to bear in mind is that the hotter gases will increase the ship's infra-red signature which under certain circumstances would make it easier to detect and track the ship and could be used as a homing point by an anti-ship missile. Several under development use thermal imaging to detect and home on to the target.

The latest gas turbine to enter service is the

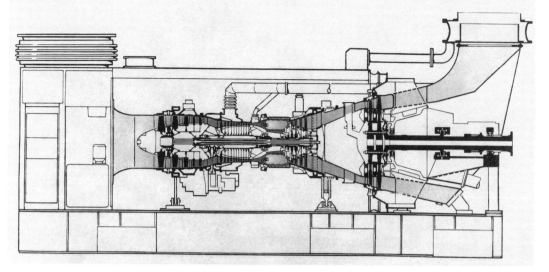

Rolls-Royce SM1A Marine Spey which is also derived from a successful aero engine. Basic power output is 18,774hp (14MW) which is less than the Olympus but considerably more than the Tyne. A complete Spey module weighs around 25 tonnes compared with 30 tonnes for an Olympus module, while specific fuel consumption is reduced by approximately 20%.

The first seagoing installation was in HMS *Brave*, a Batch II Type 22, in which two Speys replaced the Olympus units normally installed in this class and the COGOG machinery layout was retained. In this system each shaft can be driven by either one Tyne or one Olympus/Spey. With the lower powered Spey installed, HMS *Brave* is slightly slower than her sister ships but this was accepted in order to speed the installation and to gain early experience with the Spey at sea. The Batch III Type 22s are also Spey/Tyne-powered, but in these ships a COGAG arrangement is used to allow both units to power each shaft simultaneously when required and this offers a more flexible method of operation.

In the new Type 23 the Spey is also used in the machinery system but in these ships the Royal Navy has abandoned the concept of all-gas turbine propulsion which it had done so much to pioneer. Two Speys are installed, one for each shaft, to give a maximum speed of around 28kt and a cruising speed of 17kt. However, secondary power is now provided by electric motors driven by four Paxman Valenta diesel generators and the whole system is

Above:
A schematic diagram showing the layout of a Rolls-Royce SM1A Spey gas turbine module. In the centre is the gas generator which exhausts through the two-stage power turbine on the right. *Rolls-Royce*

designated CODLAG (Combined Diesel Electric and Gas Turbine). The main advantage of this is to dramatically reduce the noise generated by the ship at the low speeds (around 6kt) associated with use of the new towed array passive sonars.

The use of CODLAG and similar systems seems to point the way forward for warships whose main purpose is ASW and many new designs have been prepared using this system. However, all-gas turbine systems seem likely to prevail in other types of major warships such as destroyers and some aircraft carriers.

As a result of the development work on the marine gas turbine carried out by the Royal Navy, other navies have been quick to adopt the various systems. Consequently British companies, particularly Rolls-Royce, have benefited by gaining extensive export orders. Continuing this trend, sales of the Spey have already been made to the Netherlands Navy for its 'M' class frigates which utilise a CODOG system, while Japan has ordered several units for installation in various ships including the eight 'Asagiri' class destroyers. The latter ships are the first warships to be powered entirely by Speys, using four units on two shafts.

4 Frigates and Helicopters

As far back as 1943 the Royal Navy had seen the potentialities of the helicopter as a useful extension to shipborne airpower when an order was placed for the Sikorsky R-4 helicopter then under development in the United States. Some machines were used for trials during the war and the first Royal Navy helicopter squadron, No 771, formed at Portland in September 1945. Although a shore-based unit, it was an R-4 Hoverfly Mk 1 from this squadron which made the first landing on a frigate. The ship was the *Helmsdale*, a 'River' class frigate adapted for training purposes, and a series of trials were carried out to determine the suitability of the helicopter for anti-submarine warfare. The trials took place in late 1946 and one of the main findings was that a considerably more powerful machine was going to be needed if it was to be capable of operating under a reasonable range of weather conditions and carry a worth-while load of weapons and equipment. Although the Navy went on to develop the helicopter as a potent AS weapon, initial efforts were directed towards larger helicopters which could only operate from the decks of aircraft carriers.

In the late 1940s and early 1950s the Saunders-Roe company developed the Skeeter Light helicopter for the Army and a version of this was proposed for naval use (Skeeter Mk 5) but again power was lacking and the design was dropped. In the meantime the Fairey company had developed its Ultra Light design which was powered by a gas turbine exhausting through nozzles at the rotor tips. After this design was turned down by the Army it was demonstrated to the Navy in the hope of gaining a production order. Trials were conducted from a landing platform constructed on the stern of the Type 15 frigate *Grenville* in September 1957. Much useful data was obtained on the operation of light helicopters from small flightdecks but the Fairey Ultra Light was still too small for naval requirements.

Following its experience with the Skeeter, the Saunders-Roe company instigated design of a turbine-powered helicopter using many features of the Skeeter. The new design, designated P531-0, first flew on 20 July 1958, powered by a 300shp Turbomeca Turmo 600 engine. After the initial trials the Royal Navy ordered three P531-0/N helicopters for further trials and tests aboard ship. By this time the Navy had a firm requirement for a torpedo-carrying helicopter to operate from small warships. This was due to the fact that shipboard weapon systems could not operate at the long ranges at which modern sonar equipment could detect and track submarines. Thus the MATCH (manned torpedo carrying helicopter) concept was born, and in late 1959 the P531 prototypes carried out a series of trials to determine the type's suitability for the new role. The trials were conducted aboard another Type 15 frigate, *Undaunted*, which also had a small flightdeck constructed over the quarterdeck. As a result of these trials the P531 was ordered in quantity for

the Royal Navy from the Westland company which had by then taken over development of the aircraft from Saunders-Roe. The production version, named Wasp, was powered by a Blackburn Nimbus engine rated at 700shp and featured a larger cabin than that of the P531 prototype. As a result of the trials aboard *Undaunted*, the Wasp was fitted with a four-wheel fully castoring undercarriage instead of the skids of the earlier version. A total of 98 Wasps was delivered to the Royal Navy and, flown by detached flights of No 829 Squadron, they were operated by 'Tribal', 'Leander', 'Rothesay' and Type 21 class frigates. The first ship's flight formed aboard HMS *Leander* on 11 November 1963, with other flights forming as aircraft became available.

By the late 1960s the helicopter was established as an integral part of a frigate's armament and following presentations from Westlands a naval version of their WG13 was ordered in prototype form in 1967. This order was part of a larger deal involving Anglo-French production of three helicopter types for both countries. These were the Puma, a medium capacity troop-carrying heli-copter to be produced under French leadership; the Gazelle, a light helicopter mainly for army use and again produced under French leadership; and the Lynx (WG13) produced under Westland's leadership for both the British and French armed forces. The first naval Lynx flew in May 1972 and it was immediately obvious that the type had considerable potential. Thanks to its new 'rigid rotor' it was fast and very manoeuvrable, and could carry a wide range of weapons including Mk 44 and 46 torpedoes as well as AS12 and Sea Skua missiles. An initial order for 60 was placed and the first ship's flight formed in 1978 aboard HMS *Sirius*, an Exocet 'Leander' class frigate. Subsequently, all Type 21 class frigates, as well as many 'Leander' class were equipped with the new type while the Type 22 frigate was designed from the outset to carry two Lynx helicopters. Today the Lynx has completely replaced the Wasp aboard Royal Navy ships. The latter was officially withdrawn from the Royal Navy after 25 years' front line service on 31 March 1988, the last operational flights being aboard the Type 12 frigates *Plymouth* and *Rothesay*, both of which paid off for the last time shortly afterwards.

The Wasp had originally been brought into service as a means of carrying AS weapons out to the maximum range at which submarines could be detected and tracked by the ship's sonar, originally around 10 miles. The main improvement offered by the Lynx was a greatly improved weapon load and increased endurance. However, the work being carried out on towed array passive sonars in the 1970s, and the introduction of the equipment in the mid-1980s, gave rise to a requirement for a

Right:
The sole example of the Fairey Ultra Light helicopter which carried out deck landing trials on HMS *Grenville* in 1958. Note the compact size of the fuselage and the absence of a tail rotor which was not required as the tip nozzle-powered main rotor produced no torque.
Real Photographs

Above:
One of the three Saunders-Roe P531-O/N prototypes used for deck landing trials aboard HMS *Ashanti* in 1962. The suction pad landing gear was an experimental attempt to evolve a suitable system for operating from a small flightdeck. The idea was that the pads would grip the deck on landing while reverse pressure would cause the pads to act like small hovercraft so that the helicopter could easily be moved around the deck. Eventually a four-wheel castoring undercarriage was adopted for the Westland Wasp which was derived from the P531.
Author's Collection

Right:
A Wasp HAS1 edges sideways over HMS *Dido's* flightdeck for a landing. The Wasp had a more powerful engine than the earlier P531 prototypes and also featured a folding tailboom to assist stowage in small hangars. Note the VDS gear and the Limbo mortar well on the ship's stern.
HMS Osprey

151

Above:
The Westland Lynx is currently the Royal Navy's standard helicopter for destroyers and frigates now that the Wasp has been retired, and the Type 22 frigates can carry two of these helicopters. The Lynx is an extremely versatile machine — its speed and manoeuvrability making it useful for the anti-ship role as well as the normal ASW missions. *Fleet Photographic Unit*

Left:
The latest Type 22s and the new Type 23s have enlarged flightdecks and hangars so that they will be able to operate the three-engined EH101 Merlin helicopter, due to enter service in 1996. The EH101 has also been ordered by the Italian and Canadian Navies. *Westland Helicopters*

Right:
To plug the gap until the EH101 is ready for the service, the Royal Navy will deploy the well tried Sea King aboard some of its frigates. The HAS5 version is equipped with a surface search radar and a dipping sonar, and can carry up to four Mk 46 or Stingray torpedoes.
Westland Helicopters

helicopter which could operate from a frigate but which could patrol for several hours at ranges of up to 100 miles from the ship while carrying a heavy weapon load and its own detection equipment. In order to meet this specification Westland Helicopters, in conjuction with Agusta of Italy, formed a consortium (European Helicopter Industries) in 1980 to design and produce the new helicopter. The result is the EH101, named Merlin by the Royal Navy, which is scheduled to enter service in 1996 (1993 for the RAF version). The first prototype made its maiden flight on 9 October 1987 followed by the first Italian aircraft on 26 November the same year. A total of 50 aircraft have been ordered by the Royal Navy as well as another 25 for the RAF for use in the troop-carrying role, 42 for the Italian Navy and 35 for the Canadian Armed Forces.

The British version of the Merlin will be powered by three Rolls-Royce RTM322 turboshaft engines in preference to the General Electric T700/CT7 fitted to the prototypes. With a crew of four and carrying an integrated ASW electronics suite which will process signals from sonobuoys and other passive listening devices, the Merlin has a payload of 6 tonnes allowing it to carry a full weapon load (up to four homing torpedoes) and enough fuel for a 5hr patrol on station. This will give a major boost to the total AS capability of the parent frigate.

The Royal Navy will eventually deploy the Merlin aboard the later Batch II and III Type 22 frigates, which have an enlarged flightdeck and hangar, and the Type 23 ships. Eventually it will also replace the current Sea King helicopters

aboard the 'Invincible' class carriers and it is anticipated that the total Royal Navy purchase will be 100 machines. Present production plans envisage the first aircraft going to the RAF, and the Royal Navy will not receive its first operational aircraft until 1996. To plug the gap in the early 1990s, some ships will operate the latest version of the long established Sea King. This large twin-engined helicopter is already in widespread service with the Royal Navy but, until now, has never been deployed aboard its frigates (although the Canadian Navy, for instance, has done so for many years). The recently ordered HAS6 version features uprated Gnome H1400T engines, advanced design composite main and tail rotors, improved radar and the capability to carry and fire the Sea Eagle anti-ship missile. The first examples should be delivered in 1989 but, in the meantime, trials have already been conducted aboard HMS Cornwall with a Sea King of 826 Squadron.

Brief specifications of helicopter types operated from Royal Navy frigates are given below.

Sikorsky R-4 Hoverfly Mk 1
Rotor diameter: 38ft
Length: 35ft 3in
Max weight: 2,530lb
Max speed: 80mph
Max range: 220 miles
Powered by: One Warner Super Scarab R-550-1 seven cylinder radial engine, 180hp
Crew: Two
Total: 52 supplied to UK for use by RN and RAF

Fairey Ultra Light
Rotor diameter: 28ft 3½in
Length: 15ft 8in
Max weight: 1,900lb
Max speed: 95mph
Max range: 185 miles
Powered by: One Blackburn Turbomeca Palouste turbine, 252lb static thrust, driving two-bladed rotor through tip nozzles
Crew: Two

Saunders-Roe P531-0/N
Rotor diameter: 32ft 3in
Length: 30ft 4in
Max weight: 4,000lb
Max speed: 132mph
Max range: 242 miles
Powered by: One Blackburn Turbomeca Turmo 600, 300shp
Crew: Five seats, normal crew two

Westland Wasp HAS1
Rotor diameter: 32ft 3in
Length: 30ft 4in
Max weight: 5,500lb
Max speed: 120mph
Max range: 270 miles
Powered by: One Blackburn (later Rolls-Royce) Nimbus turbine engine, 710shp
Crew: Five seats, normal crew two

Westland WG13 Lynx HAS2
Rotor diameter: 42ft
Length: 39ft 1¼in
Max weight: 9,500lb
Max speed: 207mph
Max range: 391 miles
Powered by: Two Rolls-Royce BS360 Gem turboshafts, 900shp each
Crew: Two, can carry up to 10 troops. Later versions equipped with MAD and dipping sonar, to give limited AS detection capability

European Helicopter Industries EH101 Merlin
Rotor diameter: 61ft (18.6m)
Length: 52ft 6in (16m) tail folded
Max weight: 28,660lb
Max speed: 193mph (167kt)
Max range: 869 miles (5hr endurance on station)
Powered by: Three Rolls-Royce RTM322 turbo-shafts, 2,100shp each
Crew: Four

Westland Sea King HAS6
Rotor diameter: 62ft (18.9m)
Length: 47ft 3in (14.4m) rotors/tail folded
Max weight: 21,500lb
Max speed: 143mph (132kt)
Max range: 2hr on station with max payload
Powered by: Two Rolls-Royce Gnome H1400T turboshafts, 1,465shp each
Crew: Four

5 Notes on RN Sonar Equipment

Since the invention of 'Asdic' at the close of WW1, the Royal Navy has been in the forefront of Sonar development and, in the period covered by this book, has continued to introduce new and improved equipment. Sonars can be classified under two broad headings – Active, in which the parent ship sends out pulses of sound energy which are reflected from the target allowing range and bearing to be determined; and Passive, in which the shipboard equipment detects noise emissions from the target and enables its bearing to be determined with varying degrees of accuracy. The following list, by no means exhaustive, gives brief details of the main sonar equipments used aboard operational frigates since 1945.

Type	Year	Notes
144	1942	Developed from the earlier Type 128 fitted as standard to prewar destroyers and sloops, the 144 was intended for use with the first ATWs such as Hedgehog. Gyrostabilised transducer array carried in underhull streamlined dome. Featured automatic training and a bearing recorder. A 'Q' attachment, introduced in 1943, consisted of a small transducer fitted below the main array and angled down at 15°. This allowed contact to be maintained on deep diving targets at short range. The Type 144 was produced in numerous variants and
		the suffix 'Q' was added to indicate the fitting of the attachment (eg 144BQ).
147	1943	Short range depth finding sonar, particularly intended for use in the attack phase with the Squid mortar. A small two-ply quartz transducer was carried in streamlined 'sword' which could be raised or lowered beneath the hull. First operational fitting was aboard HMS *Hadleigh Castle*.
162	1948	Also known as 'Cockchafer'. Bottom target classification sonar using three fixed hull-mounted transducer strips – one below the keel and the others on either side. Maximum range 1,800ft. Prototype trials carried out in HMS *Helmsdale*.
164	1950	Updated version of prototype Type 160X which, in turn, was developed from the Type 144. Featured new streamlined dome housing, two separate transducers improved range and bearing recorders and a mechanism to incorporate ship's course and speed into the fire control solution for the Squid mortar. Operated in the 14-22kHz range.

Type	Year	Notes

170   1952   First set to be completely developed postwar. Utilised hull-mounted fully stabilised 'four square' transducer. Instrumentation was consolidated on a large console in the operations room and comprised a range recorder with depth attachment, bearing recorder, as well as CRT display for bearing in azimuth. This equipment was used as the attack set for the Mk 10 Limbo mortar and incorporated an analogue fire control computer. After trials in *Helmsdale* and *Scorpion* ('Weapon' class destroyer) the first sets were fitted in the original Type 15 conversions, *Relentless* and *Rocket*. Frequency range 15-30kHz.

177   1956   A long range search set, using sector scan techniques and low frequencies, and benefiting from the results of postwar research programmes. Featured a hull-mounted 2-ton, 4ft-square, transducer array which could be mechanically rotated. Effective up to 10 miles and operated on frequencies around 7.5kHz. Prototype set mounted in *Undaunted* for trials and subsequently fitted to the Type 81 'Tribal' class and early 'Leander' class frigates.

184   1963   Originally intended for use on larger ships, this equipment eventually superseded the Type 177 aboard the later 'Leanders' and was fitted to the Type 21s. It was a low frequency set using sector scan but with a 360° passive capability.

199   1960   Variable depth sonar (VDS) based on the Type 170 electronics. Off-the-shelf purchase of equipment developed by the Canadian Navy (SQS-504) and fitted in some 'Tribal' and 'Leander' class ships.

2016   1978   Developed for use aboard the Type 22 frigates but also fitted to some modernised 'Leanders' and to later Type 42 destroyers. The main array consists of 64 vertical staves arranged in cylindrical form, each consisting of a column of 12 transducer elements. Low frequency 360° scan, can track multiple targets simultaneously, improved performance in shallow water, provides torpedo attack warning and can

Above:
An interesting photograph showing the hydrophone array associated with the Type 2031 passive sonar being reeled aboard the installation on the stern of the Leander class frigate HMS *Argonaut*. *Author*

Below:
The display consoles for the latest Type 2050 sonar which is being fitted to the newest frigates. A single operator controls the whole system using a trackerball, four nudge keys and a plasma panel with a touch sensitive overlay. *Ferranti*

interface with the ship's AIO. Operations room equipment comprises three consoles, while a below-decks sonar room contains the signal processing equipment which utilises modern digital computing techniques. Early trials carried out aboard HMS *Matapan*, a converted 'Battle' class destroyer, and first production set was completed in 1978.

2031 1980 First of the modern towed array passive sonars to enter service with the Royal Navy surface ships. Developed, via prototype 2031X, from Type 2026 used aboard Royal Navy submarines. Consists of a 500m array of hydrophones towed by cable some distance behind the ship. Produced in two versions, the 2031I was initially fitted to four converted Batch 2A 'Leanders' from 1983 onwards while the stretched Batch II Type 22s received the 2031Z with improved electronics, also from 1983. Initial trials with towed

arrays were carried out aboard the Type 12 frigate *Lowestoft* commencing in 1977.

2050 1986 Designed to be hull- or bow-mounted, this active/passive set has been developed by Ferranti as a replacement for the Type 2016. Prototype trials were carried out aboard HMS *Scylla* during 1986/87 and production sets are destined for the Batch III Type 22s and the new Type 23s. In addition, older ships equipped with the Type 2016 can have their electronics and signal processing updated by replacing some components with modules from the 2050.

2057 1990+ New low frequency towed array sonar currently in the development stage and intended for use by both submarines and surface vessels. The array will be much longer than those currently in use.

6 Postwar Disposal Lists

At the end of hostilities in 1945 the Royal Navy possessed hundreds of sloops and frigates in addition to many more still under construction. The fate of those ships which played a significant role in the postwar fleet has been outlined in the early chapters of this book. However, many of the early classes were not required and most were laid up and eventually scrapped, although a few found active employment. To complete the postwar record, brief notes in the disposal of these ships are listed below.

PREWAR SLOOPS

Name	Number	Launched	Fate
Bridgwater	L01	1928	Scrapped Gelleswick Bay 1947
Sandwich	L12	1928	Sold and scrapped 1946
Folkestone	L22	1930	Scrapped Gelleswick Bay 1947
Scarborough	L25	1930	Scrapped Thornaby 1949
Hastings	L27	1930	Scrapped Troon 1946
Fowey	L15	1930	Mercantile *Fowlock* 1946, scrapped Mombasa 1950
Shorehan	L32	1930	Mercantile *Jorge fel Joven* 1946, scrapped 1950
Bideford	L43	1931	Scrapped Milford Haven 1949
Rochester	F50	1931	Navigation training ship 1946-49, scrapped Dunston 1951
Falmouth	L34	1932	Used as RNVR TS *Calliope* from 1952, scrapped 1968
Milford	L51	1932	Scrapped Hayle 1949
Weston	L72	1932	Scrapped Gelleswick Bay 1947
Leith	L36	1933	Sold for mercantile use 1946, scrapped 1955
Lowestoft	L59	1934	Mercantile *Miraflores* sold for scrapping 1955
Wellington	L65	1934	Hulked as HQ ship River Thames 1947
Deptford	L53	1935	Scrapped Milford Haven 1948

Above:
HMS *Fleetwood* was one of the few prewar sloops to see significant postwar service. Converted in 1946, she served as a radio trials ship until 1958 and was scrapped in 1959/60. *Wright & Logan*

Below:
A cluster of frigates laid up at Sheerness in 1950. In the foreground is HMS *Meon* which was later used as a

headquarters ship and was not scrapped until 1966. *Maritime Photo Library*

Bottom:
HMS *Bleasdale* was a Type 3 hunt which remained in commission until 1952. In this 1950 photograph she retains her wartime appearance and is rated as an anti-aircraft frigate. *Wright & Logan*

Name	Number	Launched	Fate
Londonderry	L76	1935	Scrapped Llanelli 1948
Aberdeen	L97	1936	Scrapped Hayle 1949
Fleetwood	F47	1936	Radio Trials ship 1946-58, scrapped 1959
Enchantress	L56	1934	Mercantile *Lady Enchantress* 1947, scrapped Dunston 1952
Stork	F81	1936	Laid up in reserve 1949, scrapped 1958
Pelican	F86	1938	Paid off into reserve 2/1957, scrapped 1958

'RIVER' CLASS FRIGATES

Name	Number	Launched	Fate
Aire	K262	1943	Ran aground near Singapore 23/12/1946. Total loss
Annan	K404	1943	RDN *Niels Ebbesen* 1945, scrapped Odense 1963
Avon	F332	1943	Portuguese *Nuno Tristao* 1949, scrapped 1970
Awe	F331	1943	Portuguese *Diogo Gomes* 1949, scrapped 1969
Balinderry	F155	1942	Placed in reserve 1947, scrapped Barrow 1961
Bann	K256	1942	RIN *TIR* 1947, converted to training ship, scrapped 1979
Chelmer	F221	1943	Laid up in reserve 1946, scrapped Charlestown 1957
Dart	F21	1942	Laid up in reserve 1947, scrapped Newport 1957
Derg	F257	1943	RNVR HQ ship Solent/Severn Divisions 1947-59, scrapped 1960
Deveron	K265	1942	RIN *Dhanush* 1945, RPN *Zulfiquar* 1948, scrapped 1985?
Duddon	K411	1943	RCN 1944-46, scrapped Blyth 1957
Ettrick	F254	1943	RCN 1944-45, scrapped Grays 1956
Exe	F92	1942	In reserve from 1947, scrapped Preston 1956
Fal	F205	1942	Burmese *Mayu* 1947, scrapped 1979
Halladale	F417	1944	Sold and converted to car ferry 1949. Fate not known
Helford	F252	1943	In reserve from 1946, scrapped Troon 1956
Helmsdale	F253	1943	Trials ship until 1953, scrapped Faslane 1957
Jed	F253	1942	In reserve from 1946, scrapped Milford Haven 1957
Kale	F241	1942	In reserve from 1946, scrapped Newport 1958
Lochy	F365	1943	In reserve from 1947, scrapped Troon 1956
Meon	F269	1943	Converted to LSH(S) 1945, paid off 1965, scrapped 1966
Nene	F270	1942	In reserve from 1945, scrapped Briton Ferry 1955
Ness	F219	1942	In reserve from 1946, scrapped Newport 1956
Nith	F215	1942	Egyptian *Domiat* 1948, sunk during Suez landings 1/11/1956
Odzani	F356	1943	In reserve from 1946, scrapped Newport 1957
Plym	F271	1943	In reserve 1946, sunk in Montebello Atomic tests 1952
Ribble	F525	1943	In reserve postwar, scrapped Blyth 1957
Rother	F224	1941	Laid up 1945, scrapped Troon 1955
Spey	F246	1941	Egyptian *Rashid* 1948, still extant 1988
Swale	F217	1942	In reserve from 1947, scrapped Faslane 1955
Taff	F367	1943	In reserve from 1947, scrapped Newport 1957
Tavy	F272	1943	In reserve postwar, scrapped Newport 1955
Tay	F232	1942	In reserve from 1947, scrapped Rosyth 1956
Tees	F293	1943	In reserve postwar, scrapped Newport 1955
Test	F56	1942	RIN *Neza* 1946-47, accommodation ship 1949-51, scrapped 1955
Teviot	F222	1942	SAN 1945-46, reserve from 1947, scrapped Briton Ferry 1955
Towy	F294	1943	In reserve postwar, scrapped Port Glasgow 1956
Trent	F243	1942	RIN 1946, converted to survey vessel 1951, paid off 1975
Usk	F295	1943	Egyptian *Abikir* 1948, Suez blockship 1956, broken up 1957
Waveney	F248	1942	Converted to LSH 1945/46, reserve 1947, scrapped Troon 1957
Wear	F230	1942	In reserve from 1946, scrapped Sunderland 1957
Wye	F371	1943	In reserve postwar, scrapped Troon 1955

'HUNT' CLASS FRIGATES

Name	Type	Number	Launched	Fate
Albrighton	(3)	F112	1941	W. German *Raule* 1959, scrapped 1969
Atherstone	(1)	F05	1939	Laid up 1945, scrapped Port Glasgow 1957
Avon Vale	(2)	L06	1940	Laid up 1946, scrapped Sunderland 1958
Badsworth	(2)	L03	1941	R Nor N *Arendal* 1946, scrapped 1961
Beaufort	(2)	F14	1941	R Nor N *Haugesund* 1952, scrapped 1965
Bedale	(2	F126	1941	IN *Godivar* 1952, ran aground 1976, scrapped 1979
Belvoir	(3)	F132	1941	Laid up 1946, scrapped 1957
Bicester	(2)	F134	1941	Laid up 1950, scrapped Grays 1956
Blackmore	(2)	F143	1941	RDN *Esbern Snare* 1952, scrapped 1966
Blankney	(2)	F130	1940	Laid up 1946, scrapped Blyth 1959
Bleasdale	(3)	F150	1941	Nore Flotilla until laid up 1952, scrapped Blyth 1956
Blencathra	(2)	L24	1940	Target ship 1945-47, laid up 1948, scrapped Barrow 1957
Brecon	(4)	F176	1942	Laid up 1946, scrapped Faslane 1962
Brissenden	(4)	F79	1942	Laid up 1948, scrapped Dalmuir 1965
Brocklesby	(2)	F142	1940	Training and Trials ship to 1963, scrapped Faslane 1968
Calpe	(2)	F171	1941	RDN *Rolf Krake* 1952, scrapped 1966
Catterick	(3)	L81	1941	Greek N *Hastings* 1946, scrapped 1963
Cattistock	(1)	F135	1940	Laid up 1946, scrapped Newport 1957
Chiddingfold	(2)	F131	1941	IN *Ganga* 1952, laid up for disposal 1975
Cleveland	(1)	F146	1940	Laid up 1945, wrecked under tow near Swansea 1957, broken up 1959
Cotswold	(1)	F154	1940	Laid up 1946, scrapped Grays 1957
Cottesmore	(1)	F78	1940	Egyptian N 1950, scrapped 1985/86
Cowdray	(2)	F152	1941	Laid up 1950, scrapped Gateshead 1959
Croome	(2)	F162	1941	Laid up 1945, scrapped Briton Ferry 1957
Easton	(3)	F09	1942	Laid up 1949, scrapped Rosyth 1953
Eggesford	(3)	F15	1942	W German *Brommy* 1958, scrapped 1969
Eglinton	(1)	F87	1939	Laid up 1946, scrapped Blyth 1956
Exmoor	(2)	F08	1941	RDN *Valdemar Sejr* 1953, scrapped 1966
Farndale	(2)	F70	1940	Laid up 1947, scrapped Blyth 1962
Fernie	(1)	L11	1940	Target ship 1945-47, laid up 1948, scrapped Pt Glasgow 1956
Garth	(1)	F120	1940	Laid up 1945, scrapped Barrow 1958
Glaisdale	(3)	L44	1942	R Nor N *Narvik* 1946, scrapped Denmark 1961
Hambledon	(1)	F137	1939	Laid up 1946, scrapped R Tyne 1957
Haydon	(3)	F75	1942	Laid up 1952, scrapped Dunston 1958
Holderness	(1)	F148	1940	Laid up 1946, scrapped Preston 1956
Lamerton	(2)	F88	1940	IN *Gomati* 1952, paid off for disposal 1975
Lauderdale	(2)	L95	1941	Greek *Aigaion* 1946, scrapped 1959/60
Ledbury	(2)	F190	1941	Laid up 1946, scrapped Rosyth 1958
Liddesdale	(2)	L100	1940	Laid up 1945, scrapped Gateshead 1948
Melbreak	(3)	L73	1942	Laid up after running aground 1945, scrapped Grays 1956
Mendip	(1)	L60	1940	Chinese N 1948, Egyptian N 1949, Israeli N 1956, LU 1972
Meynell	(1)	F182	1940	Equadorian *Pres Velasco Ibarra* 1954, for disposal 1978
Middleton	(2)	F174	1941	Laid up 1946, scrapped Blyth 1957
Oakley	(2)	F198	1942	W German *Gneisenau* 1958, scrapped 1972
Pytchley	(1)	F192	1940	Target ship 1945-46, laid up 1946, scrapped Llanelly 1956/57
Quantock	(1)	F158	1940	Equadorian *Presidente Alfaro* 1955, for disposal 1978
Silverton	(2)	L115	1940	Polish N until laid up 1946, scrapped Milford Haven 1956
Southdown	(1)	F25	1940	Target ship 1946, laid up 1946, scrapped Barrow 1956
Stevenstone	(3)	F16	1942	Laid up 1948, scrapped 1959
Talybont	(3)	F118	1943	Reserve 1946, static training ship 1959/60, scrapped 1961
Tanatside	(3)	L69	1942	Greek N *Adrias* 1946, scrapped 1963/64
Tetcott	(2)	F199	1941	Laid up 1945, scrapped Milford Haven 1956
Wensleydale	(3)	L86	1942	Damaged in collision 1944, scrapped Blyth 1946
Whaddon	(1)	F145	1940	Laid up 1945, scrapped Faslane 1959
Wheatland	(2)	L122	1941	Laid up 1945, scrapped 1959
Wilton	(2)	F128	1941	Reserve 1946-49, active 1949-52, scrapped Faslane 1959
Zetland	(2)	F59	1942	R Nor N *Tromso* 1954, scrapped 1965

Bibliography

The following books have provided a considerable amount of background information as well as the facts and figures necessary in compiling a book such as this.

Edgar J. March; *British Destroyers 1892-1953*; Seeley Service and Co, 1966.

Denis Archer (Ed); *Jane's Pocket Book of Naval Armament* (No 9 in a series); Macdonald and Jane's Publishers Ltd, 1976.

Jean Labayle Couhat (Ed); *Combat Fleets of the World* (Various editions 1978-85); Arms and Armour Press.

Capt John E. Moore RN, FRGS (Ed); *Jane's Fighting Ships* (Various editions 1945-88); Jane's Yearbooks.

H. T. Lenton; *Warships of the British and Commonwealth Navies*; Ian Allan Ltd, 1969 (2nd Edition).

Norman Friedman; *Modern Warship Design and Development*; Conway Maritime Press, 1978.

Raymond V. B. Blackman, AMINA, AIMarE; *The World's Warships*; Macdonald 1960, 1963, 1969.

Laurence Dunn, Assoc RINA; *British Warships*; Longacre Press Ltd, 1962.

H. T. Lenton; *British Fleet and Escort Destroyers* (two vols); Macdonald and Co (Publishers) Ltd, 1970.

John Young; *A Dictionary of Ships of the Royal Navy of the Second World War*; Patrick Stephens Ltd, 1975.

H. T. Lenton; *British Warships*; Ian Allan Ltd, Sixth Edition 1962.

Peter Elliott; *Allied Escort Ships of World War II*; Macdonald and Jane's, London, 1977.

Transactions of the Institute of Naval Architects, Vols 89 and 116; Royal Institute of Naval Architects, London, 1947 and 1974.

Owen Thetford; *British Naval Aircraft Since 1912*; Putnam, London, Fourth Edition, 1978.

Lt-Cdr J. M. Milne; *Flashing Blades over the Sea*; Maritime Books, Liskeard, 1980.

H. T. Lenton; *British Escort Ships*; Macdonald and Jane's, 1974.

Mike Critchley; *British Warships Since 1945 (Part 3 Destroyers)*; Maritime Books, Liskeard, 1982.

Mike Critchley; *British Warships Since 1945 (Part 5, Frigates)*; Maritime Books, Liskeard, 1984.

Willem Hackman; *Seek and Destroy*; HMSO 1984.

Norman Friedman; *The Postwar Naval Revolution*; Conway Maritime Press, 1986.

The following magazines and periodicals are devoted to warships or publish articles of interest connected with warships and their history and development. They have, again, proved useful in carrying out research for this book.

Warship published quarterly by Conway Maritime Press.

Flight International published weekly by IPC Transport Press Ltd.

Ships Monthly published monthly by Waterway Productions Ltd.

Navy News published monthly by *Navy News*, HMS *Nelson*, Plymouth.

Navy International published monthly by Maritime World Ltd.

Warship World published quarterly by Maritime Books, Liskeard.

Below:
HMS *Chichester* was converted in 1972/73 to act as a guardship at Hong Kong. She was stripped of most of her radar equipment leaving the stump of the mainmast in place and armament comprised the twin 4.5in mounting, one 40mm and two 20mm guns. *IWM MH30502*